The
Return ^{of}_{the} Dead

The Return $^{of}_{the}$ Dead

The Return ^{of}_{the} Dead

Ghosts, Ancestors, *and*
the Transparent Veil *of*
the Pagan Mind

CLAUDE LECOUTEUX

Translated by Jon E. Graham

Inner Traditions
Rochester, Vermont • Toronto, Canada

Inner Traditions
One Park Street
Rochester, Vermont 05767
www.InnerTraditions.com

Originally published in French under the title *Fantômes et Revenants au Moyen Age* by
    Éditions Imago, 25 rue Beaurepaire, 75010 Paris
First U.S. edition published in 2009 by Inner Traditions

Library of Congress Cataloging-in-Publication Data

Lecouteux, Claude.
    [Fantômes et revenants au Moyen Age. English]
    The return of the dead : ghosts, ancestors, and the transparent veil of the Pagan mind /
Claude Lecouteux ; translated by Jon E. Graham. — 1st U.S. ed.
        p. cm.
    Includes bibliographical references (p.   ) and index.
    ISBN 978-1-59477-318-1 (pbk.)
    1. Ghosts—Europe—History. 2. Zombies—Europe—History. I. Title.
    BF1472.E85L4313 2009
    133.1094—dc22
                                                                    2009016096

Printed and bound in the United States by Lake Book Manufacturing

10 9 8 7 6 5 4 3 2 1

Text design and layout by Priscilla Baker
This book was typeset in Garamond Premier Pro, with Longfellow and Gill Sans used as
display typefaces

Inner Traditions wishes to express its appreciation for assistance given by the government
of France through the National Book Office of the Ministère de la Culture in the
preparation of this translation.

Nous tenons à exprimer nos plus vifs remerciements au government de la France et le
ministère de la Culture, Centre National du Livre, pour leur concours dans le préparation
de la traduction de cet ouvrage.

Contents

PART THREE

PART FOUR

Preface

A Brief Overview of the Research

Since the publication of the first edition of this book, research has been ongoing in search of a complete definition for this complex belief system at whose heart reside the fundamental beliefs touching upon the soul, the beyond, and ancestor worship. The universal nature of the belief in a multiple "soul" has been confirmed by Régis Boyer,[1] while its Christianized variations can be found in the background of texts concerning the beyond translated by Alexandre Micha.[2] The otherworld and the dangerous dead are the subject of a splendid study by Jacqueline Amat,[3] and we have seen that this appellation of "dangerous dead" in fact covers a plurality of places.[4] Martin Illi has examined where the dead go,[5] and Peter Jezler has published a magnificent and richly illustrated book on heaven, hell, and purgatory,[6] the last two realms often being the originating points for revenants. This book, *The Return of the Dead,* will be rounded off with a fine collective work on death in daily life.[7] Revenants in medieval Christian tradition are the subject of a monograph by Jean-Claude Schmitt,[8] which, alas, reflects only the clerical point of view and does not attempt to bridge to the witnesses of paganism. Several stories of revenants have been given extensive study, notably the one concerning the revenant of Beaucaire (1211) by Henri Bresc[9] and the theme of the grateful dead by Danièle Régnier-Bohler.[10] In addition, Marie-Anne Polo de Beaulieu and Jean-Claude Schmitt have translated a dialogue that took place with a revenant.[11] To the best of my knowledge, no one has attempted to distinguish ghosts from revenants. If we expand our perspective, we can see that the beliefs studied in *The Return of the Dead: Ghosts, Ancestors, and the Transparent Veil of the Pagan Mind* are still in evidence today, particularly among the African peoples, as Stuart J. Edelstein has demonstrated for the Igbo, Yoruba, and Edo peoples (Nigeria).[12] For China, we can read the collection of ghost stories *L'Antre aux fantômes des collines de l'Ouest* (The Lair of the Ghosts of the Western Hills),[13] and we can also find numerous Breton parallels in the *Legende de la Mort* (The Legends of the Dead) by Anatole Le Braz.[14]

Ethnologists and folklorists have been especially active. The life led by the dead in tombs and the deceased who return and carry off the living or who deliver messages have been cited by Gerda Grober-Glück, Leander Petzold, and the historian Arnold Angenendt.[15] Felix Karlinger has examined the dining habits of the dead and the table that is set in hopes that the deceased will take a seat there. He has also included many stories about revenants in his book on how time is experienced in the beyond.[16] E. Campi has looked into stories concerning cowherds who became revenants, and Charles Joisten has studied processions of the dead.[17] Also, a wide presentation of revenants emerges in the folk legends (*volkssage*) of the Anvers region in the work of M. Van den Berg, who offers a classification and typology of revenants.[18]

Before going on, I must correct an oversight: anyone interested in the survival of the beliefs examined here will find substantial parallels and information in the catalog of stories on the dead by Ingeborg Müller and Lutz Röhrich,[19] as well as in the different repertoires of narrative motifs that have come out of the Helsinki School.[20]

I should also point out another path for further research: in the iconography, revenants are often diaphanous or white in color, whereas in the texts they are often black. This reversal might be explained by the desire to distinguish them from demons but does not correspond with ancient beliefs as expressed in the testimony of Tacitus, who said a Germanic people painted their bodies black and carried shields of the same color and spread terror by passing for an army of ghosts, *umbra feralis exercitus* (*Germania* 43). Black often remains the color of the otherworld in medieval romances, whether or not this otherworld is magical or deadly.

Since 1986 it has been possible to observe that these singular dead beings can be encountered everywhere, provided we know how to recognize them beneath their various disguises.[21] Some time ago I published the fruit of my discoveries for specialists, then devoted myself to the study of the transformation and mythization of revenants and phantoms. I was able to show evidence for how these dead beings remaining close to us had transformed into dwarves and elves[22]—a point confirmed and clarified by Régis Boyer[23]—and into earth spirits.[24] I was able to demonstrate that they had become nightmares and were closely tied to sorcery, to white and black magic. But the most important discovery undoubtedly resulted from the exploration of the notion of the multiple soul,[25] which allows us to explain the corporeal nature of the revenants, the fundamental opposition between them and intangible ghosts. What survives, and comes back, and manifests itself was clearly what the ancient Scandinavians called the *hamir* and what other people designate by the term *alter ego*. This hamir, in short, is the Double of the individual, something that brings us back to extremely widespread beliefs among the shamanic peoples and that, until now, could not be understood by those who restricted their search to the writings of the Roman world because it was impossible to read in strongly Christianized remnants.

The belief in the Double remains foreign to many researchers, the best example of which would be Claude Carozzi, who, in an otherwise excellent study of the journey into the beyond,[26] cites stories of the soul leaving the body in the form of an animal—bird, butterfly, or some other tiny creature—and notes the antiquity of the belief and the compound structure of humans (body, mind, soul). He speaks about a "kind of double," but he overlooks the fact that it involves a vestige of shamanism, a fact that enables resolution of the problems concerning the corporeal nature of revenants and that of the soul.[27] If the soul is wounded in the beyond,[28] this injury is transmitted to the body when the soul reenters it, just as the wound that has been inflicted upon the revenant can be found on it when its grave is opened. (See the story of Hrapp in chapter 5.)

I was criticized for not examining the Infernal Hunt, also known as Mesnie Hellequin, the band of revenants who makes an appearance on certain dates. This extremely complex subject merits its own detailed study, one on which I've been laboring for many years.[29] In 1986 my investigations had not advanced sufficiently to offer a pertinent analysis. At my disposal I had a body of texts—one that has grown nonstop since that time—and relatively ancient monographs based on false premises, as I was able to determine, which has created a good many errors.

Other critics, unfamiliar with the texts and ignorant of the research performed by scholars of northern Europe, could not grasp the mentality capable of producing all these stories about ghosts and revenants. In response to their objections, I translated and published a part of this corpus, leaving to the texts themselves the task of convincing the skeptics.[30] Some critics also expressed the wish that I would have examined other historical periods and civilizations, but interdisciplinarity has its limits. The medievalist works on a period spanning eight centuries and the texts from the entire medieval West. The vast range of reading and study from this broad time period and many places forbids incursions into areas that are not the medievalist's proper territory.

Others clearly saw the coherence of the complex; they carried water to my mill through constructive criticism and inspired further research in this subject area. I offer them my heartiest thanks for their interest and support. Finally, I want to underscore the fact that no study has emerged to invalidate my conclusions, which have been confirmed by the thesis of K. T. Nilssen.[31]

Additional Notes

Page 19: Among the magic formulas intended to keep a dead individual in his tomb and to protect him, this one was discovered on the rune stone of Gorlev (Denmark), dating from around 900 CE:

> *Thjodvi raised this stone for Odinkar*
> *F u Þ a r k n i a s t b l m r*
> *Enjoy your tomb!*
> *Þ m k i i i s s t t i i l l l*
> *I have arranged the runes as they should be.*
> *Gunni. Armund*

Another stone found in Ledberg, in Ostrogothia (Sweden), presents the formula in this form:

> *Þ m k : i i i: s s s : t t t: i i i: l l l*

This has been deciphered as: thistl (l), "thistle," mistil (l) "mistletoe," and kistil (l), "coffin," with no reason discovered for this grouping. The second line of the Gorlev inscription is nothing other than the runic alphabet. It is common knowledge that the people of an earlier time lent magic virtues to this alphabet, and Christians carved it on the steeples of churches.[32]

Pages 32–34: Putting shoes on the feet of the dead seems to have been more widespread than previously thought and not limited to Germany alone. Indeed, in the thirteenth century William Durand, bishop of Mende, notes in his *Rationale divinum officiorum* that many people "say that the dead must wear trousers and shoes with laces, thinking that thereby they will be ready for the Last Judgment."[33] At the end of that same century, shoes were given out to the poor on All Soul's Day.[34]

On the other hand, archaeology has unearthed numerous amulets in Celtic tombs, especially in those of Dürrnberg, near Hallein, which date from the Iron Age. Among them we find bronze shoes that scholars have classified as magic objects.[35] We can assume that these shoes occupied an important place in ancient beliefs and that medieval testimonies like that of William Durand are their final echo.

Pages 32–35: In her study on the shroud, Danièle Alexandre-Bidon reminds us that crosses, which were almost always Latin in the fourteenth and fifteenth centuries, were always tacked to the lengthwise seam of the shroud or else placed on the forehead or, in the early Middle Ages, on the chest. She thinks that these crosses were material records of the placement of the anointment and wonders about their role in the protection of the body.[36] In my opinion, the shroud, sanctified by the cross, possesses an apotropaic function. For the church, it was a matter of protecting the body from demonic incursions. We know in fact that one of the clerical explanations for revenants is the possession of the corpse by a devil that has slipped into and animated it. Furthermore, the individual crosses that sometimes appear on tombs lend themselves to the same analysis, as is noted by William Durand, bishop of Mende from 1285 until his death in Rome in 1296: "[T]he devil greatly dreads this sign and fears to approach the place that gleams with the sign of the cross." Yet we are able to make out another function of the cross: it prevents the deceased from leaving his grave. In this sense, the crosses on the shroud possess exactly the same virtues as iron needles.

Pages 67–68: The belief in the life of the dead in the tomb is confirmed clearly by a passage in the *Life of Saint Fridolin,* which had been inserted in the ancient *Vita* during the thirteenth century. The following events are supposed to have occurred during the sixth or seventh century.

The lands of Glaris (Switzerland) belonged to two brothers, Landolf and Urso. With the consent of his brother, the latter bequeathed his own lands to the cloister of Säckingen. Upon Urso's death, Landolf took back this donation. The abbot Fridolin took him before the court of Rankweil. The judges instructed him to present Urso before the court to give testimony about the gift.

Fridolin made his way to Urso's tomb and asked Urso to follow him. He took him by the hand and led him to Rankweil. Seeing Landolf, Urso said to him: "Alas, brother, why have you robbed my soul of what belonged to me?" Landolf returned the bequeathed properties, adding his own to them, and Fridolin brought Urso back to his tomb.[37]

This anecdote throws a stark light upon the mind-set of this time, and it confirms that the dead were still living and could return to ensure that justice was done. As for the universal faith and belief of the Christian laity in the posthumous presence or return of the dead, this seems incontestable. It is founded upon a tradition that the church barely adulterated.[38]

Page 163: There remains to be made a comparative study of the *fylgja* and the guardian angel, *fylgjuengill* in Norse (*fylgja* + *engill,* "angel"). This notion seems common to many peoples, and we can compare it to the description made by the writer of Armenian medieval traditions: "An angel assigned specifically to each individual human being. . . . When the time arrives for the life of his client to end, it is he who carries away his soul, along with his account book, for judgment. His most noteworthy role, therefore, is to take the soul, and it is at this moment that he appears as the angel of death."[39]

Page 206: The belief in revenants emerges clearly from a passage of *Erec and Enid* (verses 4854–78) by Chrétien de Troyes. When Erec comes out of his swoon in the Count of Limors's castle and flies to the aid of Enid, everyone draws away from him, believing that he is "the devil in person come among them. . . . They soon emptied the palace

with all saying, weak and strong alike: 'Flee! Flee! It is the dead man!'"
There is a striking similarity between this scene and a passage from
the *Historia Dunelmensis Ecclesiae* (III, 25) written between 1104 and
1109 by Simeon de Durham: A man named Eadulf living in the village
of Raeveneswurthe falls sick and dies one Saturday evening. The next
morning he is resurrected, causing all around him to flee in terror.[40]
The mental backdrop visible in both Chrétien's and Simeon's work is
the same: people believe that after death, it is possible to return to life.

In the *Romance of Perceforest,* the revenants that appear have been
given a very literary treatment, and magic is charged with explaining
their return:

> A knight encountered two other knights of the lineage of Dornant
> the Enchanter, slain by Gadiffer and the Tor. They and their horses
> had been dead for quite some time, yet "they seemed to have life."
> They held the maiden Olive in bondage. Once she had been deliv-
> ered by Gadiffer and the Tor, she cast a spell upon the bodies of the
> dead knights so that her liberators' victory would be remembered.[41]

By virtue of resorting to an enchantment, the belief is concealed
and the story veers into the fantastic, as Francis Dubost clearly
demonstrates.[42]

In Celtic literature, in addition to the text cited earlier (beginning on page 209), we find certain figures whose true status remains
unknown. This is the case in the Welsh *Peredur,* in which a knight
emerges from beneath a flat stone.[43] But in the *Triads of the Red Book*
in which all the marvels of Ireland are inventoried, several issues are
dedicated to the famous ghosts of the isle.[44]

Introduction

Cemeteries with broken grave stones and ruined chapels abandoned under the moonlight, shadow-infested old dwellings whose shutters groan in the wind and whose floors creak, ancient castles clinging to the tops of peaks, inns in the forest that were once the haunts of brigands, moors and marshlands covered in fog: these are the kinds of places where, customarily, we see apparitions of the dead, specters in bloody shrouds that are either speckled with dirt or dripping with seawater. For as long as humans have existed, they have spoken about the shades of the departed who return to trouble the living and create an atmosphere of anxiety and of terror—friendly and inoffensive ghosts remain a rarity. But does anyone recall that these deceased individuals once formed part of everyday life, that once upon a time, in a room in which animals and people sometimes lived together, a small light attached to a joist was left burning all night long? Does anyone remember that going out in the night to attend to a natural need amounted to exposing yourself to strange, often dangerous encounters? When someone saw a scattered flock, it was not rare to find the shepherd dead and a horrible sight: every bone in in the shepherd's body was broken; a revenant had torn him to pieces.

Language has several different terms at its disposal to designate these alarming dead, but these labels are generally viewed as synonymous, although the realities they address are different. Everyone knows *phantom*, which conjures the idea of illusion and phantasmagoria; *specter*, to which is attached a notion of fright or horror, the same inspired by the sniggering skeleton or decomposing cadaver; *shade*, which essentially reflects a poetic vocabulary and recalls the dissolution of the body into death; *spirit*, which remains vague and expresses human perplexity before inexplicable phenomena and is placed in the world of parapsychology—"spirit, are you there?" *Ectoplasm* is recent and serves to designate an immaterial form that escapes the body of an entranced medium. *Larva*, a name inherited from the Romans, is no longer used in its primary sense of referring to a deceased individual who has been denied eternal rest for one reason or another. *Revenant*, on the other hand, suggests immediately the return of a dead person. The term expresses a simple observation and does not refer to any illusion. If we establish a chronology of the use of these words, we can note a slow transition from reality—the dead person who comes back to life—to the ghost, the ectoplasm, the immaterial shape. The notion of the term *revenant* deteriorated over the course of the years and, leaving the realm of reality, entered that of spiritism. All the writings solidly confirm this phenomenon.

Literature, which has been telling us about apparitions for more than two thousand years, testifies in its own way to the evolution of mind-sets. When Sophocles describes the meeting of Clytemnestra and her late husband, when Homer narrates that of Penelope and her dead sister, when Aeschylus causes the specter of Argos to come out, and when Philostratus shows us Achilles leaving his grave and returning to it when the cock crows, we can see that the revenants and ghosts of antiquity are actors and not supernumeraries. They speak and act; they hand out both counsel and blame. This is how things proceed until the sixteenth century. Shakespeare depicts the ghost of Hamlet's father crying out for vengeance on a gun battlement at the Castle of Elsinore, and he shows us the terror that grips Macbeth at the sight of Banquo's specter.

Eventually, however, ghosts and revenants become simple literary motifs, such as the one in *The Canterville Ghost* by Oscar Wilde. They are soon transformed into movie figures, as in *Fantôme à vendre* (Ghost for Sale) by René Clair, for example, before becoming shudder-inspiring material in horror films, a mediocre exploitation of the fear they once inspired. The dead who have the misfortune to leave their graves have even been turned into figures of derision in ghost tours. Yet hiding behind their literary and other uses are age-old beliefs that have become lost in the depths of time. Writers such as Hans Christian Anderson and Charles Dickens, in *The Traveling Companion* and *A Christmas Carol,* respectively, knew how to use these beliefs for inspiration.

Modern literature is deceptive when it speaks of postmortem wanderings and hauntings. It has popularized the notion of the ghost at the expense of the revenant, and, using fantasy, it invites us to believe that our senses deceive us—a notion that may be reassuring but is merely a decoy. The revenants of olden days are not ectoplasm, three-dimensional images similar to holograms—those wonderful photos in relief. They are not diaphanous or nebulous shapes appearing at set times to repeat tirelessly the same gestures, travel the same routes, and produce the same noises always at the same place: at the scene of the crime, an accident, or an unusual death. The revenants of the distant past did not disappear at the simplest prayer, and they discouraged exorcists by not vanishing when confronted by the sign of the cross or the sting of holy water (for priests regarded them as diabolical apparitions). Protection was not to be found by tracing a circle around yourself with a sword, and when, at night, footsteps could be heard on the roof or the animals were becoming agitated in the stalls nearby, people hoped that the specter lurking in the vicinity would stay outside. The murderer was never safe and had to dread constantly the vengeance of his victim, the woman responsible for the death of a detested spouse could expect to find him waiting in her bed, and whoever failed to respect the last wish of a dying person exposed himself to the individual's future wrath.

Today, ghosts and revenants are clearly far from being well known—

and this is to be expected because historians began taking an interest in this subject only recently and because the ancient works, *Quatre Livres des Spectres* (Four Books of Specters), that Pierre Le Loyer published in Angers in 1587, are not reliable, do not have a scientific approach, and open the door to the irrational divagations that have contaminated many more recent works. The great studies on death, such as those of Pierre Ariès and Michel Vovelle, do not touch on this subject, whereas Edgar Morin has made several excellent obervations about it.[1] Serious information appears in the studies by Jacques Chiffoleau, Alain Groix, and Jean Delumeau,[2] but the two books that truly drew attention to the study of revenants are *Montaillou, village Occitan* (Montaillou, Occitan Village) by Emmanuel Le Roy Ladurie and *La naissance du Purgatoire* (The Birth of Purgatory) by Jacques Le Goff. *Montaillou* provides an important testimony of the popular belief in ghosts with whom we can communicate via a "specialist" intermediary called an *armier. La naissance du Purgatoire* shows the profound metamorphosis that revenants underwent in the eleventh and twelfth centuries. Purgatory serves as a prison for the dead, but they can manage to escape it in brief apparitions to the living, whose zeal to help them is nevertheless insufficient.[3] According to Christian belief, this space between the two worlds is the home of people who are neither completely good nor completely evil and who need suffrage: prayers and Masses in order to be able to attain Paradise. In the invention of purgatory there is the first logical explanation for the existence of revenants. Ghosts were then incorporated into the church and lost their pagan character.

Picking up where Jacques Le Goff left off and going deeper, Jean-Claude Schmitt saw this point clearly: during the eleventh and twelfth centuries, the dead were the stakes in an ideological struggle that aimed to replace the worship of the dead—which was of capital importance in pagan beliefs—with funeral rituals and adoration of the saints. The abrupt irruption of revenants and ghosts into the texts of the era is moreover connected with a modification of kinship relations.[4] Ancestor worship made way for the cult of saints, and the old revenants disappeared to the benefit of immaterial ghosts (the results of hallucinations and nightmares). Only the dead that manifested in good visions (i.e., those originating in God) had the right to be cited.

As we shall see, the source is extremely important. Toward which texts and which eras should we turn to retrace the history of revenants in order to present them in the form they were encountered by our ancestors?

Basing our research on Christian literature—*exempla*,* hagiographic legends, and narratives of visions—amounts to echoing the dominant culture that repudiated the dead escaping from their graves. These were academic traditions in which folk and pagan beliefs were by and large concealed by clerics working for the greater glory of God. Furthermore, clerical literature was a hybrid by virtue of how greatly it had been saturated by the reminiscences of classical antiquity. In fact, the writers who lined the invasion route into literature that revenants had taken are named St. Augustine, Gregory the Great, Peter Damian, and Peter the Elder.

There is equal danger in relying upon the popular entertainment literature written in the common tongue. The authors of the romances were men educated in monastic schools, and they were keen admirers of Christian culture and that of antiquity. This literature also experienced fashions; its purpose was to teach and to please (*prodesse et delectare*), not to transcribe reality.

It is tempting to refer to the vast collections of folktales, but do we have the right to project upon the past any data that was collected several centuries later? I do not think so—this would be making an interpretation in reverse. Folk traditions can and even should be exploited as soon as a chain of a typological or genetic order has connected them to facts that were confirmed long before. Folklore is in fact made up of the scattered limbs (*membra disjecta*) of a once coherent culture, as Michel Vovelle clearly sees.[5] Yet the sociocultural evolution of peoples

---

*The *exemplum* is a short narrative with edifying tendencies intended to illustrate the dangers of sin, for example.

alters information considerably. The development of knowledge transforms mind-sets ceaselessly, and inscribing revenants into the culture
that welcomed them obliges us to refuse nothing of what accompanied
them in time and society—in short, in history.

The Middle Ages as a period for exploration of revenants is the obvious choice. We must grasp the phenomenon of revenants as far back in
time as possible, before its mutations and transformation due, essentially,
to the intervention of the church. As it happens, not all the countries
of the medieval West developed at the same pace—there can be a two-
century gap between the north and the south—and not all of them offer
equal historical richness of ghosts and revenants. For example, from the
eleventh century on in France, though the church adulterated the roam-
ing dead except in rural regions, where we can see some notable resistance,
its grip was not total over certain regions whose historical development
was behind that of southern Europe. These areas long remained islands
of pagan culture—such as the Germanic countries—characterized by the
coexistence of Christianity and paganism.

Among these countries, Iceland merits full attention because of its
obvious insularity from the world. Revenants were fully at home there,
and the local writers had much to say about them. Although written in the twelfth and thirteenth centuries, the Norse texts known as
Islendingasögur (*The Sagas of the Icelanders*) relate actual events that
occurred some two or three centuries earlier. These sagas often take on
the appearance of regional or family chronicles, and they form a veritable
treasury of historical, cultural, and geographical remnants. The historic
value of the sagas has been fuel for much discussion, and the subject is still
controversial. Régis Boyer summarizes the problem of their historicity.

> We have obtained absolute certainty about what it [the saga] is not:
> a historical work, the faithful depositing of immemorial oral tradi-
> tions, a moral tale, or just some fragment of a prose epic. . . . It can
> accede to authentic oral traditions, easily base itself upon skaldic
> strophes that are older than it by sometimes several centuries, pos-

sibly even abandon itself to a surprising blend of heterogeneous elements drawn from every available source, to offer us these linear narratives that are sober to the point of dryness. . . . At the same time, it translates a vision of the world, life, and man that in the final analysis gives it its rigorous originality.[6]

The *Sagas of the Icelanders* therefore contains a kernel of truth upon which its narrators embroider. Reality and fiction intermingle—then, over the course of time, fiction takes an increasingly important part. While history is visible in the framework of the family or the clan, the sagas nonetheless contain no shortage of details touching upon everyday life, beliefs, and customs—and therefore upon revenants. They are literary testimonies, to be sure, but the image they provide of Icelandic society is simultaneously the expression, reflection, and sublimation of the real society, a mirror that changes more or less in accordance with the ends and desires—conscious or unconscious—of the authors. The second mine of information, *Lándnámabók* (*The Book of Settlements*),[7] is an invaluable tool because its information duplicates that of the sagas on more than one occasion. It relates the establishment of the first colonists on the island and the history of their descendants and sometimes provides lists of genealogies and place-names, but its dry erudition is scattered with lively anecdotes that throw a keen and penetrating light upon the concerns of the people of that time. Of the five versions we possess, I have used *Sturlubók* (the Book of Sturla), by Sturla Thordarson (1214–1284), and *Hauksbók* (the Book of Haukr), by Haukr Erlendsson, who died in 1334. These two writers drew their material from older manuscripts that are now lost.

Alas, the other countries of the Germanic language do not possess these teeming riches. Christian since the seventh century, England's ancient literature is practically devoid of revenants. By chance there are several texts in Latin that reveal their existence, at least in folk traditions. Also remaining is the language of Old English, which bears testimony in the form of glosses in the margins or between the lines of texts of classical antiquity. Here we can find the names of ghosts and revenants slowly incorporated into demons.

In the lands of the German tongue, the same phenomenon occurs: There appears not a single revenant that can be used in a scientific study before the *Dialogus miraculorum,*[8] completed between 1219 and 1223 by Caesarius, prior of the Cistercian monastery of Heisterbach, near Königswinter. Although this work—a collection of exempla—is based on written and scholarly sources (Gregory the Great's *Dialogi* and the *Liber miraculorum atque visionum* by Herbert of Clairvaux, for example), here we can find oral traditions that, though surely distorted, offer us references that are suitable for comparative study. Furthermore, the educated individuals and scholars of these countries have bequeathed an extraordinary corpus of glosses—close to four thousand pages of Latin lemma of every provenance translated into Old High German—which makes it possible to establish, in connection with the other information collected, the reality of the belief in revenants.[9] Linguistic implements form part of the mental and intellectual toolkit of a people; language reflects ideas and beliefs and is therefore an excellent means of uncovering many secrets when texts are lacking. In order to better perceive the historical reality of the fabrication, I used, whenever possible, the ancient juridical texts—laws of the early Middle Ages, the Norwegian laws of Gulathing, German communal laws, minutes of trials collected in the chronicles— and archaeological discoveries.* Alone, these specific sources reveal little, but when added to the other data, they become creditable.

I thus decided to study revenants in the Germanic countries during the period from the tenth to the thirteenth centuries. After 1300 came the time of the epigones, so that before this time, in the north at least, there was an era of transition between—let's say cohabitation of—paganism and Christianity, and the coherence of the non-Christian culture was still distinguishable. This focus does not prevent me from turning to Romanesque literature when it offers something of interest.

---

*The orthography of proper names in the Norse texts has been simplified in the body of the paper, not in the citations.

We are therefore going to descend into the world of shadow in an attempt to find answers to the five questions raised by the texts: Who comes back to this world? When? Where? How? Why? Simple in appearance, these interrogations compel us to examine the problems of the beyond without losing sight of our primary objective. We will then discover a mental world in which revenants are flesh and blood beings that speak and act as the living do. I shall not turn to the resources of psychoanalysis to advance a modern explanation for the phenomenon. This would be a violation of the spirit of the texts and a misunderstanding of the people of the Middle Ages through whose eyes I have chosen to look at ghosts and revenants.

It may seem odd to study the reality of such phenomena when they are so disparaged today and have retreated so much before the influence of the Enlightenment and the advent of reason. Industrialization dealt them a fatal blow by shattering the old familial structures and uprooting individuals, transporting them to urban environments. Until the nineteenth century, revenants could overlook the proscriptions that have struck them recently. So as not to seem ridiculous and to avoid being taken for naïfs or fools, people kept their mouths shut and their memories clouded. Oral transmission entered its death agony, and the thread was broken. A chapter of history sank into the shadows. This book seeks to dissipate those shadows by letting the people of a bygone age speak for themselves again.

PART ONE

ONE

The Fear of the Dead and the Dread of Revenants

Askeleton armed with a scythe, a hunter tending his snares, an old deformed woman, an angel: death advances on muffled steps to carry off its victim. The sudden, unforeseen, and unexpected death causes anxiety and raises questions. It is a source of anguish when it is accidental because it testifies to the irritation of the gods and takes on a religious meaning. Death by homicide caused revulsion, especially in the Germanic countries, where murder struck the sacred that all individuals carried inside. To fade away at the end of a long life is a blessing from the gods; to die prematurely is a curse.

The belief in revenants and ghosts possesses two roots: the fear of the departed and the stupefaction caused by any abnormal death. These two points are practically inseparable, but in order to appreciate the apparitions clearly, to grasp their originality, and to distinguish in them what comes from folk beliefs and what is superimposed foreign contribution, we need to have a very precise reference point. Roman civilization provides us with one.

This choice is not arbitrary. The influence of Roman institutions and religion upon the Middle Ages is well known, as is the role they played in the formation of Western thought. Through its literature, its military occupation, and the fathers of the church, Rome has left behind a considerable legacy. Passed on by the "founders of the Middle Ages" (perhaps primarily Isidore of Seville, who died in 663 and who was the final scholar of the ancient world and the first Christian encyclopedist),[1] Roman traditions mixed with autochthonous beliefs, either altering or erasing them. The church, tributary of the Roman world, also contributed to spreading the superstitions of Roman pagans, if only in order to fight them. Furthermore, for everything related to the dead, the traditions of ancient Rome offer curious similarities to the stories I collected and bolster these stories' authenticity. Yet the revenant who wanders beneath the blue sky of the Mediterranean world cannot be identical in every point to the one who haunts the mists of the North.

Rome's Example

In Rome,[2] the deceased were regarded as impure and dangerous; it was therefore necessary to gain the good graces of the dead, if not they would commit more than one misdeed. The deceased were believed to be the cause of epidemics and cases of madness and possession, which are described by the word *larvaetus,* "possessed by a larva"—in other words, being possessed by a dead person who committed a crime or departed this life under peculiar circumstances. Among the living, the dead were held responsible for epilepsy, chorea or St. Guy's Dance, apoplexy, and female sterility. If the propitiatory rites were neglected, the dead would seek revenge. One day, Ovid tells us, the worship of the dead fell out of fashion, but this had such dreadful consequences that the Romans reestablished it and once again celebrated the feasts of the ancestors (*parentalia, dies parentales*).[3]

If the dead were thought to have so much power, it is because they continued to live within their tombs. This belief has been confirmed in Rome and for a great many other peoples.[4] Evidence for this is provided by certain customs. At the end of the funeral ceremony, the living wished the deceased, "Take good care of yourself!" and then added, "May the earth be light upon you," even if the body had been cremated. The soul was called three times by the name it had borne in life. This triple repetition was like an exorcism; undoubtedly, it was meant to ward off the return of the deceased.

If we can place our faith in Roman law, the soul (*anima, animus, umbra, imago, inanis imago*) did not immediately leave the body it inhabited. The estate of the deceased could not be liquidated before the completion of some extremely complex funeral rites. Among these, the time of mourning (*tempus lugendi*) had to be over and the sacrifice of the ninth day (*novemdiale*) had to be performed near the tomb (*apud tumulum*). The widow or widower was forbidden to remarry before the end of the mourning period without any connection to the actual time of viduity. If the rights of the deceased were not respected, he or she, being outraged, injured, or dissatisfied, could return to trouble the living.

Are all the dead dreadful? No, there are only certain categories that present any danger. The ranks of these are called "the evil dead." Members of this group were those who have perished in violent deaths—murder, execution (with the exclusion of soldiers who fell in battle), suicide, premature death (*immature*)—that is, before the day fixed by fate for death. Also included were the deceased who left with no sepulcher (*insepulti*), for example drowning victims.[5]

The *insepulti*, sometimes called "those for whom no one has wept" (*indeplorati*), formed the bulk of the troop of revenants and ghosts. We must note straight off that it is easy to earn a place in their ranks because all individuals who had not received the ritual burial—the constraining ceremony that was not comparable to the simple burial of the corpse—were potential revenants. They did not reach the hells, and, dissatisfied with their fate, they did all they could to obtain reparation for the prejudice they suffered. The following story, reported by Pliny the Younger (ca. 62–114 CE), provides proof. Pliny states that he was convinced of the veracity of this anecdote.

There was a haunted house in Athens that was rented by the philosopher Athenodorus. He saw a specter wearing manacles on its feet (*compedes*) and wrists (*catenae*), and the specter beckoned him [Athenodorus] to follow him into the courtyard, where he disappeared. The philosopher got authorization to excavate this location. A chained skeleton was unearthed and given a public funeral ceremony. The apparitions then ceased.[6]

Criminals had no right to a ritual burial. Their bodies were tossed upon Esquiline Field, where, as Horace tells us, the witches would go at sunset to collect ingredients for their potions—fragments of bone, hunks of flesh*—digging through the ground with their fingernails. Victims of execution remained displayed on the Gemonian Stairs before being cast into the Tiber. The *Book of Pontiffs* forbids suicides the right of being buried in accordance with the rites, and Tarquin Superb delivered to the executioner the bodies of Roman citizens who killed themselves rather than work on the construction of a public sewer. We should note in passing that the act of suicide could be an act of revenge; the ghost returned to persecute the individual who drove him to take his life, most often an abusive lender.

Murder victims were buried, quite often at the site of their deaths, but they joined the host of revenants because, according to general opinion, the hells were shut to them. Joining them in this indefinite realm between our world and the beyond were the victims of accidental death because Roman belief regarded them as victims of the hostility of invisible forces. This was all too obvious for those killed by lightning, a motif that was picked up by medieval Christian literature, which applied it to tyrants.

---

*Horace (*Satires*, I, 8) paints a gripping portrait of the witches Canidie and Sagana digging through the dirt with their fingernails. Apulieus provides a complete catalog of the materials used by witches: "metal strips inscribed in unknown languages, fragments of sunken ships, countless pieces of corpses that had already been mourned or even buried. Noses and fingers were collected here while over there were nails from gibbets to which morsels of flesh yet clung, in another place the blood of murder victims was kept . . ." (*The Golden Ass or The Metamorphoses*, III, 17).

The dead could also be punished. Mutilation of the corpse formed a barrier to ritual burial* based on the widespread opinion that the state of the soul depends on that of the body. In times of antiquity, it was believed that it was necessary to die with physical integrity. Otherwise an individual could not live properly in the otherworld.[7] For this reason, several ancient peoples practiced the euthanasia of the elderly as a veritable act of filial piety. It was no rarity in the Middle Ages to witness the condemnation and execution of the dead. In 897, the cadaver of Pope Formosus was exhumed, held on trial, then condemned, whereupon his remains were thrown into the Tiber.

In Rome, the evil dead, especially criminals, were excluded from the city of the deceased and expelled from every religious and even familial community. Their busts did not appear in the atrium of the home (*domus*), their names were never uttered, and their memories were blackened (*damnatio memoriae*). For both city and family, it was as though the criminal never lived.

Therefore, a potentially vast number of revenants and ghosts existed: the deceased who sought vengeance or someone to avenge them or that aspired to ritual burial. They were discontented and envious—therefore, evildoing dead. These beliefs can be found among all Indo-European peoples. An abnormal death was evidence of ghosts who would return to wander as apparitions. It was therefore necessary for the deceased to rest in peace if the living wished to avoid having the dead become larvae. Introducing an undesirable guest into a dead person's tomb amounted to annoying him. The Roman who left could forbid the burial of other family members by his side. Also having potential to disturb the peace of

---

*This mutilation was sometimes performed when a debtor died with his debts still outstanding. According to Roman law, the creditor could throw the corpse to the dogs or leave it for the birds or even, if we can trust the word of Aulus Gellius (*Attic Nights*, XX, I, 47), cut it into pieces (*secare partes*), which amounted to punishing the deceased by refusing to bury the body. Seen as overly cruel, the law was changed on this point.

It is curious to note that Germanic laws left the condemned "to the beasts and crows" and to see that the Norwegian laws of Guluthing also authorized mutilation of the debtor.

the dead were magic ceremonies performed upon the dead's final resting place or in its immediate proximity as well as immoral acts performed by young libertines.* Curses and spells of execration decorated funeral monuments. These were intended to prevent acts of sacrilege—violations of the sepulcher, for example—and threatened the potential guilty parties with vengeance or—even worse—with becoming specters themselves.[8] How could individuals protect themselves from revenants? First, they could provide the deceased with a ritual burial, a difficult feat when the body was not available. The Romans erected cenotaphs, empty tombs that could procure peace for some insepulti.

But isn't this the same attitude that can be seen today—in Brittany, for example—in the cases of those who have been lost at sea? In 1958 the *proella* was celebrated in Ouessant for a young priest who drowned attempting to save a child and whose body had not been recovered. Here is how the newspaper *Le Télégramme de Brest* recounted this simulacrum of a funeral.

A white wax cross, the Christian sign and symbol for the deceased, was placed on a white linen-covered table at the drowned man's home. A small cross lay upon a cap. Two lit candles framed the cross. In front of it was a plate holding a branch of boxwood that had been dipped in holy water. When evening fell, the funeral vigil began.

The next day, preceded by the cross, the clergy arrived as they would have for the traditional raising of the body. The godfather respectfully carried the little wax cross still resting on the cap that served as a shroud. Behind him followed family and friends of the deceased.

The funeral procession made its way slowly to the church. The little cross was slid upon the catafalque and the burial service was celebrated. At the end of the service, the priest placed the wax cross in a wooden chest placed on the altar of the departed in the transept. The ceremony was over.[9]

---

*Petronious (*Satyricon*, LXXI) indicates that Trimalchio wished for one of his freedmen to guard his tomb "so that the public would not use it as a toilet."

Jean Delumeau cites this text and says: "It has long been thought, especially in all the shore regions, that those who died at sea continued to wander amid the waves and near the reefs for want of receiving a burial. . . . It was commonly believed that those who perished at sea were condemned to wander as long as the church neglected to pray for them."

If, after similar measures, it was possible to reduce the number of potential revenants, the living still needed protection against the return of the departed who entered houses once a year. The Romans were powerless to prevent their entrance on the unlucky days of the Lemuralia—May 9, 11, and 13—when they were supported by the gods: Forculus, guardian of doors, and Limentius, attendant of the threshold, seconded by Limentina as well as Forcula [or Cardea], the goddess of hinges.* The *pater familias,* the priest of the domestic altar, then had to ward off their invasion with specific rites. Barefoot, he would walk through the house tossing black beans, beating on a bronze vessel, and reciting an incantation nine times—three times three. What role do beans and bronze play here? It was popularly believed that the spirit of the dead was able to enter beans and therefore possess the person who ate them; bronze, meanwhile, is reputed to give off a sound the spirits cannot tolerate.†

Other measures were added to these rites because the dead made up a formidable mob. In midwinter, the traditional season of the dead, the feast of crossroads (*compitalia*) was celebrated in honor of Hecate or the genies of these locations (*lares compitales*), which gave the ceremony the name of Laralia. At these crossroads, the pater familias hung from the trees woolen dolls (*maniae*) or bark masks (*oscilla*) representing family members, and he asked the spirits of darkness to accept these substitutes for the people they represented.

This ritual did not vanish with the fall of ancient Rome, and there is strong evidence of its continued existence during the Middle Ages

---

*We should recall that in Greece the dead had free rein, so to speak, during the three days of the Anthesteria, the feasts celebrating the end of winter.

†During the Middle Ages it was iron that caused spirits to flee.

because humans have always lent a supernatural character to crossroads (*bivium, trivium, compitalis*). They belong to the dead first, then
to witches. "You shall swear no oaths nor light any torches in these
places," proclaimed Césaire d'Arles (ca. 542), Martin de Braga (ca.
580), a sermon of the Pseudo-Eligius of Noyon (eighth century), and
a twelfth-century homily.[10] In a Carolingian capitulary—*Capitula sub
Carolo Magno,* written around 744—it is stated explicitly that "you
shall make no binding, nor incantations upon bread, the herbs that
you would hide in the trees by the crossings of two or three paths";[11]
Pirman (ca. 753), founder of the Benedictine abbey of Richenau in
Lake Constance, states clearly that at the crossroads idols were not to
be placed to be worshipped nor were oaths to be sworn to them.[12] The
penitential known under the name of *Excarpsus Cummeani* (eighth century) established a link between divination (*haruspices*) and crossroads,
adding that such practices were sacrilegious.[13] These several examples
are intended to prove the persistence of ancient beliefs and the similarity of the mind-set of the people of the early Middle Ages and that of
the people of classical antiquity. Finally, the notion of the crossroads as
a malefic space still exists today, as is shown by the erection on these
sites of numerous crosses or niches housing statues of saints.

Preventive measures were combined with other practices—in this
instance, magical ones. Amulets, incantations, or exorcism spells carved
on wood or lead or drawn on parchment and called *characters* offered
protection from ghosts and revenants. At least, this was the claim of the
lapidaries from antiquity who, through scholarly literature, were known
to the minds of the people of the Middle Ages. On more than one occasion, they bolstered certain folk traditions. This was how jasper and dia-
mond, coral and *obsyonthe,* the thunder-stone (*ceraunius*) and chrysolite
provided protection from ghosts and night terrors, shades and visions.[14]

One detail to retain from our foray into Rome: the dead could
return and take action when the form of their deaths or the behavior of
the living did not please them. The bulk of the information collected
from Germanic sources is often barely changed from Roman belief.

Germany: The Archaeological Data

There can be no doubt that fear of the dead was more prevalent than honoring the dead. Additionally, seeking to earn their favor and good graces by satisfying their wishes finds ample supporting evidence in archaeology[15] and the reading of the old texts.

In northern Germany, the first traces of burial are found in the transitional period between the Paleolithic and Neolithic Ages. Mutilated skeletons have been discovered in mounds of domestic detritus: On the Jutland peninsula, a skull broken in several pieces has been found in Aamölle, and another in the same condition and placed at the height of the pelvis was discovered in Ertebölle.[16] In other Germanic burial sites unearthed in France, researchers have exhumed dead who were more or less folded up, with the knees and arms pressed tightly against the chest, which gives the impression that they were bound before burial. In primitive civilizations, this was a well-known custom to prevent the dead from leaving their tombs. Whether or not this was the reason for their binding, the fact that the corpses were not just abandoned implies a belief in their survival,[17] and the mutilation of the bodies clearly attests to the fear they inspired.

Megalithic tombs appeared in northern Europe between 2500 and 2000 BCE. In German and Danish they bear the name "giants' tombs" (*Hünengräber* and *jaettestuer,* respectively). This appellation establishes a link, also found in folktales and legends, between megaliths and giants. To the medieval mind, only giants, reputed to be the first inhabitants of the world, could have been capable of erecting such monuments. The gifts and funerary furnishings in these tombs imply the belief in another life. Further, these megaliths are both individual and collective: the dead are either seated or lying in them with tools, weapons, and food. It was undoubtedly believed that the dead led a life in the tomb or in the empire of darkness similar to the one they had known in our world.

Other funerary customs—burial beneath a mound, a custom that became widespread during the Bronze Age, and cremation—give us hardly any information. It was thought that the purpose of cremation of the corpse was to prevent return, but the prevailing opinion currently is that it was a purification intended to facilitate the passage of the deceased into the beyond. Death is in fact a rite of passage whose primordial roots still survive in the word *departed* or in the viatic word (*viaticum*) used to designate Extreme Unction.

Burial and cremation coexisted for a long time, but since the end of the Iron Age, toward the eighth and ninth centuries BCE—we must remember that these ages did not coincide in the north and south (the northern region was noticeably behind)—the dead were regularly interred beneath a tumulus or a mound. These mounds were solid: earth and good-size stones were piled on top of a wooden chamber framed by standing stones, as if it was necessary to prevent someone from leaving.

If all we had were these archaeological testimonies, the fear of the dead would amount to a hypothesis, and for confirmation of it, we would have to turn to the primitive customs revealed to us by ethnology and anthropology—the preburial removal of flesh, for example, in which all the soft parts of the body were discarded and only the bones were interred.* But there are texts from the eighth and ninth centuries that confirm what archaeology allows us to presume.

Proof of the Terror Inspired by the Dead

We possess extremely diverse testimonies from the Early Middle Ages to the nineteenth century proving that fear of the dead was no fancy. Even earlier, Tacitus left us an interesting observation about the mores of the Germans: "[T]he coward, the unwarlike, the man stained with abominable vices, is plunged into the mire of the morass with a hurdle put over

---

*As practiced in the fifteenth century, removal of the flesh essentially was used to facilitate the transport of cadavers. The bodies of Edward of York and the Count of Suffolk, slain at Agincourt, and that of Henri V, were dealt with in this manner, although in 1299 and 1300 Pope Boniface III had forbidden the custom. His successors granted the necessary dispensations.

*Suicide is a proof of postmortem wandering. The dead individual has no grounds for being content with his or her fate. (*Poetic and Philosophical Codex, Folio No. 2, Stuttgart, folio 65 r°, 1467)

him."[18] Discoveries made in Scandinavian peat bogs have revealed bodies covered with branches, logs, or stones. Sometimes the bodies were in a kneeling position, sometimes they were upside down or their heads had been slit, sometimes their limbs were bound. The hurdle mentioned by Tacitus corresponds to the net that the pagan Alamans threw over graves or to the branches or brambles that were arranged on top of the criminals who had been buried alive in a mud-filled ditch that had been dug beneath the gibbet. Thirteenth-century Norman law, still fairly permeated by Germanic traditions, called this form of execution the *bèche* [spade] from the medio-Latin *becca*. The last known execution of this manner took place in Coutances in 1447. It seems that burying criminals alive was practiced in other locales besides Normandy. In 1295 Marie de Romainville, suspected of theft, was, in Anteuil, "solemnly buried beneath the forks of Auteul.*

Not only criminals but also suicides inspired fear. During the fifteenth century, the communal laws of Riga (Latvia) stipulated the binding of their bodies in the grave. Those of Rügen (on the Baltic Sea) recommended placing three stones on the cadaver when it was buried—one on the head, one on the torso, and one on the feet. In northern Germany the corpse was burned, in southern Germany it was abandoned in a river, in the province of Holstein a harrow was placed with the sharp points down on top of the graves of suicides.[19] Suicides were sometimes buried where they were found, which compelled certain precautionary measures: "Near Wildegg in Argovia (Swiss Canton), a hunter hanged himself from a pear tree. He was buried at the foot of the tree, and none that passed by neglected to cast a stone on top of his tomb to forestall his return."†

Decapitating the corpse of an enemy was a custom that was confirmed early on among the Salian Franks, who impaled the human remains upon a stake. It was believed that if deprived of his head, the dead person could not seek vengeance. A judgment delivered in Lower Saxony in 1570 curiously attests to the same mind-set: When the relatives of a victim seize a murderer, they should bring him to a crossroads, turn his head toward the east, cover it with a straw sack, and decapitate him. Next, they should plant a bark-covered staff topped with a penny and bring the head back to the court.‡

---

*See A. Micha, *Étude sur le Merlin de Robert de Boron* (Geneva: Droz, 1980), 113. This mode of execution was reserved for women; no doubt out of respect for decency as hanging them upon forks risked exposing their anatomy to the eyes of onlookers.

†R. His, *Der Totenglaube in der Geschichte des germanischen Rechts* (Munster: 1929), 8. At the beginning of the twentieth century, Bernhard Kalhe visited Iceland and he saw a cairn. His guide invited him to add a stone to it, explaining that the bishop, Gwendur, had banished a revenant there some six hundred years before.

‡Ibid., 6. The purpose of the sack was to neutralize the evil eye. In the *Laxdaela Saga* (chapter 38), Stigandi is captured and his head is covered with a sack, but there are holes in it and he can cast his gaze at a nearby slope. Never again would any grass grow there. Stigandi was then stoned to death and buried beneath a cairn. In the *Saga of Gisli Sursson* (chapter 19) the sorcerer Thorgrim Nef is dealt with in the same manner.

Beliefs such as these remained rooted deeply in the folk soul:

- In the eighteenth century, the von Wollschlaägers, a family of Prussian squires, met in council to make a decision about a deceased family member regarded as a vampire. It should be noted that in Prussia it was customary for peasants to disinter cadavers that were suspect because the dirt in their graves did not sink in, to decapitate them, and then to place the head between the feet of the corpse.
- The body of a tramp was found in 1901 near Iéna in Lichtenstein. His body was stored in the garage with fire engines, where, the next morning, he was discovered entirely tied up. Young villagers stated they had done so "to drive out of him once and for all the desire to wander."

Vlad Dracula dining among his executed victims.
(Strasbourg: Mathias Hupfuff, 1500)

- In 1913, an old woman died in a village of the canton of Putzig (Prussia). The deaths of seven family members followed soon after, and it was declared that the deceased had not found rest and was drawing her relatives to her. Feeling himself going into a decline, one of the old woman's sons asked for advice from those around him. He was told to exhume the cadaver, decapitate it, and place the head between the feet. He followed this advice, and shortly afterward he said he was feeling much better.[20]

Similar stories are told almost everywhere throughout Europe:

- In the village of Amarasti, in the north of Dolj (Romania), the sons of a dead woman cut their mother in two because she was haunting the region. When the body was exhumed a second time, it was noted that the corpse was intact!
- In 1801 the bishop of Siges asked Alexander Moruzi, prince of Valachia, to prevent the peasants of Stoesti from constantly disinterring their dead to verify if they had transformed into vampires (*strigoi*).*

All these testimonies show how pertinent it is to explore the mutilation of the dead and certain archaeological data, which concern preventive and atropaic measures. Once decapitated, the dead were no longer able to act—or so it was believed—and when the head was placed at the feet of the corpse or beneath its pelvis or between

---

*Cited from Ralf-Peter Märtin, *Dracula, das Leben des Fürsten Vlad Tepes* (Berlin: Wagenbach Klaus GmBH, 1980), 163. The first story adds: "They then took the body into the forest and deposited it beneath a tree after having cut out the heart, from which blood still flowed, cut it into four pieces, then burned it. They next mixed the ashes with water and gave it to children to drink. The cadaver was cremated and the ashes buried. The deaths stopped."

Valachia abuts the southern end of Transylvania, where Bram Stoker brought back to life Vlad III Tepes Draculeo (ca. 1431–1477), nicknamed the Impaler, as the character Dracula.

its legs, the dead individual could not grab it and put it back on his shoulders. If he was bound, he was no longer capable of moving about. If he was buried beneath a pile of stones, he would be a prisoner of his tomb. Yet all these precautions were quite illusory, as we shall see.

The Persistance and Survival of the Traditions

Up to now, as we have just seen, only certain kinds of dead were truly dreadful. By and large, they are always the same as the dead we encountered in Rome; mind-sets had hardly changed in this regard. A Polish ethnologist, L. Stomma, analyzed five hundred cases of dead people who became revenants. Working on documents from the second half of the nineteenth century, he drew up the following table.[21]

Dead	Number of Cases	Percentage
Dead fetuses	38	7.6
Abortions	55	11
Unbaptized children	90	18
Women who died in labor	10	2
Women who died after giving birth but before they rose from the same bed	14	2.8
Fiancées who died right before the wedding	14	2.8
Spouses who died on their wedding day	40	8
Suicides	43	8.6
Victims of hanging	38	7.6
Drowning victims	101	20.2
Those dying violent or unnatural deaths	15	3
Other cases	42	8.4
Total	500	100

After examining this table, Jean Delumeau observes: "There must have been a link between revenants and the tragic failure of a rite of passage." Added to what we know from the Romans, L. Stomma's investigation clearly establishes the definite relationship between a flawed death and the impossibility of reaching the beyond. These dead were "blocked" in what Emmanuel Le Roy Ladurie has named an "airlock."

It is obvious that it is not viable to project Jean Delumeau's conclusions regarding the past without noting the differences between the past and more recent times. By the nineteenth century, the notion of ritual burial had disappeared—but it seems it had been replaced by the Christian cemetery as well as by ancestor worship, whose last traces in Christianity can be found in All Souls' Day and the Feast of the Dead.* Medieval humans were certainly aware that death was a passage, a departure, and that the duty of the living was to help the deceased reach the beyond. This can be deduced from the ubiquitous presence of Our Lady of the Good Death, a transparent expression of the fear inspired by an unusual death, and the *Arts of Dying Well,* which flourished during the early Middle Ages. Folk beliefs provide us with another argument, often a weakened echo of paganism that has been altered in accordance with the law of ecotypes.† If someone on his or her deathbed failed truly to die, these beliefs dictated that it was necessary to move the table or turn over or even remove a roof tile. Another tradition recommended opening the windows, plugging up everything that was hollow in the house, and turning all hollow objects upside down in order that the soul may leave freely and not linger anywhere. Finally, peace could be brought to the dead by tossing three clumps of dirt on their grave.[22]

---

*The entire liturgical triduum overlays in fact the ancient worship of the ancestors.
†Themes and motifs and thoughts and concepts change as a consequence of historical evolution, the civilization that welcomes them in, and the time. This law of ecotypes takes into account evolution, the permanent adaptation of mind-sets, and legends. The absence of any development in this area indicates that the point being examined is a vestige, a fossil, a dead tradition that no longer corresponds to reality.

A good death is a guarantee of posthumous rest.
(Savonarola, Predica del arte del bene morire, *Florence, 1495)*

Requiescat in pace [Rest in Peace] is no empty phrase or rhetorical flourish; this oath is fraught with meaning. It is in fact a conjuration proving that the thread holding the human being to his former life is hard to break, especially during the weeks immediately following the death. It was believed that if a woman died in labor, wood from an almond tree or a book should be put in her bed. It was necessary to unmake the bed entirely then remake it, otherwise she would not be able to rest peacefully before a span of six weeks. In lieu of this, it was said that her bowl should be rinsed thoroughly to keep her from coming back. If the linens of a dead person were not washed quickly, he or she would not find rest. Further, it was believed that a woman who died before leaving the bed in which she gave birth should be given scissors, needle, and thread to prevent her from coming back in search of them.[23] What survives in all these prescriptions is the idea that the deceased would complete their labors in the next world. We should also note the role played by water, which appears to provide a natural obstacle to unwanted returns.

It was believed that the dead retained their nature and feelings—at least this is what we can deduce from the following story reported by Caesarius of Heisterbach.

There were two peasant families that lived in the bishopric of Cologne and that detested each other more than anything else. Each had a leader, a man who was haughty and proud and eager to ignite hostilities and fan hatreds, a man who prevented all attempts to bring about any reconciliation between the two families. Divine will ordained that both men died upon the same day. As both were members of the Neunkirchen parish, their bodies were placed in the same grave, because God wished them to serve as an example of the dangers of discord.

What next befell was a great wonder and a thing unheard of: in the presence of all, the two corpses turned their backs upon each other and struck each other with their heads, their backs, and their heels with such violence that one could have said they were two bad horses that had never been tamed.

Subsequently, one of them was pulled from the grave and buried in another tomb, a little farther away.[24]

The references to divine will should not cause us to cling to any illusions. Caesarius is writing an exemplum whose intention is obvious.

Nonetheless, he is referring to folk traditions whose trace can be found in a story from the nineteenth century that relates the following anecdote.

> In Eutin (Schleswig-Holstein) there lived two priests who could barely stand one another and were always quarreling. After both had died, they were often seen at night, clad in long white habits, leaving their graves and hurling themselves upon each other, exchanging blows in a terrible brawl. The dogs would then begin to howl and such a din was caused that nobody could sleep. At one o'clock, each priest returned to his tomb. This went on for many nights.[25]

It was undoubtedly to prevent similar manifestations that the Germanic peoples developed such exact and restrictive funeral rites.

TWO

The Funeral Rites

We need only lend an ear to hear what the Scandinavian sagas have to say about the dead and rites and the beliefs surrounding them. This, then, makes it possible to retrace the final path that we travel.

The Deceased

Death is omnipresent and comes in many forms that are often violent or strange. The narrators speak little about what triggered the illness; it is simply indicated in one sentence: "I was never bedridden in my life, says the man, and I believe I will not be getting back up."[1] This presentment always proves to be exactly true.

Death strikes the sailors who are driven upon the reefs by storms. "Next morning Thorodd and his men put out from Nes with their dried fish, and they were all drowned off Enni," says the *Saga of Snorri the Godi*.[2] Odd events are sometimes announced.

That same autumn Thorstein went to Hoskuld Island to fetch provisions. One evening in the autumn, as Thorstein's shepherd was tending sheep north of Helga Fell, he saw the whole north die as the mountain opened up, with great fires burning inside it and the noise of clamour and feasting over the ale-horns. As he strained to catch particular words, he was able to make out that Thorstein Cod-Biter and his crew were being welcomed into the mountain. . . . In the morning some men brought news from Hoskuld Island that Thorstein Cod-Biter had been drowned on a fishing trip.[3]

Death could strike at a bend in the road: An adversary might have loomed up from a grove or valley or from behind a hill, armed with a stake, an ax, a sword, or a bow. Woe to he who had a sore quarrel with his neighbors or who refused to pay the compensation* requested by the court for a homicide—intentional or not. He should have planned on losing his life, for vengeance was an obligation and the victim's relatives would be dishonored if they did not achieve it.

As in the entire medieval West, death reaped both those who bore arms and those who tended to their normal business, and sometimes it gave no explanation.

Thorolf [Twist-Foot] went home in a rage, for he could see how difficult it was going to be for him to get what he wanted. It was evening when he reached home, and he sat down on the high-seat without uttering a word to anybody. He ate nothing all evening and stayed in his seat when the rest of the household went to bed. In the morning, when they got up Thorolf was sitting there, dead. . . . Everyone in the house was numb with terror, his death was so gruesome.[4]

The Funerary Toilet and the Handling of the Body

Generally speaking, the deceased was laid out on straw, a plank, or stones, after his or her eyes and mouth had been closed and the nostrils had been clogged. For those preparing the body, it was necessary to protect themselves from the evil eye and to prevent the dead person's spirit from leaving the corpse. The head was swaddled in a cloth, sometimes shoes called *Helskór,* "the shoes of Hel"—a custom confirmed by

---

Wergeld, "the price of a man," the monetary compensation paid by a murderer.

discoveries made in the peat bogs of northern Europe—were placed on the feet of the dead so that she or he could more easily make a way to the afterlife. Then a hole was made in the wall of the house and the cadaver was taken out through that opening, which was then resealed. This was to prevent the deceased from returning to the house by the same path by which he or she had left it.

We cannot find all these elements collected together in a single text. The most complete seems to be in the *Eyrbyggja Saga*. When Thorolf Twist-Foot dies, his son Arnkel is sent for:

When Arnkel went into the living room he crossed the hall to get behind Thorolf, warning people to take care not to get in front of the corpse until the eyes [mouth and nose] had been closed. He took Thorolf by the shoulders but had to use all his strength before he could force him down. After that he wrapped some clothes around Thorolf's head and got him ready for burial according to the custom of the time. He had a hole broken through the wall behind Thorolf

*Executions often produced revenants; the blindfold over the eyes protected those present from the evil eye. (*Poetic and Philosophical Codex, *Folio No. 2, Stuttgart, folio 65 r°)*

and the corpse was dragged outside. After a yoke of oxen had been hitched to a sled, Arnkel laid Thorolf on it . . .[5]

Customs like these are confirmed by the *Saga of Egil Skallagrimsson* (chapter 58),[6] but only the *Saga of Gisli Sursson* mentions the shoes of Hel (chapter 14): "Thorgrim went to Gisli and said, 'It is a custom to tie Hel-shoes to the men that they may wear them on their journey to Valhalla.'"[7]

This isolated Nordic testimony could inspire doubts concerning its authenticity, but fortunately we have another one—German, from Caesarius of Heisterbach. The information is slightly distorted in his *Dialogus miraculorum:* "A priest's mistress, feeling her death close at hand, asked a pair of shoes be made for her and placed on her feet after she died. The sequel to this story depicts her as a revenant."[8]

Caesarius had no possible knowledge of the Icelandic saga. This allows us to conclude that the belief is ancient and Germanic and not a simple literary motif.

The funerary toiletry implies that the fingernails and toenails of the dead were clipped. The sagas do not mention this, satisfied merely to report that "the body was dealt with according to custom," but we have two testimonies. Archaeology informs us that nail clippings have been discovered in the tombs of northern Europe,[9] and Snorri Sturluson (1179–1241), the great Icelandic poet, says this in his *Prose Edda,* when he describes the "Twilight of the Gods" (Ragnarök):

> Then it also will happen that the ship Naglfar will loosen from its moorings. It is made from the nails of dead men, and for this reason it is worth considering the warning that if a person dies with untrimmed nails he contributes crucial material to Naglfar, a ship that both gods and men would prefer not to see built.[10]

Not all the rites I have so far mentioned survived. There is still confirmation for closing the eyes of the dead, even if its first meaning has been lost. The same is true for the blocking of the cadaver's orifices. In the area surrounding Givet and in Champagne the custom still existed at the beginning of the twentieth century. The nostrils and the anus were also corked with wax, but this was viewed as no more than a simple measure of hygiene, not a method concerning the spirit of the dead person.

The body, completely dressed, was placed on a plank, in a chariot, or on a sled to be taken to its final resting place. The use of a shroud in which the body was placed naked became widespread following the introduction of Christianity. This was called "veiling the cadaver" (*hylja hrae*). Generally, the shroud was closed with a pin. This practice was the same throughout the medieval West; in the excavation of the Cemetery of the Innocents in Paris during the nineteenth century, a large number were found. This pin was a preventive and apotropaic measure. It was thought to prohibit the dead individual from coming back. In the *Eyrbyggja*, Thorgunna appears naked after her death because her shroud had not been stitched shut.[11] In Lorraine a point was made to sew the shroud shut so that the deceased could not leave the grave to make nocturnal visits. In other places, the two big toes of the cadaver's feet were bound together, and in yet others the departed's hands were tied together with a rosary. All of these customs reflect, in fact, the ancient custom of binding the dead.

The Vigil

Before being taken to the mound or tomb, a vigil over the dead person was sometimes kept. The Norse texts tell us next to nothing explicit about this practice; therefore, we need to turn to the ecclesiastical literature written in Latin. It informs us that vigils were accompanied by singing and dancing. Around the year 1000 CE, Burchard of Worms prohibited what he called "singing diabolical songs" as well as playing games and capers in the presence of the dead, because these were pagan customs.[12]

In England the penitential attributed to Archbishop Theodore, who died in 690, forbids any festivity in the presence of a deceased individual, and we encounter the same ban in the penitential of Ecgbert (ninth century) and in the canons that Aelfric, abbot of the monastery of Eynsham (Oxfordshire), wrote around the year 1000.[13] The vigil as practiced by the ancient Germans therefore included rites incompatible with Christianity.

Folk traditions hung on to them for a long time, though, and Jan de Vries cites games and dances accompanying funeral vigils in Westphalia.*

From the House to the Burial Site

In more remote times, the cadaver did not follow any specific path when taken to the mound or the grave. With the spread of Christianity and wider acceptance of burial in Christian ground, a notion of a path reserved for the dead was put into place. In certain regions—in Westphalia and in the province of Groningue, for example—this route was most recently called Hel's Path. The term is an ancient one and can be found in the *Poetic Edda*—"Men tread the path of Hel"[14]—to illustrate the fact that the dead must take a certain route to reach the afterlife regions.

Reserving a road for the dead was undoubtedly a form of the fear the dead inspire. In nineteenth-century Estonia, it was still said: "The funeral procession should not cross a field, even if it is fallow." Death was contagious, and the field would become sterile.

A Useful Precaution

Once the body had left the house, it was necessary to burn the bedding of the deceased. Confirmation of this measure can be found in Ireland, northern Germany, and the Netherlands,[15] and it is not merely a prophylactic measure if we can believe the *Eyrbyggja Saga*. When Thorgunna expresses her final wishes, she says:

> But my bed and all its furninshing I want burnt to ashes, for they'll never do anyone much good. I am not saying this because I grudge

---

*Jan de Vries, *Altgermanische Religionsgeschichte* [Germanic Religion], 2 vols. (Berlin: W. De Gruyter, 1956), vol. 1, 191. The Council of Arles (524) put it this way: "The laity who keep vigil over a dead person should do so with fear and trembling, and with respect. May no one risk singing diabolical songs, spinning, or dancing, as the pagans are wont to do under the devil's influence. . . . If someone wishes to sing, let him start singing the *Kyrie eleison!* Otherwise, may he hold his tongue." This is the same information seen in Burchard of Worms (in endnote 13), but without any allusion to meals and drinking bouts.

these things to anyone who could use them, but I must be firm about it. I wouldn't like to be responsible for all the trouble people will bring on themselves if they don't respect my wishes.[16]

Her wishes were not respected, and more deaths and strange occurrences resulted.

The Burial

In addition to the testimonies provided by archaeology and what the sagas tell us, we have at our disposal a document of the highest order—one by the Arab traveler Ibn Fadlan, who, in 822 CE, attended the funeral of a Swedish chieftain and left us a detailed account.

> The dead man was placed in his boat that had been pulled up on the bank. At his side were placed his weapons, intoxicating beverages, bread, meat, onions, a dog cut in half, horses that had been cut apart with swords, two oxen that had suffered the same treatment, a rooster and a hen, and a slave who had been put to death after having sexual relations with six men. A fire was then kindled on the craft that, once it had been reduced to ashes, was covered by a "round hill," in other words, a mound in the middle of which was erected a beechwood post on which the dead man's name was carved.[17]

Not all the departed enjoyed such a luxurious funeral, but burial inside a boat was quite common. When archaelogists opened a tumulus at Snape Common, near Alderburgh (Suffolk), remains of a boat and objects dating from the sixth century were found. A similar discovery was made at Sutton Hoo, near Woodbridge, in the same county. In a smaller mound close to the first one mentioned, which was opened in 1938, traces of cremation were discovered.[18]

The sagas have preserved the memory of the burial and cremation customs current in ancient times, and Snorri Sturluson says:

As to funeral rites, the earliest age is called the Age of Burning, because all the dead were consumed by fire. . . . The Age of Cairns began properly in Denmark after Dan Milkillate had raised for himself a burial cairn. . . . But the burning of the dead continued, long after that time, to be the custom of the Swedes and the Northmen.[19]

Egil's Saga (chapter 58) indicates that Skallagrim was buried beneath a mound with his horse, his weapons, and his blacksmith tools.[20] In the *Saga of Grettir the Strong* (chapter 18), Kar the Old is placed in his tumulus, seated in a chair surrounded by his riches. In another story, the dead man is seated in a boat.[21] The funeral gifts imply the belief in another life, a point we shall concern ourselves with later in the book.

Most revealing is the custom of fastening the dead into their graves with the help of a stake. In his *Decret,* written between 1012 and 1023, Burchard, bishop of Worms, mentions it in connection with the deaths of newborns and women in labor.

You have done what certain women customarily do under the devil's instigation: If a very small child dies without baptism, they take the body into a secret place and pierce it through with a rod. They say that if they did not do this, the child would come back and could cause harm to a great many people.

If a woman does not manage to give birth to her child and dies in labor, in the very grave both mother and child are pierced with a rod that nails them to the ground.[22]

The precaution is taken here against those who died prematurely, but it is sometimes used for someone who died "normally." Among the ancient Scandinavians, this custom was known as "to inter beneath the stake," and it is cited in Norwegian laws.[23] We have an excellent description of it in the *Vinland Sagas* concerning Eric the Red, the discoverer of North America. Gigrid has just died and the narrator steps in.

It had been common practice in Greenland, since Christianity had been adopted, to bury people in unconsecrated ground on the farms where they had died. A stake was set up over the breast of each corpse until a priest came, then the stake was pulled out and consecrated water poured into the hole and a burial service performed, even though this was only done much later.[24]

This text reveals how Christianity superimposed itself upon pagan beliefs: The stake and, later, holy water were to prevent the deceased from leaving the grave. The same result was also obtained by burying the dead in consecrated ground—which is to say, protected from the *demon,* the word in fact designating everything that could relate to spirits and superstitions. I have attempted to compare interment beneath the stake to another solidly confirmed practice: nails were hammered into the feet of a corpse to prevent any posthumous roving. On the shores of the Baltic Sea, I came across an interesting variation. The Estonians customarily drove into the doorsill the same number of nails as there were dead in the household. It is well known that the threshold is a sacred space. The French preacher Berthold de Ratisbonne, who died December 3, 1272, indicated that an individual who died in a state of mortal sin should not be taken from the house through the door. A passageway must be dug beneath the threshold, and, without touching it and with the help of only a rope, the body had to be pulled through this opening.[25] This would be another way of preventing a dead person from getting back into his home by the way used to remove him from it.

Among the German peoples, the stake, and then its euphemistic forms—nails, for example—have always represented an elementary precaution intended to prevent postmortem manifestations. In England, until 1824, a stake was used to hold the suicide in his grave dug at a crossroads. We should note the simultaneous emergence of two motifs here: with no awareness that they were doing so, English legists applied an ancient measure consisting of two points, the second being to facilitate access to the otherworld for the deceased because, for the dead, the crossing of the roads is one of the entrances to the hells.

The Dead Man's Share

The sagas do not speak of a practice that archaeology has revealed to us. Since the third century CE, in Denmark, on the isle of Gotland (in Sweden), and in southern Germany, coins were placed in the mouths of the dead. In Hassleben (Thuringia), for example, a skeleton had in its mouth an aureus of Gallienus (253–68 CE). It was initially thought that this was a custom borrowed from ancient Rome: the coin would have been used to pay Charon, the ferryman of the hells. Yet this hypothesis was shown to be erroneous; the correct conclusion was supplied by ancient German law. The coin was the symbolic representation of the dead individual's designated contribution. The departed had the right to keep one-third of his wealth, which originally should have permitted him to lead a decent life beyond the tomb. The meaning was lost during the Middle Ages, when the laws made numerous allusions to this portion, but the souvenir held on strongly in folk traditions.[26]

Here it was said, "Money had to be placed in the mouths of the dead so they do not return in the event they were concealing a treasure," and there it was declared, "The person who buries his money is destined to return as long as it has not been found." An entire set of tales and legends has grown out of these notions, and on more than one occasion specters have taken on the duties of guardians of buried treasures.

There are details in the sagas that indicate the medieval person's concern for this matter. They explicitly tell whether the dead individual was buried with his riches. Skallagrim and Höskuld are not accompanied by any treasures.[27] It is possible that this custom was abandoned to avoid the violation of graves, something heroes were not loath to do.

One evening very late when Grettir was preparing to return home, he saw a great fire shoot up on the headland below Audun's place and asked what new thing that might be. Audun said there was no pressing need for him to know. "If they saw such a thing in our country," said Grettir, "they would say the fire came from some treasure." "He who rules that fire," answered the man, "is one whom it will be better not to inquire about." "But I want to know," Grettir said. "On that headland," said Audun, "there is a howe, wherein lies Kar the Old, the father of Thorfinn. Once upon a time father and son had a farm-property on the island; but ever since Kar died his ghost has been walking and has scared away all the other farmers, so that now the whole island belongs to Thorfinn, and no man who is under Thorfinn's protection suffers any injury." "You have done right to tell me," said Grettir. Expect me here tomorrow morning, and have tools ready for digging." . . .

Grettir appeared early the next morning, and the bondi, who had got all the tools for digging ready, went with Grettir to the howe. Grettir broke open the grave and worked with all his might, never stopping until he came to wood, by which time the day was already spent. He tore away the woodwork; Audun implored him not to go down, but Grettir bade him attend to the rope, saying that he meant to find out what it was that dwelt there. Then he descended into the howe. It was very dark and the odor was not pleasant. He began to explore how it was arranged and found the bones of a horse. Then he knocked against a sort of throne in which he was aware of a man seated. There was much treasure of gold and silver collected together, and a casket under his feet, full of silver. Grettir took all the treasure. . . .[28]

The violation of graves is frequently referred to in the annals, and the *Book of Sturla* recounts that of an anonymous tomb: "Leif was on a military expedition in Iceland and discovered a large tomb. He entered and all was dark except for the glow of a sword a man was holding. Leif slew this man—the dead man, in fact—and took his sword and much money."[29]

Tombs are pillaged everywhere in Europe, and various recent news items show that the lure of profit is stronger at times than loathing or respect for the dead.

Funerary Festivities

Once the departed had been buried, it was necessary to throw a banquet in his honor. In northern Europe, the "beer of the inheritance" was then drunk and the heirs did not truly gain the dead person's bequests until after this feast, where there were made toasts in honor of the dead. In the *Saga of the Vikings of Jomsburg,* for example, King Sveyn Forkbeard is forced to postpone his father's funeral banquet four times. "The point had been reached," says the narrator, "when Sveyn would no longer be regarded as the rightful king if he did not celebrate his father's funeral banquet before the third night of winter,"[30] meaning the end of October. A man is legally dead when his heirs have followed this custom. The heirs sometimes would wait for the return of relatives traveling abroad. On other occasions, in the case of murder, they waited for vengeance to be done—a man who had been slain could not rest in peace until he had been avenged.

The ceremony should have taken place on the third, the seventh, and the thirtieth days following the death of the individual. The remains of meals—bones, pieces of pottery, carbonized wood—have been discovered in Frankish and Burgundian necropolises. Furthermore, the anathemas of the church can leave no doubt as to the reality of these practices. Hincmar of Reims speaks of them around 852 CE—alas, without much precision—but the fifth canon of a synod that took place on April 21, 742, prohibited these cult meals in honor of the dead. *The Indiculus superstionum et paganiarum* (eighth century), of which we possess only the table of contents, titles its second article "On Sacrileges Committed among the Dead, in Other Words, Singing Funeral Songs."[31] What's more, the first article of this capitulary focuses "On the Sacrilegious Practices at the Tombs of the Dead." St. Ambrose (fourth century) spoke even then of pagans "who visit the tombs of martyrs with their ale horns and make libations until late in the evening, convinced they shall not be heard otherwise."

Unfortunately, the Christian texts blend very diverse traditions whose sole common factor is reference to the dead, and they declare ceaselessly the same thing: this custom is sacrilegious. In 737 CE, when Gregory III fulminated against the Hessians because they performed sacrifices to the dead, the Hessian practice could have been a case of ancestor worship,[32] and all our witnesses from the eighth to the eleventh century repeat: "Thy shalt not offer sacrifices to the departed in the presence of their bodies or upon their tombs."[33] In Charlemagne's *Capitulare primum* (796 CE), royal authority bolstered the religious prohibitions. One sole fact is incontestable: a funeral banquet took place, sometimes accompanied by singing. It was renewed at regular intervals, notably during Jól, which was replaced by Christmas, and then formed part of a worship encompassing the living and the dead in the same community. As on every occasion when they mention a practice known to everyone, the sagas say little that is explicit. Here is one example:

Thorodd and his crew had perished at sea and the waves had not surrendered their bodies: When the news came to Frodriver, Kjartan and Thurid invited their neighbors to a funeral feast, at which they used the Christmas ale. On the first evening of the feast, when all the guests were seated, Thorodd and his companions came into the room drenched to the skin. Everyone welcomed Thorodd and his men and thought this a happy omen because in those days it was believed that drowned people had been well received by the sea-goddess, Ran, if they came to their own funeral feast. At that time a good many heathen beliefs still prevailed, though people were baptized and supposed to be Christians.[34]

The stage is almost set; the examples we've examined already allow us to see the important role played by the dead, premonitions, and the pagan substratum. Before introducing those I call false revenants, I still need to say a bit about the mind-set of the people who have bequeathed us such strange stories about ghosts and revenants.

THREE

The Church, Ghosts, and Revenants

It was difficult for Christians nourished on the Bible and the church fathers to accept that people could appear after their deaths. For these believers—and this was before the notion of purgatory had been established—only two possibilities existed for the deceased: they went either to heaven or to hell. Confronted with worship of the dead, which was of capital importance in paganism, the church was compelled to react and impose its own answers to questions concerning the afterlife. The two theologians who played the most important role in the history of ghosts and revenants are Tertullian and St. Augustine, whose interpretations fed the clerical commentaries of the Middle Ages.

In his treatise *On the Soul,* written around 210–11 CE,[1] Tertullian debates the fate of the soul after death and reviews the beliefs of his time. One of the interesting features of his report shows us how these beliefs were passed on to posterity due in particular to the Christian scholars who fought against them.

For his part, St. Augustine justifies the belief in the dead without rest, and in this sense he is one of the "fathers" of ghosts and revenants. He follows the same intellectual course as Tertullian, and he poses the problem of perception: Are these apparitions the creations of slumbering, somnolent, or feverish men?

When purgatory was established,[2] this third place naturally became the residence of the dead who were not resting peacefully. Henceforth these individuals were regarded as imprisoned souls, or the damned. It was believed that the elect show themselves at times, but they are easily identified because they are radiant with happiness and beauty, and the clerics were incapable of confusing them with the sinners suffering the punishments of purgatory.

Tertullian and the Legacy of Antiquity

The treatise *On the Soul* is a goldmine of information on Roman beliefs concerning the dead. Tertullian reviews and critiques them.

Says Tertullian, Plato and other philosophers asserted that the soul sometimes remains a prisoner of the body after death. They took as proof the fact that some bodies do not decompose, and the hair and nails continue growing after death (*On the Soul*, 51, 2). While indicating awareness of these facts, Tertullian denies the interpretation given them. He cites an example he himself had witnessed: when the body of a young widow was being readied to be taken for burial, the cadaver was seen joining its hands together while the priest spoke the orison, and he put them back along her sides when the prayer was over. This story made its way through the exempla and can even be found in the chronicles. In the continuation of the chronicle by William of Newburgh (1136–1198), the author clearly states that a dead person behaved the same way in 1275,[3] which clearly shows the kind of importance assumed by traditions.

For Tertullian, the movements of a corpse did not indicate the presence of the soul in the body, and he provides a second example before reaching his conclusion.

> Then there is that well-known story, among we Christians, about a body in a cemetery that moved of its own volition to afford room to

another body being buried at its side. Even if similar things are told among the heathen, we can say that God shows signs everywhere as consolation to his people or as testimony of his existence to those who are not believers. Whatever may be the origin of such events, they should rather be regarded as signs and miracles, and they cannot be the rule.[4]

This interpretation heralds that of the clerics of the Middle Ages whose explanations sometimes perform the same pirouette: nothing is impossible for God.

Tertullian next attacks the belief that the infernal regions deny entrance to those who have died prematurely as well as to those who were victims of violent death, granting a special place for those who had been executed by cruel torture. He then asks the following rhetorical question.

I beg you to decide between two things: Are the infernal regions good or evil? If they are evil, then the worst souls deserve to be cast therein; if they are good, why should you deem them unworthy of housing those who died at an early age, those who left life before marriage, in short those who by virtue of their age were innocent and pure?[5]

Tertullian then sets up the opinion that would be embraced during the Middle Ages: revenants were demons or dead people possessed by a devil. He attacks necromancy, which he accuses of being imposture and idolatry and a magic art that provoked confusion of the senses. But all these "black arts" triggered only the appearance of shapes, delusions, and reflections because the demon blinds humans (*On the Soul*, 57, 1–6). Therefore, all apparitions can be boiled down to diabolical tricks and *illusions*—this term being key in Christian explanations. It derives from the verb *inludere*, "to play with." The demon is playing with us by sending images we mistake for reality.

It is only a step from illusion to dream, and Tertullian sets foot in a realm the church has always distrusted, and he prepares the ground for an interpretation that St. Augustine would develop: the dead person who appears in a dream is no more real than the living person you may see there. "It is not because something appears that it is real but it is real because it has been realized."[6] In short, in Tertullian's opinion a revenant must have a body. Otherwise, it is an illusion—he uses the word *phantasma,* the origin of the word *phantom*—an imposture. Yet we should note that by his reasoning we could infer that every physical revenant is a reality!

St. Augustine

In his booklet *On the Care of the Dead,* written between 421 and 424 CE, Augustine examines the apparitions of the departed with more subtlety than Tertullian, and he first directs his gaze at the unburied dead.

> Stories are told of certain appearances, which brings up a question that should not be disregarded as negligible. It is said that either in dream or in some other manner, some dead men have shown themselves to the living who did not know where the bodies of these dead people lay unburied. The dead people directed them to it and requested that the sepulcher that was lacking be provided.
>
> To respond that these visions are false shall appear to be in imprudent contradiction with the testimonies written by fellow Christian authors—and by allusion, to scholarly tradition—and the conviction of those people who assure they experienced them. The true answer is as follows. It is not to be thought that the dead are acting as real or conscious beings when they seem to say, show, or ask in dream what it is claimed. For the living also appears in dreams to the living and they know not that they do.[7]

Augustine therefore asserts the reality of the apparitions while denying that the defunct play any role in this phenomenon, thereby further developing Tertullian's argument. But a problem remains: How is it possible for the deceased to show themselves? Augustine then asks:

> Why would it be surprising that the dead, knowing or feeling nothing of it, be seen in dream by the living and tell them things that upon awakening are found to be true? I would be inclined to believe that these apparitions are the work of angelic intervention, permitted or commanded by God. It communicates to the dreamer that these dead bodies require burial, and all without the knowledge of the former owners of these bodies.[8]

Everything comes back to God, and the apparitions assumed the meaning of divine messages that the angels transmit to us by different means. This idea gained ground, and Peter Damian is not mistaken when he writes around 1147–57: "Divine clemency instructs the living by means of the dead."[9]

By postulating angelic activity, as Tertullian did two centuries earlier, Augustine took an important step—one that would permit medieval theologians to resolve a part of the problem of apparitions: good angels bring good dreams, those coming from God; fallen angels cause fallacious dreams and delusions.

Can we trust our senses? Augustine responds in the negative.

> Such, however, is human infirmity that when someone sees a dead man in a dream, he thinks it is his soul he sees, whereas if he sees a living man, he is perfectly convinced that it is not his soul or his body that he sees but his image. As if it were not possible for dead men to appear in the same manner as the living, not in the form of their souls but in a likeness that replicates their features.[10]

Revenants were thus stripped of all physicality. All that really appeared were images, reflections, and true copies that would later be called *ghosts*. But St. Augustine's reasoning is based on one postulate: the dead appear only in dream, which is false, but this clever trick makes it possible to hold these apparitions in check as oneiric phenomena and strip them of any wide scope. Yet it is appropriate to note that Augustine managed to forge the essential weapon for exegetes and theologians seeking to eradicate worship of the dead and the beliefs connected with death. All of it would be nothing but vain dreams. Furthermore, citing personal examples to support his argument, Augustine concludes by citing the words from Ecclesiastes 3:21: "Things higher than you, seek not; and things stronger than you, search not; but what the Lord has commanded you, on those things bethink you always."

Gregory the Great: Relay for Augustine's Ideas

In his *Dialogues*,[11] Gregory the Great (ca. 540–604) borrowed Augustinian theories and illustrated them with the help of anecdotes and exempla demonstrating the importance assumed by suffrages—the dead could be helped by Masses, fasting, and alms—but at the same time his work proved that ghosts and revenants existed in large number. We learn from it that Germanus, bishop of Capua, encountered the deceased Paschasius, a deacon who had chosen to support the false pope Lawrence. Paschasius was working at the public baths of Augulum in the Abruzzo region, atoning for his sin.[12]

In the sixth century, baths were regarded as places where sinners could serve out their sentence, purifying themselves, and a second exemplum clearly shows this. Gregory retells the story of the bishop Felix, who encountered a soul being punished for his sins and, not knowing the situation, gave him two singing breads* that the other refused, saying:

> "This bread is holy and I cannot eat of it for I who you see here was once master of these baths, but because of my sins, I was sent back here after my death. If you wish to be of service to me, offer these breads to almighty God, as an intercessor for my sins. You shall

---

*[Bread consecrated by the priest singing a blessing over it. —*Ed.*]

know your prayers have been answered when you no longer find me here." With these words he vanished, thereby revealing that he was in reality a spirit taking on human appearance.[13]

The originality of stories like this, which are solidly situated in time and geography, thereby reinforcing their credibility, is to localize the places of atonement where a particular sinner lived. This opinion precisely allowed non-Christian revenants to find their way into the writings of the fathers of the church to be used for edifying purposes once their nature had been slightly retouched. The dead showed up where they had lived and sinned, a thought barely removed from pagan beliefs: murdered people haunted the site of their deaths, and the same is true for all those whose deaths were abnormal. The possibility of expiating sins on earth disappeared at the same time as the birth of a purgatory that welcomed those who were neither completely good nor terribly evil—which is to say, in the end, almost everybody. With purgatory, the dead were banished into the beyond. If they wished aid or suffrages, may God permit them to show themselves in dream to the living!

The Commemoration of the Dead

The notion of suffrages helpful to the dead gave birth to the directives serving to eliminate worship of the dead, a core feature of paganism. It was adulterated and recuperated with great subtlety and, wherever possible, the saints replaced the good ancestors—the objects of a cult connected to the third function (fecundity/fertility*)—and liturgical feasts replaced the pagan festivals.

---

*[This refers to the trifunctional ideology that gives structure to caste-societies and is characteristic of all cultures of Indo-European origin. According to Georges Dumezil, the scholar who discovered this trifunctional ideology, the first function concerns magical and judicial sovereignty (embodied in the Norse Odin and Tyr, or the Vedic Mitra and Varuna), the second concerns military activities (war gods like Thor), and the third function concerns fertility and pastoral activities (Frey and Freya). In the social structure these three functions are represented by the clergy, warriors, and farmers; craftspeople; and herdsmen, respectively. —*Trans.*]

Between the Carolingian era and the eleventh century, the books of life, scrolls of the dead, and obituaries attest to a straight-line evolution that took place from the ideas of St. Augustine and Gregory the Great: death does not put an end to the relations between the living and the dead; the deceased need the help of the living, and the living have a sacred duty to help their relatives and close friends who have gone on to the otherworld. The remembering of the departed—which, for pagans, took the form of cult meals and which, for Christians, meant the liturgy—was set by the monks of Cluny.[14] It was they who set the feast of the dead on November 2, as recounted in the following exemplum:

> St. Odilon, abbot of Cluny, on learning that it was common to hear in the neighborhood of a Sicilian volcano the cries and howls of demons complaining that the souls of the departed were being torn from their grasp by alms and prayers, commanded that his monasteries celebrate, following the feast of all the saints, a commemoration of the dead, which was subsequently approved by the entire church.[15]

Inseparable from the implementation of purgatory and suffrages is the irruption of the departed in the exempla and clerical literature, which was becoming increasingly more numerous. Augustine and Gregory had provided good models with their anecdotes, and they bequeathed a narrative structure along with all the elements of assessment. These were relayed into the twelfth century by Alcher de Clairvaux, who, in his treatise *On the Spirit and the Soul*,[16] examines the nature of the dead, and by Peter the Elder, whose *De miraculis* (composed 1145–57) informs us that, among other things, the visions and apparitions of the dead constitute the *miracula* characteristic of his time.[17]

It would take too long to trace the evolution that transformed revenants and ghosts into souls undergoing punishment for their sins, and I refer readers to Jacques Le Goff's admirable work *The Birth of Purgatory*; the excellent study by Otto Gerhard Oexle;[18] and, to cite a medieval testimony, Jacobus de Voragine (Varazzo), who completed his *Golden Legend* before 1267. In *The Birth of Purgatory,* which enjoyed a phenomenal diffusion, Jacques Le Goff compiles the most significant texts of the exemplary tradition and devotes a long chapter to the feast of the dead.[19]

He recalls why Odilon instituted the commemoration of the deceased and specifies that there are three kinds of souls that can know redemption by virtue of suffrages—those of men who had not completed their penitence, those of sinners whose penitence was too light because of priestly ignorance or neglect, and those of people possessed by too great a love for temporal goods. These were tortured by evil angels in purgatory, which was located close to hell. Jacques Le Goff also borrows the Gregorian tradition and asserts that in certain cases some souls were banished to specific places, by virtue of a saint's intervention, to undergo a lesser punishment, to more easily find salvation, or even to serve the living as an example and inspire us to mend our ways. He includes one final detail of great importance: some souls atoned at the sites of their sins, which explains why people could meet revenants. All sinners were not in purgatory or hell!

With the help of different anecdotes borrowed from his predecessors, Le Goff clearly shows that the principal function of apparitions of the dead is to instruct the living. The tortures endured by the souls in purgatory were sufficiently frightening, it was thought, to coax the stray sheep back onto the right path. Consider this disciple of Silo (Siger de Brabant), who wears a cloak of parchment covered with sophisms and woven of flames on the inside: the student lets a drop of sweat fall upon his master's outstretched hand, which it pierces through like an arrow. The wound provides confirmation of the story's veracity and the reality of the encounter.

A great lesson emerges from the disciple of Silo in the chapter entitled *De commemoratione mortuorum:* helping the dead is a duty; if you fulfill it, you can expect the dead to come to your aid the day you need them. This notion is not simply Christian, it takes up and slightly alters the pagan traditions evident among both the Germans and the Romans. The dead must be honored, their memories celebrated, and invitations must be given them to attend feasts and festivals, otherwise there is a risk they will be wrathful and seek revenge.

The Christian Interpretation of Revenants

On the margins of clerical and monastic culture appeared revenants who were difficult to Christianize because they did not conform to the exegetic outlines in force. They lived in oral and folk tradition, the last remnants of a paganism that was slowly dying but still anchored firmly in local mind-sets. The church was therefore faced with a problem it could not afford to ignore: How was it possible for the dead to wander and stroll about? Thanks to Augustine and Tertullian, the church had responded to the question of the existence of phantoms who were oneiric and not corporeal, but what steps could it take when the physicality of the apparitions was beyond question?

Within the sphere of influence of Tertullian and Augustine's contemplations, the following explanation emerged during the course of the twelfth century: God sometimes authorized fallen angels to slip into cadavers and animate them. An obstacle to this possession could be erected by virtue of the last rites and the burial of the dead in consecrated ground. As a precautionary measure, the corpse could also be sprinkled with holy water and bathed in the fumes of incense. William Durand (1230–1296), bishop of Mende, expressly recommended the latter because aromas sent spirits fleeing,[20] a belief that humans have held from the dawn of time and whose existence has been confirmed throughout the Mediterranean basin long before the birth of Jesus. By the end of the twelfth century, all revenants were regarded as victims of possession.

Also in evidence during the thirteenth century, but certainly possessing much older roots, was the belief that compared revenants to changelings—children that have been substituted at birth.[21] In the case of revenants, the devil was presumed to have substituted a likeness for the body of the person believed dead. Yet if we compare the writings left us by Thomas de Cantimpare (ca. 1273)[22] to that of a story told by Walter Map in his *De nugis curialium* (ca. 1181–93),[23] we can see that these demons were in fact individuals from the depths of mythology. It should be admitted that *diabolus, daemonium,* or *daemon* are terms that present quite a nuisance to researchers but were quite practical for the clerics of the Middle Ages because they designated all the beings of non-Christian beliefs. The explanation of revenants by possession is therefore not the correct one; it is but one among others that enjoyed success because it was more credible in that era.

Now we will draw up a brief overview of the means used to resolve the problem of revenants. They were discarded as the products of dream, and their wandering nature was attributed to demons that invested some corpses. The essential concept here is the term *incubus,* which covers everything touching on this domain—human perception was implicated because it was possible the senses had been blinded by somatic disorders. Over the course of my examination, I have discovered other means of resolution of the problem of revenants, which have proceeded from those I have mentioned here. We must keep in mind that from the twelfth century on, the revenant was considered a kind of demon—it was stripped of its physicality and became a ghost, an image, a simulacrum of the body, and it was transformed into a soul that was suffering a punishment or that had been damned. We must keep this in mind if we want to distinguish folk traditions from Christian traditions that are more or less well camouflaged. Writing the history of ghosts and revenants in the Middle Ages implies a continuous back and forth between these two elements—folk tradition and Christian tradition—and between the two cultures that have been blended to make the revenant a reality. The *interpretatio christiana*[24] overlies all the writings and muddies the trail. It is therefore necessary to get past it and not allow it to take any further advantage of us.

PART TWO

FOUR

The False Revenants

After analyzing the texts, it is possible for us to make a distinction between false and true revenants. The issue of true revenants—dead people who return of their own volition for their own reasons—will be examined in chapter 5. The false revenants that are the subject of this chapter, however, are the dead that make an immediate appearance after their decease, as if they continued to live for a span of time, or the dead who seem to have been called back to life under certain circumstances. Here, we will examine these two groups of false revenants: first, the dead who were carried to the grave against their will, then the departed who came back to life in self-defense, because their sepulcher has been violated, or because they have been forced to return through necromancy.

The Recalcitrant Dead

Losing life certainly cannot be pleasant, but being buried in exile, removed from the community of the living, was, it seems, intolerable. This was the true death—exile in a timeless retirement. It is easy to deduce the considerations related to this death from the references that pepper the narrations here and there. Someone named Hrapp asks his wife to make sure that he is buried standing up beneath the kitchen door so that he can watch over the household. Karl Thorsteinsson has himself buried at the edge of a river so that he can watch the coming and going of the ships. Ingolf requests that his body not be placed in the family mound but by the side of the road so that the girls of Lake Valley would remember him.[1] It is therefore not surprising to see such deaths followed by strange phenomena.

Sigrid died during the night; a coffin was made in which to place her body, but things occurred which caused someone to be sent to fetch back her spouse.

> Then Thorstein Ericksson sent word to his namesake (Master Thorstein) to come to him, saying there was no peace at home because the farmer's wife was trying to rise up and get into the bed with him. When Thorstein entered, she had reached the sideboards of the bed. He took hold of her and drove an ax into her breast. Thorstein Eriksson died near sundown.[2]

The text presents two important pieces of data: the dead can be intimidated,* and they can return to seek out or designate those who are soon to die. We have another account of this incident, and it is interesting to compare the two narratives. Note that Sigrid is named Grimhild here:

> It was not long until the sickness came to Thorstein's house, and his wife, Grimhild, was the first to fall ill. She was a very large woman, with the strength of a man, yet she bowed to the illness. Soon after that, Thorstein Eriksson was stricken, and both of them lay ill until Grimhild, wife of Thorstein the Black, died.
>
> After she had died, Thorstein the Black left the room to seek a plank on which to put her body. Gudrid, the servant, then spoke, "Don't be away long, dear Thorstein," she said. He promised to do as she asked.
>
> Thorstein Eriksson then spoke, "Strange are the actions of the

---

*Note that the iron of the ax blade brings an end to the strange phenomenon.

mistress of the house now; she's struggling to raise herself up on her elbow, stretching her feet out from the bedboards and feeling for her shoes." At this, Thorstein the Black returned, and Grimhild collapsed that same instant, with a cracking sound coming from every timber in the room. Thorstein then made a coffin for Grimhild's body and took it away and secured it. He was a large, strong man, and needed to call upon all his strength before he managed to remove his wife from the farm.[3]

This final touch recurs frequently in the sagas: Sometimes even a pair of oxen can barely manage to pull the cart in which the deceased have been placed. Sometimes the body makes itself so heavy that it has to be buried wherever it seems to want to remain. In the following instance, Arnkel is bringing Thorolf Twist-Foot to his final resting place: "After a yoke of oxen had been hitched to sled, Arnkel laid Thorolf on it, and they began driving it through Thorsardale. It was hard work hauling Thorolf to his burial place."[4] This resistance does not presage anything good, and the narrator adds: "When they got him there, they built a solid cairn (*rammliga*) over him," which clearly shows that everyone feared his return.

The recalcitrant dead are not people that are easy to move and the coffin offers no resistance to their pressure.

One night, Audun went in search of Thorgils. Gyda, his mother, had died in a bizarre fashion, causing the flight of the entire household. It should be said that she had witchlike powers. Audun wished to bury her and was looking for help. Thorgils and he went to the farm, built a coffin, and placed Gyda's body inside. "Let's carry the bier," said Audun. "Put it in the ground and place over it the heaviest objects we can find." Because two precautions are always better than one, they encircled the bier with iron bands before starting off.

They had barely gotten any distance from the farm when the coffin groaned, the iron bands burst into shards, and Gyda emerged. Audun and Thorgils grabbed her, and to hold her, they were forced to use all their strength, and they were both hearty men. Incapable of carrying her any further, they burned her body.[5]

Let's look at a different example. In the *Saga of Hallfred Troublesome Skald,* one evening the hero, accompanied by Audgisl, goes to the home of a man named Önund, who treacherously slays Audgisl and seeks to do the same to Hallfred. Yet he misses in his attempt and loses his life. Hallfred locks Önund's body in his cabin. During the night, Önund shakes the door, but Hallfred leans against it, keeping it closed. This went on all night.[6]

Why do the dead sometimes refuse to leave their homes to be buried? It is cold in the tomb, an anonymous skald sings,[7] and a well-known Icelandic folksong says that Thorgunna, whose acquaintance we have already made, declares while her coffin is being interred in Skalaholt: "My feet are cold."[8] In northern Europe, the dead keep the memory of and taste for life. The second Song of Helgi, Murderer of King Hunding, explains this in gripping fashion. Sigrun enters the mound of her late husband whom she engages in dialogue.

> 44 *First I want to kiss the lifeless king,*
> *before you throw off your bloody mail-coat;*
> *your hair, Helgi, is thick with hoar-frost,*
> *the prince is all soaked in slaughter-dew,*
> *Hogni's son-in-law has clammy hands.*
> *How, lord, can I find a remedy for this?*
> 45 *You alone, Sigrun, from Sefafell,*
> *cause Helgi to be soaked in sorrow-dew;*
> *you weep, gold-adorned lady, bitter tears,*
> *sun-bright southern girl, before you go to sleep;*
> *each falls bloody on the breast of the prince,*
> *cold as dew, burning hot, thick with grief.*
> 46 *We ought to drink this precious liquid,*
> *though we have lost our love and our lands!*[9]

Cold and regret are the lot of the dead, as seen in Charles
Baudelaire's *The Kind-Hearted Servant.*

> *The dead, ah! the poor dead suffer great pains,*
> *And when October, the pruner of old trees, blows*
> *His melancholy breath about their marble tombs,*
> *Surely they must think the living most ungrateful,*
> *To sleep, as they do, between warm, white sheets,*
> *While, devoured by gloomy reveries,*
> *Without bedfellows, without pleasant causeries,*
> *Old, frozen skeletons, belabored by the worm,*
> *They feel the drip of winter's snow . . .*

Odd postmortem manifestations are most likely the origin for a type
of legend that enjoyed great success in the Christian literature written in
Latin: the story of the dead person who opens his eyes and shares what
he has seen. Caesarius of Heisterbach is the author of the following:

In France, a monk who had led a blameless life died in a Cistercian
monastery. He was carried into the oratory. The next night the
monks were singing psalms in the presence of the body, as was
their custom, when the dead man rose up from his stretcher, looked
around, and called out to his brothers. All fled in terror; the only
one to remain was the father superior. The deceased spoke to him:
"Have no fear, I am your brother. I was dead and I live again.
Summon the abbot!" He then recounted how angels had brought
him to Paradise, where he had not been allowed to enter because
he was not wearing the habit of his order. His clothes were changed
and he surrendered his soul to God.[10]

If we remove the edifying tone from this Christian tale, this dead
individual is moving and speaking before burial in the same way that
occurs in the Norse stories.

The Christian Explanation for Holding Vigils over the Dead

The custom of keeping vigil over the dead is ancient, as we have seen, but it did not always perform the same function. Its purpose among the Romans, according to Apulieus, was to prevent witches from mutilating the body. Among the ancient Germans, the vigil was a feast to honor the deceased.

Borrowing the testimony of the Anglo-Norman cleric Wace, who around 1160 finished *The Ascending Chronicle of the Dukes of Normandy*—also known as the *Roman de Rou* (ca. 927)—we discover an extremely curious explanation. Wace recounts why Richard I commanded that vigils be held over the dead in Normandy.

One night, Richard entered into a chapel where a cadaver was lying on a bier. While he prayed, the dead man stretched out his arm and stood up. Hearing the noise, Richard looked around, "saw the body large and tall, the devil's likeness," drew his sword, and struck it. He told others of his adventure and instituted the funeral vigil.[11]

Wace revisits this subject in greater detail in the third book of his chronicle, and he first makes clear that "many phantoms he [Richard] saw and found," which places the episode under the sign of the revenants: One night, Richard enters a monastery that Wace gives to understand is a cemetery chapel (verse 328). "Inside there was a corpse upon a bier." He begins praying when he suddenly hears the body stirring and the bier cracking behind him:

el mustier oï ariere
moveir le cors, cruistre la biere.

He commands the body to lay back down and, crossing himself, speaks the following exorcism.

Per hoc signum sancta cruces,
libera me de malignis,
Domine Deux salutis.

By the sign of the Holy Cross
deliver me from Evil
O Lord, God of Salvation.

He then entrusts his soul to the hands of the Lord and grabs
his sword, but the dead man stretches out his arm "as if he wanted
to seize Richard." Richard strikes him and, later, he proclaimed in
the churches and markets that a deceased should never be left alone
before burial:

As eglises fist commander
e as marches dire e crier
que mais n'ai cors seul guerpi
de si que l'en l'eit enfui.[12]

The anecdote bears a striking resemblance to those in which Sigrid
and Gyda move as if alive. Wace is surely making use of folk traditions,
perhaps even Norse ones, which is not at all surprising because the
Normans have exhibited a long-lasting loyalty to their traditions.

For the auditors or readers of the era, it was obvious that a spirit—
preferably a diabolical one—had taken possession of the body. Moreover, another Anglo-Norman romance, *Foulke Fitz Warin,* from the
second half of the thirteenth century, which retraces the history of
the Foulques family until the death of Foulques III (1256), introduces
the giant Goemagog. He had drowned and a demon took possession
of his body, bringing about such a reign of terror in the land that no
Breton dares live there anymore: ". . . *e un esprit del deble meyntenant*
entra le corps Goemagog e vynt en ces parties e defendy longement, ce qe
unque Breton n'osa habiter."[13]

Vigil over the dead was kept in the twelfth century to prevent a spirit from taking possession of the body of the deceased. This was the Christian interpretation of the pagan data clearly reflected in the Norse sagas. Cadavers were malefic—which is why, according to a custom evident in several dioceses of thirteenth-century France, during the night they were placed in the church with the doors closed. The ecclesiastical authorities forbade the keeping of mortal remains in the home; they had to be transported to the church and left there until the funeral services. In the Tours diocese, for example, one document even states this: "A vigil should not be kept overnight in the church . . . because of the malefic activities that occur there," which refers to acts of necromancy and legends like that of King Richard.

Other Postmortem Manifestations

The departed did not always refuse to go to the grave, but they sometimes exhibited curious behavior, both beneficial and malefic.

After the death of Styr the Murderer, his body was placed in a lean-to before it was buried. During that night, overcome with curiosity and wanting to see what Styr looked like, Gudrid and her sister entered the building. Styr then rose from where he was lying and spoke a strophe, a common habit for revenants and ghosts who generally express themselves in verse. Gudrid lost her reason and died that morning, victim of the malignant nature of the deceased.[14]

Another narrative is even more interesting because it depicts a dead woman respecting the law and lending assistance to the people transporting her corpse. Thorgunna wanted to be buried in Skalaholt. The road is long and a storm is raging, as is often the case when a strange death occurs. Her body has been placed in an unstitched shroud and placed in a coffin.

Eventually they came to a farm called Nether Ness in Statholtstungur and asked to stay the night, but the farmer refused to give them hospitality. It was getting very late, and they thought they could go no farther, as it seemed unwise to risk fording the Hvit river at night, so they unloaded the horses, carried the coffin into a storehouse near the door, walked into the living room, and took off their clothes, intending to spend the night there, without food if necessary.

The household went to bed before it grew dark. They hadn't been long in their beds when they heard loud noises coming from the larder, and some of them went to see if thieves had broken into the house. When they came to the larder, there was a tall woman, stark naked, not a stitch of clothing on her, getting a meal ready. The people of the household were too scared when they saw her to come anywhere near. As soon as the corpse-bearers heard about it, they went to see for themselves what was going on. The woman was Thorgunna, and everyone thought it best to leave her in peace. When she finished doing what she wanted in the larder, she carried the food into the living room, laid the table, and served the meal. "Before we part, you may end up very sorry that you didn't treat us more hospitably," said the corpse-bearers to the farmer.

"We'll gladly give you food and anything else you need," said the farmer and his wife.

And as soon as the farmer had made them welcome, Thorgunna walked out of the room and didn't reappear.

Now a lamp was lit in the living room, and the travelers were . . . given dry things. They sat down at the table and made the sign of the cross over the food, and the farmer had every corner of the house sprinkled with holy water. The travelers ate their food and it did them no harm at all.[15]

The text has a wealth of lessons to teach us, and these are noteworthy because of their sober telling. Whoever refused to give hospitality to the bearers of a corpse had to pay a three-mark fine, a steep sum at the time. Thorgunna therefore rises to underscore the rights of her bearers. She is naked because her shroud is neither sewn shut nor held closed by a pin. The sign of the cross as well as the holy water are exorcisms, but Régis Boyer points out that "making a sign" over food and drink was also known by Nordic pagans.[16] In this text, it was used to neutralize any potentially malefic effects of the meal. Furthermore, Thorgunna's apparition is sufficient to let the inhospitable farmer realize the danger he courted by not respecting the customs.

The Self-defense of the Dead

Once they were in their tombs, the dead had little taste for being bothered. Yet there are rare stories in which the deceased gives his or her visitor a warm welcome. On the majority of occasions, men violate graves in the hopes of lucre. I have already cited several examples of such occasions, and we will pick up the thread of one of them again in chapter 5, in which Grettir enters the tomb of Kar the Old.

> [Grettir] went back toward the rope, but on his way he felt himself seized by a strong hand. He left the treasure to close with his attacker and the two engaged in a merciless struggle. Everything about them was smashed. The howedweller made a ferocious onslaught. Grettir for some time gave way, but found that no holding back was possible. They did not spare one another. Soon they came to the place where the horse's bones were lying, and here they struggled long, each in turn being brought to his knees. At last it ended in the howedweller falling backward with a horrible crash, whereupon Audun above bolted from the rope, thinking that Grettir was killed. Grettir drew his sword Jokulsnaut, cut off the head of the howedweller, and laid it between his thighs. Then he went with the treasure to the rope . . .[17]

I will underscore the expression "tomb-dweller" (*kumblbúi*) or "howedweller" (*haugbúi*) as most revealing of the times. We should also note how Grettir deals with the cadaver of this living dead: he separates the head from the body and removes it in such a way that the corpse cannot reattach it to his neck.

The stories of tomb raiding do not include many details; they range from a brief narrative in two lines, as in the *Book of Settlements*—"Leif entered the tomb, saw the gleam of a sword, and killed the man who held it"[18]—to a complete tale with a wealth of details, such as this detail from the *Saga of Hörd, Grimkelsson:*

> Hörd decided to pillage Soti's tomb. He and his men began digging out the cairn, but the day would always end before their work was done, and the next morning the mound was as if no digging had ever taken place. This fact indicates that the dead individual was defending himself by virtue of the powers, perhaps magical ones, at his disposal. It was only at the time Hörd gained possession of a wonderful sword lent by the god Odin that the cairn did not seal itself back up. Hörd dropped a rope through the hole they had dug and descended into the tomb while trusted friends held it. He found himself in a dark and empty room, and he asked Geir to join him with tapers. Both then opened the door leading into the second funeral chamber. They then heard a rumbling, like that created by an earthquake. The guardians of the rope then fled in terror and the tapers went out.
>
> In the half-light, Hörd and Geir spotted a boat laden with riches. Soti, who was horrible to look upon, was seated at the stern. He spoke to his unwanted guests, and when Hörd made a move to start taking his gold, they engaged in a terrible battle—one so violent that Hörd felt his flesh knotting over his bones. Fortunately, Geir relit the tapers. Touched by their light, Soti was stripped of his strength and collapsed to the ground. Hörd then stole his gold ring from him, which Soti cursed, but when Geir mercilessly brought the torch close to him, Soti disappeared, burrowing into the ground.[19]

Sometimes the dead person simply asked that his wealth be taken and he be left in peace. This is what happens when Hromund enters Thrain's tomb. But Hromund does not hear it that way. Instead, he insults the deceased, hurling the dead's cowardice in his face, and when battle is joined, Hromund finds himself in a precarious position. He manages to extricate himself and seizes hold of Thrain's sword, and he sends Thrain's head flying.[20]

Sometimes it even happened that the dead person defended the pillager of his tomb. When Skeggi of Midfjord takes possession of weapons in the tumulus of Hrolf Kraki, Bödvar tries to hurl himself upon him, but Hrolf, the dead man, intervenes.[21] This is a rare event, and the majority of texts inform us that the dead have little taste for people meddling in their business.

Here are yet two more examples. The first example is this: One day an old woman enters the church of Holar, where the dead are buried. While she is praying, the dead emerge from their coffins and throw themselves upon her.[22]

This anecdote was noted down by the monk Gunlnlaug Leifsson in the *Saga of Jon Ögmundarson,* bishop of Holar, who died in 1211. To say the least, it is a curious tale and reveals the superposition of two cultures: Christianity (church, prayers) and paganism (the dead taking action). I can venture one explanation for this strange behavior: there may well have been dead pagans who were scorched by the prayers of the living and who were seeking to escape the sting of the orisons. Other writings do in fact tell us that pagans could not tolerate Christian discourse.

The second anecdote was collected in the sixteenth century in the Paderborn region, where it had been handed down orally.

Around the year 1516, an old woman who wished to attend the first Mass said in honor of the dead went to Saint-Laurent Church. Being mistaken about the time of the Mass, she arrived at midnight, found the doors open, entered, and saw an elderly, unknown priest officiating at the altar and a large number of people seated. The majority of them were strangers to her, and some were even lacking heads, but she recognized several as people who had recently died and whom she had known well.

Terrified, she sat down. Seeing naught but the dead, she thought they must be the souls of the dead and wondered if she should stay or not. A woman broke away from the crowd of the faithful, came over, and grabbed her by the side of her cloak. The old woman recognized her as one of her neighbors who had died three weeks earlier. "My good woman," this neighbor said, "may God protect us. How did you get here? For the love of Christ and the Virgin, take care! At the time of the consecration, flee as fast as your feet will take you, and do not look back if you value your life." The old woman followed her advice and hastened out of the church at top speed. Hardly had she stepped outside when she heard a great fracas: the specters had come in pursuit of her. Catching up to her in the cemetery, they grabbed her by the cloak, but she shook off the cloak and escaped.

Later the next morning, she returned to the cemetery in search of her cloak. She found it torn to pieces and saw on every tomb a piece of cloth.[23]

Here again I can venture an explanation. These could well have been dead who had been neither saved nor damned and feared to see their torture prolonged if their Mass was disturbed. The presence of decapitated individuals in the assembly suggests that these dead had been executed no doubt for some crime.

The Revenant Despite Himself

Not all the dead resist burial, and not all, fortunately, return to haunt the areas where they lived, but the deceased can be compelled to return through necromancy.

Divination through the dead is, among all the Germanic peoples, a well-attested phenomena—as it is among those of classical antiquity—

but the information on this has been transmitted to us by Christian, scholarly literature, which is by and large a tributary of Roman traditions. It is therefore often difficult to find indigenous data and to distinguish it from foreign contributions.

From the fourth to the twelfth centuries, the term *necromanticus,* quickly distorted into *nigromanticus* and *necromantia,* recurs with remarkable consistency in the literary efforts of educated Christians. Lactantius (Lucius Caecilius Firmianus), who wrote between 197 and 222 CE, incorporated necromancy into the demonic arts: "Demons were the inventors of astrology and soothsaying and divination and those productions that are called oracles and necromancy."[24] This opinion pops up again with Isidore of Seville; Rabanus Maurus, the "teacher of Germany," who died on February 4, 856; Hincmar of Reims (ca. 802–882); Ivo of Chartres (ca. 1040–1116); Hugues de Saint Victor (died in 1141); John of Salisbury (1115–1180); and Gratien, who died before 1179; as well as in many anonymous texts.[25] Isidore defines necromancy this way: "They are called necromants, those who by incantations resuscitate the dead to ask them about the future."[26] Following St. Augustine, the bishop of Seville then confused necromancy and hydromancy, divination by water, which was an error already committed in antiquity by Varro. "The reuse of traditions is evident when Rabunus writes: 'Hydromancy serves to summon the shades.'"[27]

Much closer to autochthonous traditions, Pierre le Mangeur (ca. 1100–1170), who owes his nickname [Peter the Book Eater] to his love of reading, states: "Necromants summon the dead by means of chants or sacrifices."[28] Predominating among all the Germanic peoples is the belief in incantation, song, and chanting. The glosses in Old English say: "Necromancy means invocation of demons, incantation, sorcery" (*necromantia .i. demonum invocatio galdre wiccecraefte*) or else more simply, "divination using the dead; incantation (*galdre mortuorum divination*).[29] The glosses in Old High German confirm the reality of necromancy, which they call *hellruna, hellrun,* terms formed from *hel,* "the hells, death," and the verb *rûnen,* "murmur," and a margin note points out that this practice means "calling the spirits back from the hells."[30] The Old English *galdre* (*galder/galster* in Old High German; *galdr* in Norse) designates the incantation that compels the dead to return. A very beautiful poem from the *Edda, The Incantation of Groa,* allows us to witness a work of necromancy: Svipdag, the son of Groa, calls back his dead mother because he wants to learn the magic charms that will assure a fine and rich life.[31]

During the early Middle Ages, necromancy was not simply a literary motif. In 1080, an English council spoke of people who consulted the dead.[32] In Norway, the Christian laws of the Gulathing designated the practice by the phrase "to be seated outside to awaken the troll" (*utiseta at vekja troll upp*).[33] Utiseta, in fact, characterizes a form of magic that translates poorly.

Let us now take a look at what the texts tell us. The oldest testimonies are found primarily in the *Poetic Edda* and in its prose reworking by Snorri Sturluson. Necromancy is the prerogative of the god Odin, whose nicknames (*cognomina*)* obviously attest to his relations with the departed. In *The Orb of the World,* Snorri states explicitly that the god Odin awakens the dead in the ground.[34] When Odin loses his son Baldr, he compels a dead seer to come back to earth in order to learn his fate:

> *Then Odin rode by the eastern doors,*
> *where he knew the seeress's grave to be;*
> *he began to speak a corpse-reviving spell for the wise woman,*
> *until reluctantly she rose, spoke these corpse-words.*[35]

All these spells begin in the same way: Svipdag sings, "Awaken, Groa, awaken good woman." "Awaken, Angantyr, Hervör awakens you," it says in the *Saga of Hervör.*[36]

---

*They are derived from words like *draugr,* "dead man, revenant," and *Draugadróttinn; hanga,* "hanged man," as in *Hangagud, Hangadróttinn,* "God of the hanged men, Lord of the hanged men"; and *vatr,* "warriors killed in battle," as in *Valfödr,* "Father of warriors fallen in battle."

Saxo Grammaticus, whose first books of the *Gesta Danorum* date from 1202 to 1216, informs us of an additional detail.

The giantess Harthgrepa wished to learn what the future held in store for her protégé Hadingus.[37] A dead man lay in the farm where both of them were spending the night. Harthgrepa carved magic spells on a piece of wood and ordered Hadingus to place it beneath the dead man's tongue. In a fury the deceased uttered the following verses:

> *May the cursed one who called me from hell perish*
> *and let him atone in Tartarus for summoning a spirit!*

The corpse spoke these words three times, and his vengeance was not long in coming: spirits tore the giantess to pieces.

Saxo designates the deceased using a circumlocution: "Individuals of his same race" (*ab originibus suae consortibus*).[38]

The texts are unanimous on one point: the dead do not like being summoned back. Groa bemoans that Svipdag awakens her; the seeress reveals Balder's fate against her will; the farmer made to speak by Harthgrepa gets his revenge; and Angantyr, in the *Saga of Hervör*, tells his daughter that she is mad to take such action and threatens her.

> *Then Angantyr sings:*
> *Hervör daughter*
> *Why do you call me*
> *With evil runes?*
> *You draw a curse down upon you.*
> *Mad you have become*
> *And bereft of reason*
> *That you seek to awaken the dead.*[39]

We should note that only Saxo Grammaticus and the anonymous author of this saga depict women indulging in necromancy; this magic art seems to have been reserved for men—indeed, *necromanticus* has no feminine form.

Around 1200, the *Saga of the Faröemen,* whose plot takes place between 1000 and 1035, introduced another form of necromancy, this time in the context of a veritable police investigation. Thorgrim the Wicked murders Sigmund to steal his gold ring. Thrond, who knows magic, has doubts about Thorgrim's version of events, pays him a visit, interrogates him, and, confronted by Thorgrim's denials, turns to necromancy to thwart him.

Thrond had a great fire kindled in the room and had four lattices set up in such a way as to form four corners. Then he drew nine squares on the outside of each lattice and took a seat between the fire and the lattices. He asked that no one speak to him, and all fell silent. He sat this way for some moments.

After a while, a man entered the room. It was Einar from the Hebrides. He approached the fire, stretched his hands toward it for a brief instant, then turned and walked out again.

A short while later, another man entered the room and also stretched his hands toward the fire momentarily, then walked back out. They recognized him as Thorir.

Immediately afterward, a third man entered the room. He was a big man, all covered with blood and carrying his head in his hands. Everyone knew him for Sigmund Brestisson. He hesitated in the room for a moment, then left.

After this, Thrond rose from his chair, gave a deep sigh, and declared: "Einar perished first, dead of the cold or drowned, for he was the weakest. Thorir must have succumbed next, and undoubtedly Sigmund carried him, and that must have worn him out even more. He must have made it to shore at the end of his strength, and these men must have slain him, because he appeared to us blood-covered and decapitated."[40]

Thorgrim the Wicked's home was searched, and Sigmund's ring was discovered.

The use of spells and runes carved on wood persisted in Iceland until relatively recently, and during the nineteenth century Jon Árnason collected in a magic book what should be done to awaken a dead person and bring him back in order to use him as an emissary (*sendingr*) or a zombie (*upvakningr,* "awakened one"):

> After writing an Our Father backward on a page in blood, "you should carve runes on a staff and go to the cemetery at midnight with these two things, and go to whatever tomb strikes your fancy. However, it would be more prudent to attack the smaller graves. You should then place the staff on top of the grave and roll it back and forth while reciting the Our Father backward at the same time, following how it is written on the page, as well as some magic spells that few people know, except for witches. During this time, the revenant will slowly rise from the tomb, because this is not something that takes place quickly, and revenants will be praying greatly and saying: "Let me (rest) in peace."[41]

Eight centuries separate this text from the poems of the *Edda,* but the information has not changed: incantation, runes, the unwillingness of the dead individual to return, danger. Wouldn't it be the better part of valor to select a small grave—in other words, that of an individual whose stature and strength would not be too formidable?

FIVE

The True Revenants

Tue revenants, which is to say the deceased who returned of their own volition for personal reasons, can be divided into two large categories, depending on whether they appeared to men in dreams or when they were awake. A distinction must therefore be made, as in the source material, between corporeal, three-dimensional revenants and the evanescent, immaterial beings known as ghosts. It is also helpful to see the role played by daydreams and dreams in the Middle Ages. Without understanding this, it will be difficult to grasp the reasons compelling the church to intervene in this area—as well as the consequences of that intervention.

Dream

The ancients bequeathed the Middle Ages a very elaborate oneiromantic [dream decoding] system, and the most important key to dreams was the *Onirocriticon* by Artemidorus of Daldis (second century CE), in which regular dreams are distinguished from visionary dreams. The first concerned the present reality, and the latter concerned the future and consisted of two sections—the theorematic dream (the one whose fulfillment represents in every aspect what was shown) and the alle-gorical dream (the one that expressed something by any kind of angle).[1] Around 400, Macrobius fine-tuned the theory that the church would later embrace as its own. There are, he says, five categories of dream: There are dreams due to worries, dreams due to fears, and dreams due to the hopes of the dreamer or even to an excess of food or drink (called *insomnium*). The dream of a person who is half-awake is called *visum* or *phantasma*. This divinatory dream, or *oraculum,* was sought through incubation, by spending the night in a sacred place—for example, a temple. The dream whose prophetic content comes true is the *visio*. Last, the enigmatic dream, *somnium,* is the one that is rightly called an interpretation.[2]

Gregory the Great, pope from 590 to 604, reused this outline, but he makes a distinction between six categories of dreams that, in fact, overlie three large types: dreams due to food or hunger, dreams sent by demons, and dreams whose origin is divine and attested by the Bible.[3] Only these last were tolerated, and they formed the framework for visionary literature. Oneiromancy was reduced to the rank of idolatry and was forbidden in 789 by the *Admonitio generalis,* then in 802–803 by the capitulary *Capitulare missorum item speciale.*[4] Gregory II (669–731) fulminated against the Germanic seers in particular and loudly proclaimed that dreams could not predict the future.[5] In 829 the Council of Paris reiterated all these prohibitions, which, after that time, could be found everywhere in the ecclesiastical literature.[6]

Dream held an important place in everyday German life, and the authors of the sagas pepper their narratives with comments such as "such a man had many dreams," or even "he knew how to interpret dreams." In *The Orb of the World,* Snorri Sturluson depicts the anxiety of King Harald the Black, who never dreams. Harald asks for advice on how to remedy what he regards as an infirmity.[7] In the *Saga of the Vikings of Jormsborg,* written around 1200 but reporting on events some two centuries older, there is one extremely revealing episode: Gorm asks for the hand in marriage of Thyri, the daughter of Jarl Harald. She does not accept immediately.

If you are so set upon wedding me, when you return home you shall
have immediately constructed a house that is large enough so that
you can find it pleasant to rest there. . . . . That is where you shall
sleep for the first night of winter and then for three nights in a row.
Next, send men in search of me to tell me your dreams and whether
you had them, and I will then tell you whether this marriage shall
take place. If you do not dream, it is not worth the trouble of con-
templating this marriage.[8]

In the *Saga of Gisli Sursson,* whose plot takes place during the second half of the tenth century, the hero dreams two nights in a row but
refuses to tell anyone what he has seen. Shortly after, his friend Vestein
is murdered. Gisli then declares: "I did not tell anyone my two dreams
because I did not want them to come true."[9]

Old Norse literature is rich in all manner of dream, but the alle-
gorical dream is predominant. Recall that of Charlemagne in *The
Song of Roland* (beginning at verse 2541): the emperor sees bears
and leopards, serpents and basilisks, dragons, demons, and griffons
tearing his soldiers apart, a theme that will enjoy enormous success
throughout the medieval West. For the German-language countries, recall Kreimhild's dream in the *Song of the Nibelungen:* "She
dreamed that she had reared a falcon, a strong, ferocious, and handsome bird, but which two eagles tear apart with their claws right
before her eyes."[10]

The falcon is Siegfried, her future husband. Dreams such as this
one are legion in medieval texts. The *Saga of the People of Lake Valley*
tells this: Gudmond has a significant dream, and he visits Finni, the
oneiromancer, and offers him a ring to interpret this vision. Shortly
thereafter, Gudmond dies. In the meantime, Einar dreams that a
magnificent ox arrives at Mödruvellir—Gudmond's domain—enters
every building on the farm, sits upon the high seat, and dies there.
The ox is Gudmond, who died in his high seat.[11]

Almost as numerous are the theorematic dreams, one of the most beautiful examples of which is found in the *Story of Burnt Njal* or *Njal's Saga,* written around 1280 using elements going back to around the year 1000:

> I dreamt, methought, that I was riding on by Knafaholes, and there I thought I saw many wolves, and they all made at me; but I turned away from them straight toward Rangriver, and then methought they pressed hard on me on all sides, but I kept them at bay, and shot all those that were foremost, till they came so close to me that I could not use my bow against them. Then I took my sword, and I smote with it with one hand, but thrust at them with my bill with the other. Shield myself then I did not, and methought then I knew not what shielded me. Then I slew many wolves, and thou, too, Kolskegg; but Hjort methought they pulled down, and tore open his breast, and one methought had his heart in his maw; but I grew so wroth that I hewed that wolf asunder just below the brisket, and after that methought the wolves turned and fled. Now my counsel is, brother Hjort, that thou ridest back west to Tongue.[12]

Gunnar, Kolskegg, and Hjort set off on their journey and fall into an ambush, where Hjort loses his life.

A small group of dreams feature the intervention of a living individual who appears to another person in dream. In the *Saga of Hallfred the Troublesome Skald* (chapter 6), a poet who lived between 950–965 and 1000, King Olaf visits his skald in this way and asks the skald to join him. On another occasion (chapter 10), the skald advises Olaf not to take part in a duel.[13]

The last category of dreams features the appearance of sendings from the otherworld, either the fylgja, the pagan equivalent of the Christian guardian angel, which is called the fulgjuengill—from *engill,* "angel"—or the dead.

Ghosts

It is in the realm of dream that the influence of the church left its deepest imprint. Yet the church did not always successfully conceal the pagan substratum. In the *Saga of Olaf the Saint*,[14] referring to Olaf II Haraldsson, who died in 1030, the recuperation of indigenous ghosts is particularly clear-cut. Here are two examples.

> Two inhabitants of Vik kidnapped a priest, gouged out his eyes, cut out his tongue, and broke his limbs. He was left for dead, but a poor woman took in the mutilated victim. One night, this priest dreamed that King Olaf came to him, passed his hand over his eyes and broken limbs, then yanked so violently on the root of his tongue that he cried out. When the priest awoke, all his injuries were healed.[15]

> Pagans captured a young Dane and took him to the Wendes.* He escaped and was recaptured and brought back. Shackled and chained, he was tossed into a dungeon. Other prisoners, fellow Christians, advised him to pray to St. Olaf, which he did. The following night, Olaf came to him in a dream and asked him to rise. On awakening, the young Dane recounted his dream to his companions in misfortune, and they asked him to stand up to see if the dream he spoke of was true. He obeyed; the chains no longer held him down.[16]

This type of dream helps illustrate Christian thought: nothing is impossible for God and his saints (St. Luke). If we refer to *The Golden Legend* by Jacobus de Voragine or de Varazzo (before 1264), we will find saints healing every kind of affliction, angels freeing the faithful from their chains, and many other marvels.[17] The two examples cited above take place in these exempla—as does a third in which King Olaf comes to the aid of a poor wretch.

---

*[An ancient Slavic tribe. —*Ed.*]

One day, Alvald, a cripple, was sleeping out in the open. In his dream he saw a majestic man coming to him and advising him to go to London, to the St. Olaf Church. On awakening, Alvald heeded his dream. When he reached London Bridge, he asked for directions. A man approached him and led him to the church. The sill was high and Alvald could only cross it by rolling over it, but his disability disappeared at once. His companion had also vanished and he never set eyes on him again.[18]

The church had created nothing *ex nihilo*—it was by and large inspired by autochthonous traditions, which in their turn borrowed quite a few literary motifs from the church. *The Book of the Colonization of Iceland* provides a splendid illustration of the blending of pagan matters and Christian particulars.

When Asolf grew old, he became an anchorite. His hut was located where the church now stands. He died in Holm, and that is where he is buried. When Halldor, son of Illugi the Red, lived there, a cowherd got into the habit of drying her shoes on a tuft of grass that grew out of Asolf's tomb. She dreamed that Asolf scolded her for wiping her shoes on his home. She reported the fact to Halldor, who paid little attention to the matter.

But when the bishop Hrodolf left Baer . . . , three monks remained there after him. One of them dreamed that Asolf told him: "Send your servant to the home of Halldor in Holm. Buy from Halldor the clump of grass that is on the path to the stable, and pay him one silver mark for it." The monk did this. The servant was able to purchase the clump of grass, and next he dug into the ground and found the bones of a man. He gathered them up and took them to the house. The next night, Halldor dreamed that Asolf came to him and said that Halldor's two eyes would pop from his head if he did not buy back the bones for the price he had sold them. Halldor bought Asolf's bones and had made for them a wooden chest, which he then placed above the altar.[19]

Let's take a closer look at this anecdote. The cowherd disturbs the rest of Asolf by soiling his sepulcher—a theme we encountered earlier in Roman beliefs—and the deceased demands a halt to this sacrilege. The second part of the story touches on another subject: Asolf is a Christian and does not want to rest any longer in unconsecrated ground. He arranges matters so that someone will take care of his mortal remains. We can note the autochthonous element beneath the edifying intention: Asolf threatens to move from words into actions—something that is hardly Christian and lets us grasp that the dead still have the power to act. More difficult to explain is the procedure for buying the anchorite's bones. It brings about the intervention of a monk and the owner of the area. The monk gives the departed satisfaction by having his remains exhumed, but then why does Asolf oblige Holldor to buy them back? There can be only a pagan explanation: The dead man is connected to his land, the place where he spent his life, and does not wish to be separated from it, like a tutelary spirit. Furthermore, the monk's servant does not provide him with an appropriate "ritual" sepulcher—one that only a free man can apparently grant. This is a very pagan trait corresponding to the Nordic mind-set of the time.

The church therefore recuperated, adapted, and transformed folk traditions. Those who need convincing need only compare the story of Asolf to an episode from *Laxdaela Saga* (Saga of the Habitants of Salmon Valley), one of the principal Icelandic sagas, written around 1230–60 and relating events that occurred during the ninth, tenth, and eleventh centuries.

One night, young Herdis dreamed that a woman came to him. She was wearing a woolen cloak and a cloth covering her head. He found her appearance quite unpleasant. The woman said to him: "Tell your grandmother that I am not at all pleased with her, for she kneels on top of me every night and waters me with drops so hot [her tears] that I burn all over from them. I'm telling you because

I like you better. . . ." Herdis then woke up and told Gudrun his dream. She took the apparition to be a good omen.

Next morning Gudrun had some boards torn from the floor of the church where she habitually kneeled to pray, and then she saw to the digging up of the ground beneath the boards. There they found some black and alarming-looking bones, a brooch, and a large magic wand. People guessed from these that it must have been the tomb of a sorceress. The bones were taken far away and buried in a place where few people went.[20]

What better way to make pagans realize, even when dead, the power of the true faith?

Ghosts sometimes appear in gripping forms that resemble specters: Gunnlaug Viper-Tongue appears to Illugi the Black, all covered with blood. An sees the ghost of his brother, which is all bloody, and a sword is piercing his chest. When Blundketil appears in a dream to announce his death to his son, it seems to the son that Blundketil is covered in flames: he had died when his house burned down.[21] The oneiric revenant often took on the appearance he wore at his final hours. To permit listeners or readers to identify these revenants with no mistake, the writers of the sagas placed signals in their stories: These deceased individuals are black and are terrifying or are majestic and shining. Ghosts are sometimes anonymous, and it is necessary to be able to distinguish them from the living who appear to other living individuals.

These nocturnal manifestations do not happen by chance. On each occasion of visitation, the dead person is driven by a specific purpose. For example, the *Book of Settlements* reports this:

"Asmund was buried beneath a cairn in Asmundarleidi—he was laid in a boat with his slave close by. The slave had taken his own life, not wishing to outlive Asmund; he was put on the other end of the boat"—which clearly shows what kind of importance was granted the rank of individuals. "Shortly afterward, Thor dreamed that Asmund said he was having problems because of the slave. . . . The mound was then dug up, and the slave was removed from the boat."[22]

That the dead sometimes were not able to cohabit the same tomb is confirmed by another story: Brynjar appears in a dream to Thorstein and asks him to remove the body of his brother, who had been buried with him, because he can no longer tolerate his violent nature.[23] All the examples I've cited here show clearly that the departed continued to live inside their tombs.

The dead therefore needed the help of the living, and this is even truer when they were attacked by the church. Hans-Joachim Klare cites the example of a revenant, a wizard, who appears three times, twice to request protection against a bishop and the third time to bid farewell.[24] In a later, legendary version of the *Saga of Harald the Merciless,* a ghost appears in dream to a bondi—a peasant who is a freeman—and explains to him that he has been driven away from his dwelling by fire. He asks that a boat be lent to him, for which he will provide a security, so that he can carry away his things. The bondi accepts the bargain, and on the next morning, when he goes to the landing, he sees that his boat has been used. On the prow he finds gold dust.[25]

The dead had no liking for being robbed. In "The Story of the Cairn Dweller," preserved in the *Book of the Flat Island* compiled around 1300, Thorstein receives a visit in dream from a dead man from whom he stole a sword. The ghost is wielding an ax and threatens him.[26] On the other hand, the dead knew how to display gratitude. Hall steals a sword from Skefil's cairn and lends it to Thorkel, who takes his place in a duel. After the battle, Thorkel has someone return the weapon to the mound, whereas Hall wishes to keep it. That night, Thorkel dreams that Skelfil visits him to thank him for returning his property and to let him know he would have been in danger if Thorkel had not done so. Skefil then congratulates Thorkel for his bravery and offers him the sword. Upon awakening, Thorkel finds it next to him.[27]

The dead were therefore omnipresent and could intervene in the lives of human beings, as is shown in the *Saga of the Faröemen* (from around 1220). Leif Thorisson has been killed, and Thurid and Thora suspect Sigurd. They ask Leif Özurason to avenge him. When he does nothing, they give him the cold shoulder:

> It is told that once Thurid saw her husband, Sigmund Brestisson, come to her in a dream, as if it was something that really happened. He spoke to her: "You are not deceiving yourself," he said, "it is truly me that has come here with the permission of God himself. Do not be hard or wicked toward Leif, your son-in-law, because he will be given the opportunity to avenge the outrage you have suffered." After which, Thurid woke up and told her daughter Thora her dream, and they treated Leif more gently than before.[28]

The comment "with the permission of God" is a pretense intended to gain acceptance for something smelling of paganism. Generally, the revenants visiting in dreams did not worry about such details. Sigmund appears, predicts the future, and compels the living to change their behavior, and this is no isolated case. In the *Saga of Gull-Thorir,* which dates perhaps from the fourteenth century, Agnar reveals the future to Thorir and advises or reprimands him after Thorir has attempted to raid his tomb, but it seems that it may not have been of his own volition.

These stories help us better understand the stories of visions that teem in the exempla: Christ, the Virgin, and the saints have no problem replacing the ghosts and playing the role of advisor or helper. The souls in purgatory experienced no difficulty coming back to demand indulgences and prayers so that they might rest in peace—just as the Norse ghosts came asking for help to enjoy the rest offered by their cairns. The assistance of the departed become a cliché of religious literature, but some narratives are of great beauty, such as this one from *The Golden Legend:* "A man always recited the psalm *De profundis* for the dead every time he passed a cemetery. One day, when he took refuge there, being pursued by his enemies, the dead immediately arose, each holding the tools of their trades in hand, and they defended him vigorously, forcing his terrified foes to flee."[29]

The great lesson of pagan and Christian texts can be spelled out in a few words: "Help the dead; they will return the favor."

Scandinavian Revenants

A selection of texts provides us with the information necessary to form a precise idea of ordinary revenants, those who do not necessarily have to wait for night to fall in order to put in an appearance, those who talk and fight, and those who continue to have influence upon the living.

An Epidemic of Revenants
The *Saga of the People of Floi,* written around 1300, takes place in southwestern Iceland and notes the following facts.

> It was during the period of Jól (Christmas). The weather was beautiful on Christmas day and people spent the entire day outside. The second day, Thorgils and his men went to bed early; they were already asleep when Jostein and his companions noisily entered the hut. They went to bed. They had barely stretched out when someone knocked at the door. One of Jostein's men leapt up saying: "It is undoubtedly good news," went outside, was taken by madness, and died the next morning. The same thing happened the next night: a man went mad declaring he saw the man who died the night before hurling himself at him. An epidemic then struck Jostein's crew and killed six people. Jostein was then carried off by the illness. Their bodies were buried in the sand, and Thorgils cautioned his men to be on their guard.
>
> After the Jól feast, all the dead returned, Thorgerd, Thorgil's wife, fell ill and succumbed, soon followed by all the men of Jostein's crew. They had reached a point where no one could go outside. Thorgils then had all the dead burnt in a pyre and revenants no longer did any wrong to anyone.[30]

These events took place during a fishing expedition to Greenland around the year 970 CE, between the Christmas feast and the beginning of the month of March. Thorgils had been shipwrecked with his companions, and they had built a hut, but their food was rationed, which no doubt explains the epidemic that struck almost everyone. The dead came to designate and abduct those meant to follow them, and only the complete destruction of their bodies prevented total carnage. It is clear that what we have here is the somewhat unreal interpretation of an actual event. We see the fantasies of men reduced by a critical situation and interpreting events in accordance with their beliefs. The strange and unexplained death of the first man and his sudden madness could not help but bring hauntings to mind, given the criteria of the era.

The Nocturnal Wanderings of Bjorn's Father

The same saga relates another incident whose components are extremely revealing of the survival of ancestral ideas that owe nothing to a literary style or genre.

Thorgils arrived one day at the home of a powerful man named Bjorn. He was given a warm welcome, and the house was splendid, yet everyone there went to bed early. Thorgils asked why and learned that Bjorn's father, who had died recently, was haunting the premises, and everyone was scared of him. During the winter, he often heard someone outside knocking on the roof. One night, he rose, grabbed his ax, and went out. He saw a large, wicked revenant standing in front of the door. He raised his ax, but the specter took flight in the direction of his mound. When he saw that Thorgils had pursued, he turned back to meet him. They fought hand to hand because Thorgils had dropped his ax. The battle was so brutal and ferocious that the ground broke up beneath their feet. Finally, because it had been given to Thorgils to live longer, the revenant fell on his back with Thorgils on top of him. Thorgils took a deep breath, picked up his fallen ax, and sent the head of the revenant flying, telling him: "You'll never again harm anyone." In truth he was never seen again. Bjorn treated Thorgils with great honor because he had restored peace to his home.[31]

This passage from the saga provides many teachings. The revenant seeks to attract people outside and makes noises like a rapping spirit (poltergeist), but he manifests on top of the roof and does not seem capable of operating inside the house, a fact that merits attention. In all superstitions, the roof plays an important role. In Rome, it was believed that the man who returned from a long journey during which he was thought to have died should not enter his house by the door but through the roof, in which an opening had been contrived. Plutarch gives us the following explanation for this fact in the form of an etiological legend.

Following a naval battle off the shores of Sicily, many Roman citizens considered dead returned to their country. One of them, finding the door of his home closed, went to sleep next to it. During his slumber, a dead man appeared and advised him to enter his home through the roof. This he did, and he lived for a long time afterward.[32]

Some ghost stories from Germanic peoples give the impression that the dead are incapable of crossing a threshold, therefore the house was considered a good refuge if the door was closed. We can compare this information with the fact that, in later beliefs, witches left their dwellings through only the chimney. The person reciting a fifteenth-century charm asked the night demons to leave by the roof. There are certainly some very old elements here, perhaps connected with the genie of the threshold. Unfortunately, the Germanic texts offer us no specific details on this point.

The second noteworthy piece of information is the flight of the revenant in the direction of his mound. The tomb was the dwelling of specters; they left it to return to where they once lived rather than wandering off in search of adventure.

Finally, we must consider the battle that pits Thorgils against Bjorn's father. The hero is not grabbing at nothing, as in later stories—the revenant is a three-dimensional being and is endowed with great strength. The text says expressly that Thorgils is a very robust man when he confronts this dead man. In northern Europe, the dead that manifested in places other than dreams were therefore not ectoplasms, reflections, images, or illusions. This is a fact that we will see again.

Hrapp

In the *Laxdaela Saga* (Saga of the Habitants of Salmon Valley), from which we have already borrowed a great deal of information, we find new proof of the corporeal quality of revenants as well as some extremely ancient particulars.

> There long lived in Hrappstadir a man named Hrapp, who was quite an unpleasant character and hard to get along with. Feeling his death coming on, he asked his wife to bury him upright in a grave dug beneath the kitchen door. "I want to be able to keep an eye on the household," he told her. His final wishes were respected after he died, but he often came back, murdering the majority of his people and causing great wrongs to his neighbors. His domain, Hrappstadir, was deserted and his widow left for the West. The farmers of the region visited Höskuld to ask him to put an end to Hrapp's wandering and misdeeds. Höskuld took several men and went to Hrappstadir and had the body of the wicked dead man exhumed, and it was taken to a place little frequented by cattle and far from any traveled roads. After this, Hrapp's hauntings almost came to an end.
>
> Olaf the Peacock, the son of Melkorka, bought Hrappstadir and built his home in Hjardarholt. The stalls for the cattle were located a fair distance from the farm, in the forest. One day, his cowherd came to him asking that someone else fulfill his duties. Olaf then told him: "I will come with you this evening when you go to tether the oxen."

When evening fell, Olaf took his spear and left the house with the cowherd. A light snow had covered the ground. They came to the stables and found them open. Olaf told his man to enter, "I will drive in the cattle and you can tie them up." The cowherd headed toward the stable, but before Olaf even had time to think, the man was leaping into his arms. "Why are you so frightened?" Olaf asked. "Hrapp is at the door," the cowherd answered. "He tried to grab me, but I've had my fill of wrestling with him." Olaf approached the door and struck at Hrapp with his spear. Hrapp seized the spearhead with both hands and twisted it so sharply that the shaft snapped. Olaf than tried to rush upon him, but Hrapp sank into the ground, where he remained.

The next morning, Olaf went to Hrapp's tomb and had it opened. They found his body there, which had not decomposed, and the corpse was still holding the spearhead. Olaf built a pyre and the

The bodies of revenants do not decompose in the tomb.
(Poetic and Philosophical Codex, *Folio No. 2, Stuttgart, folio 233 r°)*

corpse was reduced to ashes, which were then gathered and cast into the sea. Hrapp's hauntings never again caused any harm to anyone.[33]

Though revenants were dead, their bodies never decayed. Yet one detail contradicts the fact that the specter was not an ectoplasm. Hrapp sinks into the ground to get away—and this is not an isolated case. There is no secret passageway, and the ground bears no trace of the strange disappearance. Furthermore, the snow bears no footprints, which indicates that Hrapp gets into the stables the same way he left them. The saga writer notes that he disappears ". . . as he had come." The ground seems to pose no obstacle then to the travel of revenants.

We will leave this point hanging for now—more light will be shed upon it later—and note that the complete destruction of the body followed by the dispersal of its ashes in liquid puts an end to the haunting—but only if these ashes are not ingested by a living being. This detail can be compared to the fate of certain criminals in Frisia during the Middle Ages. They were buried at low tide on the shore that was left exposed by the sea going out (Wattenmeer).[34] In Scandinavia, witches were either burned after having been stoned or tied to a reef that would be covered by the sea at high tide.[35] Water seems to have been regarded as a defensive measure against haunting, but this measure was ineffective against the drowned.

Thormod or the Badly Married Revenant

The *Saga of Havard of Isafjord* has come down to us by virtue of seventeenth-century manuscripts, but Sturla twice alludes to it in his reworking of the *Book of Settlements*. The narrative appears to have circulated orally until the thirteenth century, when it was collected and set down in writing. The information it provides must be regarded with prudence, yet it only confirms what we already know from other sources.

Thormod was a man little liked and of a difficult nature; his wife was named Thorgerd. Shortly after he died and was buried, his wife visited Havard, who welcomed her warmly and asked her what was new. She told him of Thormod's death and added: "Things have not grown any better because of this, for he returns to his bed every night. I want you to help me, Havard, because while my people were loath to deal with Thormod before, now they are on the verge of all fleeing." Havard advised her to go to Laugabol, the domain of his son Olaf. She took this advice, and Olaf agreed to accompany her.

When evening came, Olaf lay down upon the bed closest to the door and pulled a cover over himself. Once night had fallen, Thormod entered. When he saw that the bed where ordinarily no one slept was occupied, he tugged on the fur cover. Olaf held on to it and it ripped. Seeing he was being resisted, Thormod leapt upon a bench while Olaf, grabbing his ax, tried to strike him. He was already too late, and Thormod leapt on him, clasping him with all his strength. All around them pieces were flying, and suddenly the lamp hanging from the transversal beam of the roof, which had been glimmering weakly, was extinguished. Thormod's assault intensified in its violence. The two combatants found themselves outside. There was a large stack of logs in the courtyard. Thormod's heels bumped into a log and he fell over backward. Olaf hurled himself upon Thormod and gave him a good going over, then he went inside the house again. Recognizing his footsteps, the entire household got up. A lamp was lit, and Olaf, whose body was covered with the injuries it had received from Thormod's fists, was given a massage.

One day, Olaf went to his sheepfold; it was a harsh winter and the sheep needed close watching. On that night, the weather had been particularly bad. When Olaf left the sheepfold, he saw Bard, wished him welcome, and asked him what he was doing out so late. "Earlier," Bard told him, "I went to check my sheep; they had gone down to the beach. They could get back up in only two places, and each time I tried to bring them up, a man barred their passage. I would like you to come with me."

Olaf went with him to the beach and saw the man. It was

Thormod. He rushed toward him and they began fighting on a snow-covered hill. Olaf managed to break Thormod's spine. He went into the water and started swimming, dragging the corpse behind him, which he then abandoned to the depths. Ever since that time, sailors traveling through these waters have been ill at ease.[36]

In this story, Thormod returns home through the door and, apparently, attacks Olaf because he is occupying Thormod's bed. Thormod does not resign himself to his death—he is avenging himself on his people and the clan that did not welcome him, and once night has fallen, he returns to his home. We should also note that his strength increases in total darkness.

Yet one point in this story is odd. Olaf does not kill Thormod during their first encounter but is satisfied with giving him only a correction. This is undoubtedly done to make Thormod realize that he is not wanted and should leave the living in peace. This effort at intimidation, which has no effect, clearly seems to have formed part of the belief in ghosts and revenants. There is another saga that depicts a ghost whose haunting ceases when he is confronted by general hostility. This indicates that the troublesome dead were assumed to have the same reactions as the living.

During their second meeting, Olaf finishes off Thormod and abandons his cadaver to the waves of the sea, but while this put an end to the deceased's nocturnal roving, the final remark in the story indicates clearly that Thormod has not lost all power. He inspires fear in all those who sail near his final abode. This could of course be an explanation, colored by the marvelous, for a particularly dangerous section of the sea for sailors. There is nothing new in this, in his *De nugis curialium,* written between 1181 and 1193, Walter Map says:

A young cobbler fell in love with a noble woman of Constantinople. To rise in station, he enlisted as a soldier. In the meantime, the lady died. The young man then entered her tomb, had sexual relations

with the dead woman, and heard a voice commanding him to
return, at the right time, to seek what she gave birth to. When that
span of time was complete, he returned and was entrusted with a
human head that had the eyes of a Gorgon. The head was cast into
the sea where, since that time, dangerous eddies occur.[37]

A Hard-headed Revenant: Thorolf Twist-Foot

The *Eyrbyggja Saga,* written around 1230, is a kind of rural chronicle depicting the life of the inhabitants of Cape Thor, Eyrr, and Swan
Fjord (western Iceland). The plot basically covers the years 884–1031
and contains a veritable treasury of ethnographical features.

Thorolf Twist-Foot was a wicked man who lived in Hvamm. He
died seated on his high seat and was buried beneath a pile of stones,
but he did not rest in peace. Once the sun had set, it was not wise
to remain outside. The oxen that had pulled his cadaver became
enthralled by sorcery, and any cattle that drew close to his tomb
went mad and bellowed themselves to death; any bird that lit upon
his tomb perished instantly.

Thorolf slew the shepherd of Hvamm, who ran into him close
to his sepulcher, and the shepherd's body was left black as charcoal
with every bone broken. No one dared pasture any livestock in the
valley. It was soon discovered that the common room was haunted.
When winter came, Thorolf often appeared at the farm, and when
the mistress of the house eventually died, she was buried along-
side Thorolf and the shepherd. The people then fled the farm, but
Thorolf began haunting the entire valley, and it was soon deserted.
He killed men, and it was seen that the dead traveled with him. Yet
wherever his son, Arnkel, was to be found, Thorolf and his band
caused no harm.

That spring, Arnkel set off with eleven men. They reached
Thorolf's cairn, opened it, and found his corpse there—hideous
to look upon and suffering no decay. They placed the corpse on a

sled, hitched two oxen to it, and carried it up to Ulfarsfell Ridge. Arnkel wished to bury Thorolf farther away at Vadilshofdi, but the oxen went into a panic, broke free of their yoke, and fled into the sea, where they perished. Thorolf was so heavy that the men could barely lift him up a nearby knoll, where they buried the recalcitrant dead man. Across the promontory, Arnkel had a wall built that was so high none could cross but the birds. Thorolf rested peacefully there as long as Arnkel remained alive.

Once Arnkel was dead, however, he resumed his evil wanderings. He killed men and beasts in Bolstad, left the lands of Thorodd desolate, then went to haunt Ulfarsfell, where he terrified everyone. Faced with the complaints of the farmers, Thorodd gathered his men and they all climbed up to the revenant's mound. They opened it and found Thorolf there. He still had not decomposed; he was black as hell and fat as an ox. When they tried to move him, they could not even budge him. They removed him from the tomb with the help of a lever, then rolled him to the riverbank, where a pyre was built. They put the cadaver inside, though it proved difficult to burn. When the fire caught, a great wind scattered his ashes to various locations. The men cast them into the sea and returned home.

A cow often went down to the bank where Thorolf had been cremated, and she licked the stones upon which ashes were still scattered. A mysterious dapple-gray bull mounted the cow, which gave birth to a large, dapple-gray calf. When Thorodd's wet nurse heard this beast bellow, she was terrified and said: "Those are the howls of a monster, not a living being," and requested on several occasions that the animal be killed. Thorodd refused and one day the calf killed him.[38]

This text offers a wealth of teachings: It gives us a revenant who spares only his son—which is to say, he respects the blood bond—and he resists in his way being buried far away. Thorolf has power over animals, kills livestock and birds, murders men, and is capable of increasing his weight to prevent the transport of his body. The destruction of his cadaver—we should note that he did not decompose—does not put an end to his wickedness. All it takes is a few of his ashes to be ingested by a cow for him to take body again in a calf whose color—dapple-gray—has, for the Germans, always been a sign of the supernatural. Thorolf therefore appears as a veritable predator. All living things are a target for his persecution, and he stops only when the entire region has been deserted, leaving him its uncontested master—something he could not achieve before he died. His story also provides us with a valuable clue regarding what Christian writers called the Infernal Hunt or the Wicked Hunt: the dead gathered as a band under the leadership of the person responsible for their deaths. This detail has already appeared in the first text we looked at, taken from the *Saga of the People of Floi,* in which a mysterious entity knocks at the door of Thorgil's and Jostein's hut, summoning the first dead man who will next attract more companions to him.

Picked up anew by the clerics, the Wild Hunt enjoyed great success: sinners, criminals, unbaptized children, people who had died without the sacraments or who died unrepentant all found a place in this procession led by a one-eyed giant who was often black. But in addition to this Christian recuperation, we have another explanation provided by Walter Map.

Invited by a dwarf, King Herla followed him into a cave with his companions. After his host's wedding celebrations were over, Herla took the return path, heaped with gifts, horses, dogs, and falcons. The dwarf led Herla out of the cave and gave him a small bloodhound, forbidding any of Herlas's band to set foot upon the ground before this dog leapt down out of the arms of the one carrying it.

Encountering a shepherd a short time later, Herla realized that the three days spent with the dwarf represented two hundred years of mortal time. Some of his companions got down from their horses, forgetting the dwarf's order, and crumbled into dust. Herla forbade the others from setting foot on the ground until the dog had jumped down, but the dog never jumped down and King Herla continues pursuing his mad rounds in the company of his army.[39]

Among the very wide array of the motifs of providence, dogs and horses play an important role—for they are the two animals whose remains are most often found in funeral mounds.

Klaufi, the Decapitated Revenant

The *Saga of the Men of Svarfadar-dale,* a place named after Thorstein the Troublemaker (*svarfadar*), has come down to us in a reworked version dating from 1300. Its subject matter is, once again, much older, as testified by the *Book of Sturla* and the *Book of Thorleif Jarl Skald.* The principal action pivots around the quarrels of Thorstein and Ljotolf, and it is based in large part on oral traditions.

> Yngvild arranged the murder of her husband, Klaufi. Her brothers slew him and hid his body in a haystack. That very evening, when Yngvild was in bed, Klaufi rose up before her. She called her brothers; they attacked the revenant, decapitated him, and placed his head by his feet.
>
> One evening, Karl the Red was sitting near the fire when some verses were heard. "One might say that was the voice of our cousin Klaufi," he said. "Perhaps he wants something." Karl and his men gathered their weapons and left for Hof. There they saw a gigantic man carrying his head beneath his arm. It was Klaufi. He invited them to follow him, and they made their way to Steindur. Klaufi knocked on the door with his head. Karl entered the farmhouse and spoke with Gris, his brother-in-law, but then Gris left under some pretext. Karl then heard the voice of Klaufi telling him to be on his guard. Karl got up, went out, and found Gris oiling the iron head of his spear. He drew his sword and killed him.
>
> As Karl and his band were leaving the farm, Klaufi loomed up and warned him of the imminent arrival of enemies. They saw the

brother of Gris, Ljotolf, with a large retinue. Combat began raging until Klaufi waded in, striking all around him with his head, which he was holding in his hand. Ljoltolf's men took flight. Ljoltolf tried to do likewise, but every time, Klaufi blocked his path and kept him there until Karl could arrive. Ljotolf called Skidi for help. Skidi heard his shout and tried to leave his home, not far from the site of the confrontation with three of his men—but Klaufi blocked the door. Skidi took a burning log, planted it on the roof in front of the door and went out with his men. Klaufi went away and they were able to help Ljotolf escape.

Winter ended and spring arrived. Karl and Gunnar were standing outside. Karl raised his eyes to the sky and grew pale. "What's wrong?" asked Gunnar. "I saw my cousin Klaufi on a gray horse. He was traveling through the air at the head of a retinue in which I thought I recognized myself." Klaufi's voice was then heard saying: "Cousin Karl! You will join me this evening." That very same day Karl fell beneath the blows of Skidi and his men.

Ljotolf, meanwhile, was found one day in a field. He had died in a very strange manner: he was transfixed by a large knife made from the metal of the sword Klaufi once owned.

Klaufi then began assaulting men and livestock. His grave mound was opened and he was exhumed. His body suffered no decay. He was placed upon a pyre, and after he was incinerated, his ashes were placed in a small lead box sealed by two iron hooks, which was then cast into a hot spring. Never again was anything heard of the revenant. The rock on which the cadaver had been burned split in half.[40]

Decapitation followed by removal of the head does not therefore always suffice to put an end to hauntings. Because he had been murdered, Klaufi cannot find rest, and only cremation combined with the immersion of his ashes can put an end to his wanderings. When Klaufi sees his murderers, Gris and Ljotolf, perish—the death of Ljotolf should in all likelihood be attributed to Klaufi—it only changes the nature of his abnormal manifestations. The revenant begins attacking all living things rather than just several particular individuals and generally behaves like the traditional specter. This saga also confirms that light serves as a weapon against ghosts and revenants. Skidi drives Klaufi away from the door by lighting it with a burning log. One final detail deserves our attention: Klaufi seeks out Karl in the form of a prophetic apparition astride a gray horse, an animal psychopomp who guides souls into the otherworld. He therefore behaves here like a fylgja,[41] the tutelary spirit connected to a man or clan, the sight of which signals an imminent death.

The Revenant's Curse

With *Grettir's Saga,* we enter one of the two fundamental texts for the history of revenants because the chapters devoted to the apparitions of Glam recapitulate and expand most of the information that we have uncovered up to this point. A summary of the tale will help in the explanation of the details.

Thorhall lived in Thorhallsstad in Forsaeludal, up from Vatnsdal. He had great difficulty in getting a shepherd to suit him because the place was haunted. When he went to the Thing [Assembly] of summer, where matters of litigation and general interest were handled, he visited Skapti, a man of law, and explained his problem to him. Skapti advised him to hire as his shepherd Glam, a solidly built man with odd features, large gray eyes, and wolf-gray hair. Thorhall thus offered Glam the position of watching his sheep during the winter, specifying that the region was haunted. "I am not scared of ghosts," answered Glam, who agreed to start his duties on winter first nights—*at vetrnóttum,* meaning October 14–16.

Glam arrived at Thorhallsstad at the agreed-upon time. He was fairly unsociable and stubborn and everyone disliked him—and furthermore, he was irreligious. On Christmas Eve he asked for something to eat, but Gudrun, Thorhall's wife, first refused to give him any food because for Christians this was a day to fast. Glam became angry and threatening, and he got what he wanted. Once his hunger was sated, he left to take care of his sheep. It was very dark. There was driving snow and the wind was howling and it became worse as the day advanced. The shepherd's voice was heard in the early part of the day, but he did not return in the evening, as was customary. Because the blizzard was still raging, no one dared venture out to search for him. Christmas night passed and still no Glam. When it was broad daylight, some men set off to look for him. They found the sheep scattered and saw climbing out of the valley footprints made by feet that were as large as the bottom of a barrel. There seemed to have been a violent scuffle: the ground was torn up and rocks were torn from it, and there were large bloodstains on the earth. They followed them and spotted Glam. He was dead, black as Hel, and swollen to the size of an ox. They tried to carry him to the church but could manage only a short distance. They returned to the farm and informed Thorhall that the evil spirit that had long been lurking there must have slain Glam.

The next day, they returned to get Glam's body, but the oxen yoked to the cadaver were unable to drag it any farther once the downward slope gave way to level ground, so the men went back home. On the third day they went back, accompanied by a priest. They spent the entire day looking for the body, with no success. The churchman retraced his steps home, and immediately the men found Glam's cadaver. They piled stones on top of it and left it there.

It was not long after Christmas that people began to notice that the shepherd was not resting peacefully. He returned quite often, and many, filled with terror, left the valley. At night, Glam walked on the roofs of the houses of the people dwelling there and even lurked about in the daytime. As the days grew longer, however, the haunting became less frequent.

Thorhall hired a new shepherd, Thorgaut, who said he had no fear of revenants. When winter came, he took care of the sheep, and he found the sound of Glam walking upon the roofs a source of amusement. On Christmas Eve he left to stay with his flock. It was dark and snowing heavily. That evening, Thorgaut did not return. No one wished to go out looking for him because night had fallen. On Christmas morning, a search party set out and found him dead with his neck broken and all the bones in his body torn apart. He was carried to the church, and no one ever suffered on his account.

Glam committed so many wicked deeds that none remained at Thorhallsstad but Thorhall, his wife, Gudrun, and a faithful cowherd. One morning, Gudrun heard a terrific noise and bellowing in the stables. She called Thorhall, who rushed into the stables. He found the cattle goring one another with their horns and his cowherd slain. His back had been broken over the flat stone separating two stalls. Thorhall then left his domain, taking with him all he could carry. Glam killed all the remaining livestock and then began ravaging all the farms in the valley, slaying everything, man or beast, which crossed his path. The haunting lessened with the onset of spring, and Thorhall moved back to his farm, but with the arrival of autumn, Glam appeared again, which affected Thorhall's daughter, Thorid, so greatly that she died of it. Many avenues were tried, but without success.

Grettir heard talk about these happenings—it must be said that it was the chief topic of every conversation—and he made his way to the home of Thorhall, who gave him a warm welcome, especially when he learned of his visitor's intention of spending the night. He gave Grettir fair warning, adding that if he kept his life, he would be sure to lose his horse no matter what happened, "for no one can keep his beast in safety who comes here." The horse was stabled in a secure building, and the night went by without Glam appearing. Grettir decided to spend a second night there. Full of hope the next morning, Thorhall went to check on Grettir's horse. He found that the door to the building had been staved in and the animal dragged outside and every bone in its body broken. Grettir remained at Thorhallsstad a third night.

When evening came, he lay down completely dressed on a bench, covering himself with a large cloak made from animal pelts. In the great common hall, which had been torn apart and was barely habitable, a lamp was left burning.

A third of the night had gone by when a great commotion started. Someone was climbing on top of the house, banging on the roof with his heels, then making his way down on the side where the door was located. Grettir then saw Glam poking his head in and slowly entering. When Glam stood upright, his head almost touched the ceiling. He spotted what looked to him to be a package on the bench, moved over, and grabbed the cloak in which Grettir had enclosed himself. He pulled, but Grettir resisted, and the garment was torn in half. Taking advantage of Glam's surprise, Grettir leapt upon him and seized him bodily, trying to topple him, but Glam gripped Grettir's arms so tightly that it staggered him. Glam tried to drag Grettir outside, but he resisted mightily, knowing that it would be harder to defend himself outside of the building. From their struggle, pieces were flying in the room. The two combatants finally tumbled out of the building, with Glam landing under Grettir. Clouds were covering the moon intermittently, and when Glam collapsed, he turned his eyes toward it when it was unobstructed by any cloud. Seeing the revenant's eyes, Grettir's strength failed him and he could not draw his short sword. Then Glam spoke: "It is my will that you will never be any stronger than you are now. . . . Henceforth murders and ill deeds await you. . . . You will be outlawed and your lot shall be to dwell ever alone. And this I lay upon you: that these eyes of mine shall be ever before your vision. You will find it hard to live alone, and at last, it shall drag you to death." Glam fell silent and the enchantment paralyzing Grettir vanished. He drew his short sword, cut off his adversary's head and laid it between his thighs. With the help of Thorhall, he burned the body. The ashes were collected in an animal hide and buried in a place far away from the haunts of man or beast.[42]

This story is exemplary for its sobriety and permits answers to be provided for several questions. What time of the year do revenants manifest? In winter, especially around Christmas, when the nights are longest. Associated with haunts and darkness, bad weather plays an important role, and a link undoubtedly exists between storms and revenants. Doesn't the Wild Hunt, an army of ghosts, frequently serve as a personification of a tempest?

How are hauntings triggered? This saga responds to this question much like the *Saga of the People of Floi:* an external power—in our text, a harmful spirit (*meinvaettr*)—kills an individual in a strange manner, and in accordance with an extremely ancient belief, this abnormal death gives rise to manifestations that are out of the ordinary. It is interesting to note that Glam seems predestined in some way to become a revenant. Otherwise, the narrator would not emphasize the gray color of his eyes and hair—a color that, as pointed out earlier, has a supernatural connotation.

The people slain by Glam do not return, which we know to be certain because of Thorgaut's death. This means that the haunting by Glam has a specific purpose, but the story does not mention it, and only comparison with other sagas can teach it to us.

The Christian elements of the story merit a note. Glam is a pagan, and the text suggests that he was punished for not respecting the Christmas Eve fast. Perhaps Christianity may have been able to protect him from the evil spirit. The opposition between paganism and the true faith is underscored when the priest's presence prevents the discovery of Glam's body. This opposition was already apparent in the corpse's passive resistance to the efforts made to bring it to the church for burial to prevent any postmortem manifestation. The observation on Thorgaut—"He was carried to the church and no one ever suffered on his account"—leaves no doubt about this. In the mind-set of that era, consecrated ground was understood to be an apotropaic means.

In fact, what we are dealing with here is a pagan text that has been slightly Christianized, which corresponds quite well with the time when the events it describes took place—the beginning of the eleventh century, because Grettir died in 1031. We should also take note of a touch that seemingly has no importance but has a very pagan echo: Glam kills horses. The importance of this animal in pagan festivals and worship, as well as in pagan views of death, is well known. When Grettir violates Kar's tumulus, he trips over horse bones; when Klaufi announces to Karl his imminent death, he is riding a gray courser. The church went on the offensive against beliefs concerning horses and forbade the eating of horsemeat, a measure that has had a long life because horse butchers are still completely absent in Scandinavian and Anglo-Saxon countries.

Finally, the text clearly confirms the belief in revenants. Why else would Grettir have placed Glam's head between the thighs of his corpse before he left to alert Thorhall? This was a necessary precaution; he was not completely certain that he had rendered Glam totally harmless, and for even more certainty, he cremated the body. The battle against Glam is quite informative, but it also raises questions that, for the moment, remain unanswered.

The Trial of the Revenants

The *Eyrbyggja Saga,* from which we have already borrowed the story of Thorolf Twist-Foot, presents an extraordinary succession of strange events linked to a series of hauntings, creating a matchless atmosphere that consists of reactions to well-known—yet stupefying—phenomena of the era. There is not just one revenant story here but at least three: that of Thorir Wooden-Leg, that of Thorgunna, and that of Thorodd. Presenting them separately breaks the thread of the story that was constructed in accordance with the principle of interweaving and does not allow a faithful accounting of the very revealing ambience of Icelandic beliefs around the year 1000.

Now that same night that the corpse-bearers came home after Thorgunna had been buried in Skalaholt, as men sat by the meal-fires at Frodriver, all who were in the house saw how a half-moon was shining on the paneling of the house wall—and it went backward and widdershins (*andsoelis*),* round about the house, and it did not vanish away while folk sat by the fires. So Thorodd asked Thorir Wooden-Leg what that might bode. Thorir said it was the Moon of Weird,† "and the deaths of men will follow thereafter." For a whole week this backward shining endured, and the Moon of Weird came in there evening after evening. Shortly after this, a shepherd returned to the house sullen and ill tempered and seemingly absent—folk thought he had been bewitched. After the second week of winter had passed, he returned home one evening and went straight to bed. He was found dead the next morning and was buried at the church.

Revenants then appeared. One night, Thorir Wooden-Leg went out to satisfy a natural need. When he tried to go back inside, the shepherd was barring the door. Thorir tried to flee, but the other seized him and threw him hard against the door. Thorir was nonetheless able to make his way back into the common hall. In places his body was as black as charcoal. He fell sick, died, and was interred at the church. After that, folk began seeing him in the company of the shepherd.

After Thorir's death, one of Thorodd's servants fell sick and

---

*All operations of black magic were performed *andsoelis.* In the *Saga of the Chiefs of Lake Valley* (*Vatnsdaela Saga,* chapter 36), Groa walks around his home in the direction opposite that of the sun, looks back toward the top of the mountain and shakes a cloth, and returns and closes the door. An earthquake strikes the farm and everyone dies. See also the *Saga of Grettir* (chapter 79) in which Thurid the Wizard enchants the tree trunk that will cause the death of the hero.

It is odd to encounter the same practice in Scotland in 1590: an assembly of witches took place in North Berwick, and the participants walked around the church *widdershins,* "in a counter-sunwise movement."

†*Urdarmáni*—from *máni,* "the moon" and *Urdr*—name of one of the three Norns. [The other two Norns are *Verthandi* and *Skuld. —Trans.*] R. Boyer notes that the moon is always a sign of death or evil spells (*La Saga de Snorri,* 215). We should add that Isidore of Seville (*Etymology* VIII, 9, 9) writes that some women have power over the moon, a bit of information we find again in the *Indiculus superstitionum* no. 21 (*de eo credunt, qui a femine lunam comendet*). For more on this astral body in German beliefs, see *Handwörterbuch des deutschen Aberglaubens* VI, col. 477–534.

died three nights later, soon followed by six more people. This was around the time of Advent. On several occasions now, noises were heard from the storeroom where the dried fish were stored, but when people went to check, they found nothing. Shortly before Jól, Thorodd and six men sailed to Ness to get more fish. That same evening, in Frodriver, a seal head began pushing through the floor of the fire pit. A servant grabbed a club and struck it, but the seal continued to rise out of the ground, staring fixedly at Thorgunna's bed canopy. A farmhand took up the task of clubbing the seal, but it continued to rise until its flippers emerged, whereupon the man fainted in terror. Kjartan, Thorodd's son, then grabbed a long-handled hammer and violently struck the seal's head, "driving it down like a nail into the floor."

The next morning, Thorodd and crew were lost at sea, and their bodies were not recovered. Kjartan and Thurid invited their neighbors to the funeral feast. The first evening, when all were at table, Thorodd and his men entered the common room, dripping wet. They were given a good welcome because it was believed if the drowned showed up to attend their own funeral feast, it was because Ran, the sea goddess, had received them well. The revenants said nary a word and did not respond to greetings. They settled themselves at the end of the room, near the fire, and remained there until it burned out. This went on every night of the funeral feast.

After the guests left and the fire was lit as usual, Thorodd and his men entered the common room, dripping with seawater. They took seats by the fire and began wringing out their clothes. Thorir Wooden-Leg and the six who had succumbed to illness then came in. They were covered with earth and also sat near the fire. This went on throughout the entire Jól season.

The noises from the dried-fish storeroom had grown louder and more frequent. It sounded to everyone as if the fish were being torn apart. The time had come to use the stored fish for food, and a man went in to get some. There he saw a hairy tail sticking out of the pile. He grabbed it and called out for others to come help him. They all pulled the tail, but it slipped away from them and was never seen again. All that remained of the fish was the skin—however, no sign of any living thing could be found in the storeroom.

Shortly afterward, Thorgrima Witch-Face, Thorir Wooden-Leg's wife, fell ill and soon died. On the very evening of her burial, she was seen in Thorir's band. Since the appearance of the tail in the storeroom, the illnesses had come back. Six people then died, with the others fleeing because of the haunting. There had been thirty servants there at the beginning of winter; eighteen had died and five had fled so that by the month of *goi* (between mid-February and mid-March) there were only seven left.

Kjarten left for Helgafell to ask counsel from his uncle Snorri, who advised him to burn Thorgunna's bed canopy, set up a door court,[43] and then institute proceedings against the revenants. He also asked a priest to accompany Kjarten back to Frodriver. On his return trip home, Kjarten invited the people of the neighboring farms to accompany him. Everyone arrived in Frodriver on Candlemass Eve.

Kjarten summoned the revenants to justice. The members of the door court were named, the charges were duly laid out, witnesses were brought forward, the cases were summed up, and sentences were handed down. Thorir rose first, speaking a few words. When he was condemned in turn, the shepherd stood, said his piece, and left the common room. Then it was the turn of Thorgrima and all the rest. Each let it be known they were leaving against their will. Thorodd stated: "We are hardly welcome here; we'd best be on our way!"

Kjarten and the others then went back inside, and the priest went to every corner of the house with holy water and relics. After this, the haunting ceased and Thorid recovered her health.

The starting point of this entire affair is a fatal error: Thorgunna's bed canopy is not burned immediately. Thorgunna has forewarned Thorodd of the danger that lurks if any of her bedding is kept. Thurid opposes her husband's desire to burn the canopy to ashes, and this is where the epidemic begins. The death that carries off the shepherd is a result of illness; however, the narrator reports general opinion: sorcery is suspected. Let's try to untangle the entwined and contradictory data.

During the Middle Ages in the Germanic lands, illness was regarded as an entity, as in Snorri's *Edda* in which Frigg, Baldr's mother, has all ills swear an oath to spare her son,[44] or else the oaths are sworn by creatures from popular mythology. Dwarves, alfes (Nordic elves), and the *cauquemars* [nightmares] (*Mahren,* or Norse *mara*) who either rode humans or shot arrows at them: these were the origins of all ills.[45] In Old English fever was *riderod,* from *rîdan,* "to ride," and in Middle High German, quartan fever was called "the four-day ride" (*der viertage rite*). In Norse, hives were called "Elf tan" (*álfarbrunni*), and two epizootic diseases were called "dwarf blow" (*dvergslag*) and "dwarf shot" (*dvergskot*). On the English side of the Channel, a charm that appeared before the year 1000 and was intended to cure horses began with these words: "Whatever the elf upon the horse may be, this has the power to heal him."[46] An unidentified illness brings vampires to mind: "elf suction" (*aelfsogoþa*). *The Redeemer* (Heliand), a poem in Old Saxon composed around 830, informs us that "wicked genies" (*dernea wihti*) send illnesses, and Old High German glosses give *wiht* and *elbe* (elf) for the Latin words *lemures* and *demones*.[47]

The dead were therefore responsible for these ills, as the glosses reflect. But what are dwarves and elves doing here? It should be known that these beings from common mythology—combined with the Mahren of elsewhere—were close kin to the departed if they are not the deceased themselves.[48] The mention of alfes or elves should not be considered an error: originally auspicious and kind, they were victims of a Christianity that saw them as pagan demons, and Christianity considered them part of a wide array of diverse figures that it grouped under the name "dwarves" (*dvegr, zwerg, dveorgh*).[49] Dwarves were wicked, harm-causing dead—but they were no longer distinguished from the alfes to whom are attributed the causes of certain illnesses.

Therefore, the shepherd stricken by illness was, according to the beliefs of the time, the victim of external intervention—injury caused by an arrow shot or a horsebackriding accident—or the internal presence of a larva that could be the dead woman whose bedding was not burned. This latter interpretation explains both his return and why being buried at the church does not prevent him from returning to slay Thorir Wooden-Leg. One detail reveals clearly that the dead shepherd incarnates and spreads illness: "[I]n places his body [Thorir's] was as black as charcoal." The apparent epidemic carries off six people at Advent—four weeks before Christmas, a date fraught with meaning, for isn't this the date when pagans celebrated the great feast of the dead?

Advent therefore brings with it two kinds of haunting: acoustic and the work of an animal. The noise from the storeroom heralds the imminent death of Thorodd, whose ship goes down when he goes to Ness to take on a load of dried fish. At this point, two different stories intersect: that of the epidemic, which is connected to Thorgunna's death and is heralded by the appearance of the Weird Moon, and that of the drowning. These two then merge into a single narrative, as the text shows: "Since the appearance of the tail in the storeroom, the illnesses had come back."

Throughout the entire winter, the noises and the appearances of the seal in the fire pit go hand in hand. Just what does the animal in the fire do? He rises up and stares at Thorgunna's bed canopy. He is therefore connected with Thorgunna's death and the illness that follow. The same holds true for the noises, whose general function is to announce death, whereas the seal seems to want to remind Kjarten and Thorid that the bed canopy should be burned. Once this has been done, Thorid recovers!

I must emphasize that in northern Europe, revenants existed in animal form. Hrapp, whose wanderings we have seen, takes the shape of a seal that swims around Thorstein's boat because Thorstein is the one who takes possession of Hrappstad, his future domain that once belonged to Hrapp. The boat sinks and there is only one survivor.[50]

In the *Eyrbyggja Saga* retold above, the seal must be the ghost of Thorgunna. Like a living reprimand, it appears in Frodriver and signifies to the men the mistake they have made.

Things are clearer for the two groups of revenants. All the specters—those of Thorir Wooden-Leg's band and those of Thorodd's crew—keep the appearance they had during their final hour: The dead who drowned are wet and the departed who were buried are covered with dirt. All come to warm themselves before the fire, and they commit no wrongs. Yet Thorir and his companions enter the house only after Thorodd's funeral banquet, as if they do not want to disturb a ceremony to which they have not been invited. This is explained quite clearly by the juridical and religious tone of the funeral banquet,[51] and law and religion were inseparable for the ancient Germans. This meal, a family feast that could not be attended by whoever wished to come, permits the liquidation of the deceased's legacy. By waiting for it to be completed, Thorir and his companions are respecting traditions and law.

The dead therefore behave like the living insofar as they comply—though perhaps with ill will—to the sentence they are given. There is nothing more extraordinary than this door court in which the revenants are judged and condemned to haunt the common room; strength remains with the law. In the nineteenth century, ghosts were no longer so docile: In Lower Saxony, the prior of Loccum was banished because he came back. He haunted a bridge, and his body was carried off into the forest.[52]

English Ghosts and Revenants

With the exception of the stories told by Walter Map, English literature does not have a wealth of revenants. Yet Providence did not want oral traditions to vanish and for anyone to believe even for a single minute that ghosts were absent from England. Toward 1400, a clerk from Byland Monastery (Yorkshire) found several virgin sheets of parchment in a manuscript and transcribed things he had heard told around him:

some thirteen stories of appearances of the dead.[53] Although heavily Christianized, they have preserved substantial vestiges of ancestral beliefs that fairly closely match the Nordic data. The stories are of uneven length and quality. Conceived as exempla, they are structured around notions of punishment and atonement. Here, a Newbury deacon comes back for having stolen some spoons (story number VI), and there a servant steals some meat from his master and subsequently goes wandering during the night following his death (story number VII). The majority of these narratives, however, depicts revenants as metamorphosing, and this is what gives the collection its originality. Alas, this anonymous cleric writes with a sparse vocabulary. He speaks only of spirits (*spiritus*) that resemble this or that (*quasi, in figura*). He never uses the words *lemures* or *larvae*, which clearly shows he is echoing folk and oral traditions. It was in fact between the end of the fourteenth century and the beginning of the fifteenth that the Middle English *goost*, the root of today's *ghost*, began being used for *spiritus*, a Latin word applying to God (*spiritus sanctis*), angels (*spiritus boni*), demons (*spiritus maligni*), and the dead (*spiritus defunctorum*). The spirit in this work is not, however, an image or a phantasm, as is ordinarily the case in the exempla. It possesses a body and is three-dimensional.

Story Number I: The Horse-like Revenant

A certain man rode on his horse, which was also carrying a pack of beans. The horse stumbled on the road and broke its leg. Seeing this, the man took the beans on his own back and as he was going along the road he saw before him what looked like another horse standing on its hind legs, with its forelegs raised up. The man was terrified and begged the horse in the name of Jesus Christ not to harm him. After this the animal went along with him as a horse, and very soon afterward it appeared in the form of a rolling truss of hay with a light in the middle of it. The man said to it: "Go away, because you will bring me ill-luck." Then the spirit (*spiritus*) told him his name and the reason for his haunting, and how he could

be helped, and added: "Allow me to carry the beans and help you."
And so he did as far as the river, but he would not cross over. . . .
After this he [the man] had the spirit absolved and masses sung and
thus freed him from his ghostly state.[54]

We should take note of the archaic data from this anecdote: The
spirit appears in horse shape reminiscent of an apparition called Grant
at the beginning of the thirteenth century,[55] and wishes to carry the
sack of beans. It so happens that beans are used as an exorcism in the
Roman *Lemuria*. Finally, he does not want to cross running water,
which, in primitive thought, as is well known, always represented the
border between this world and the otherworld.

Story Number II: The Tailor and the Revenant

It is said that a certain tailor by the name of . . . Snowball was riding
back to his house in Ampleforth on a certain night from Gilling,
and on the way he heard what seemed to be the sound of ducks
washing themselves in the stream. Soon after he saw what appeared
to be a crow flying around his head and down to the ground, with
its wings dragging on the ground as if it was about to die. The tailor dismounted to pick up the crow and as he did so he saw sparks
of fire coming out of this same crow. Then he made the sign of the
cross and begged the crow, in the name of God, not to bring him
any misfortune along that road. At this it flew away with a great
shriek to a stone's throw distant.

So the man mounted his horse again and shortly afterward the
aforesaid crow flew toward him and struck him in the side, knocking him off his horse, and flat on the ground. He lay thus stretched
out on the ground in a sort of trance or faint, very frightened. At
last he got to his feet, and with firm faith he fought the crow with
his sword until he was weary and it seemed to him as if he was
striking a peat-stack in a marsh, so he held him off, and in the name
of God said: "Protect me from whatever power this thing possesses

to harm me and make it go away." And the crow flew off again with a dreadful shriek as far as an arrow could fly.

Then the ghost appeared to the same tailor, who made the sign of the cross on his breast with his sword. This time it stood before him in the form of a dog with a chain on its neck. When he saw this the tailor began to think about it, and with his spirit full of faith said: "What is to become of me? I will beg him in the name of the Holy Trinity, and by the power of the blood of Jesus Christ of the five wounds, to speak to me and not to harm me in any way, but to stand still and answer my questions and tell me his name and the cause of his trouble and a suitable remedy." And so he did. The ghost when addressed gasped and groaned terribly and said: "I did such and such a thing and for my deeds I was excommunicated. Go therefore to a certain priest and seek absolution for me. And I must have nine times twenty masses celebrated for me, and you shall choose one of two things. Either you return to me alone on a certain night, bringing back the reply from those of whom I have spoken, and I will tell you how you can be healed, and do not fear the sight of a wood fire in the meantime. Or your flesh will putrefy and your skin will weaken and fall away from you completely in a short time. You shall know, therefore, that because you have not heard mass, not the gospel of John 'In the beginning . . .' and have not seen the consecration of the body and blood of Christ, I have been able to appear to you now, otherwise I would not have the power so to do."

As he spoke with the tailor, the ghost appeared as if burning with fire, and the man could see through its mouth into its inside, as it formed its words in the intestines (*formavit verba sua in intestinis*), and did not speak with its tongue. The tailor asked permission of the spirit to have another companion with him, but the spirit replied: "No, but you shall have above you the four evangelists and the triumphal name of Jesus of Nazareth because there are two other ghosts who dwell here, one of whom cannot speak, being bound by an oath, and appears as a fire or a thorn bush, and the other has the form of a huntsman, and they are very dangerous to meet. Furthermore you shall promise by this tombstone that you will not reveal my bones except to the priests celebrating mass for me." . . . The tailor promised by the stone not to reveal this secret as explained above. Finally, he begged the spirit to go away as far as Hoggebek until he returned. But he replied, "No, no, no," with a howl. The tailor said to him, "Then go to Bilandbank." And it was agreed.

Now the same man was taken ill for some days, but as soon as he was well he went to York to the aforesaid priest who had previously excommunicated the ghost, and begged absolution. The priest refused to absolve him, and he called another chaplain for consultation. Then he called a second, and the second a third to consider the subject of his absolution. . . . At last, after various discussions between the two sides, the tailor satisfied them, and paid five shillings, and received the absolution, written on a scroll, having sworn that he would not harm the dead man but secretly bury the scroll in his tomb beside his head. . . .

When this [was all done], the tailor went to the agreed meeting place and made a great circle with a cross, which had over it the four gospels and other sacred words. Then he stood in the middle of the circle, placing four reliquaries in the form of a cross on the edges of the same circle . . . and awaited the arrival of the same ghost. And at last the ghost came in the form of a goat, and went three times around the aforementioned circle, saying "Ah, ah, ah." Whereupon he fell prone on the ground, and rose up in the form of a man of great size, horrible and skinny. . . .

When the tailor asked if his labor had been at all successful, the spirit said: "God be praised, yes, and I was standing behind you at the ninth hour when you buried my absolution in my tomb and were afraid. And no wonder, for three devils were also present, who were punishing me with all kinds of torments after you had summoned me. . . . [N]ext Monday I, with thirty other ghosts, will go into everlasting joy. You therefore shall go to a certain river and will find a broad stone, which you will lift up, and under that stone you will pick up some sandy rock. Then you will wash all your body with water and rub it with the rock, and within a few days you will be healed."[56]

The story does not stop here, but before examining the epilogue, it is necessary to make a point: The folk and even pagan elements in this story are many. The shape of the crow adopted by the spirit reminds us that Odin (Woden, Wotan), the god of the dead, owned two crows. The pile of hay is not possible to explain by the current research, but, conversely, the circle is commonly used in conjurations and exorcisms, and the mention of Monday, a day placed under the sign of the astral body of the dead, reflects pre-Christian beliefs. The goat could be the local form of small tutelary earth spirits that the cleric incorporates with fauns or satyrs. One fact is certain: the spirit assumes a body, and when it strikes the tailor, it unhorses and injures him. Finally, the man owes his salvation solely to the vigor of his faith. Now let's take a look at the end of the story.

The tailor then asked the spirit the names of two of the other ghosts and was told: "I cannot tell you their names." But when he was asked again about their situation the ghost declared that one of them was worldly and warlike and not of this country, and had killed a pregnant woman and would not be cleared till the day of judgment. "You will see him in the form of a bullock with no mouth, eyes, or ears, and in no way will he be able to speak however much he is asked. And the other is a priest, who is in the shape of a hunter blowing his horn, and he will be questioned and cleared by the Lord, thanks to a certain boy not yet grown up."[57]

This is how, depending on the seriousness of the sin, spirits speak or keep silent and can be embodied in an animal that has been stripped of its essential functions (hearing, speech, and sight). We can note that they are not in purgatory or hell, a fairly surprising position in a text as Christian as this. The information is fairly confused, as if the cleric remembered only part of what he had learned—that is, whatever could provide him with material for a moralistic and edifying purpose. For this reason many points remain obscure. The "fire" brings to mind will o' the wisps.[58] In any event this fire is a specific indication of the presence of a dead man.

Story Number IV: The Vengeance of James Tankerlay

The old men relate that a certain James Tankerlay, formerly rector of Kirby, was buried in the presence of his favorite Bellelande, but thereafter used to go out by darkness and one night put out the eye of his concubine. And it is said that the abbot had his body removed from its grave complete with its coffin, and ordered Roger Wayneman to convey it to Gormyre. While this man was throwing the coffin into the river the oxen almost sank into the water in fear.[59]

This final point brings to mind the story of Thorolf Twist-Foot. It is curious to note that James Tankerlay gouges out one of his concubine's eye, which I regard as an act of revenge, even if the text does not indicate the reasons. It is also interesting to see once again that water is considered to be the best obstacle to a haunting.

Story Number XI: The Child in the Shoe

It is worth recalling that a certain man from Cleveland, Richard Rowntree, leaving his pregnant wife, went to the tomb of St. Jacob [James] with a large number of others, and one night they spent in a certain wood near the king's highway. So it was that one of the number kept watch for a certain part of the night for fear of night prowlers, and the others could sleep more easily.

And it happened that on the particular watch that the aforesaid man was on guard, he heard a great sound of passing travelers along the highway, and some were riding on horses, sheep, and oxen, and some on other animals; and all of them were on the creatures, which provided their mortuaries when they died. At last he saw what looked like a baby rolling along in a sort of shoe over the ground. And he questioned the child: "Who are you, and why are you rolling along thus?" And it replied: "You should not ask me, for you are my father and I am your son born prematurely, buried without baptism and without name." When he heard this, the traveler took off his shirt and put it on his son, and christened him in the name of the Holy Trinity, and took with him that old shoe as testimony of this incident. And indeed that child, when thus named, rejoiced greatly and even stood upright on his feet instead of rolling on the ground as before.

Now having ended his journey, the man called together his neighbors and asked his wife for his shoes. She showed him one, but could not find the other. Then her husband held out the shoe in which the boy had been rolling along, and she marveled at this. At which the midwife confessed the truth about the death of the boy and his burial in the shoe. And thereafter the husband and his wife were divorced . . .[60]

Three elements merit being singled out here: the presence of a band of dead people similar to the Wild Hunt, the notion of a premature birth with no baptism, and the theme of the attribution of a name. Richard does not baptize his son; he gives him a suitable garment and a name—that is all. But the child reacts as if he has been saved, a point that underscores the emergence of an ancient German belief: a newborn has no legal existence and is not part of the family or clan as long as he or she remains nameless, the patronym being the fundamental bond connecting him or her to the ancestors and the living.*

---

*Infants who died before receiving baptism have always inspired fear. Along the Moldau, it is said the small revenants encountered must be baptized and given a name: "If you are a boy, your name shall be Adam and if you are a girl, your name shall be Eve."[61]

It would be monotonous to continue telling all the stories in their entirety, so here I point out those elements that confirm the facts presented earlier in this study.

- Revenants can avenge themselves. The sister of Adam de Lond the Elder has been responsible for the dispossession of her husband and children's property. She appears to her brother and asks him to return the property deeds with which she had entrusted him. He refuses, and she tells him: "You shall know therefore that I cannot rest until your death, but after your death you will walk instead of me" (story number XIII).
- Revenants can be captured. A woman captures a ghost and carries it on her back into a certain house in the presence of several people. One of them recounts how the woman's hands sink deeply into the spirit's flesh, as if it were rotten, not solid but illusory (story number V). Robert the Younger leaves his grave at night, and the youth of the village decide to put an end to his terrifying wanderings. They station themselves at the cemetery, capture the dead man, and hold him until the priest can arrive (story number III).
- Revenants are connected with animals that play an important role in German paganism. William of Bradeforth meets a gray horse one night at a crossroads. Beseeched in Christ's name, the spirit does him no harm (story number VIII).

The general ambience all these stories produce is different from that of the sagas, but the basic beliefs are the same and compel us to accept the fact that the ancient traditions were still alive and well at the beginning of the fifteenth century; Christianity had not been successful in eliminating them. We certainly do not have the kind of data available to us that would allow an exact assessment of the facts, but we will see how the information contained in other texts can illuminate these.

German Ghosts and Revenants

The German-speaking countries do not offer the same teeming wealth of revenants in their texts written before 1300 as the Scandinavian texts. Yet at this juncture, a quick glimpse shows us that the same idea of ghosts was held there. The stories from that side of the Rhine display the use of revenants for moral and didactic purposes as well as their transformation into shades and spirits. Several characteristic examples are enough for our investigation.

The Incandescent Revenant

While continuing work on the Chronicle of Frutolf von Michelsberg (ca. 1103) Ekkehart IV of St. Gall (ca. 1126) notes, without attempting to explain it, a curious event that took place in 1120.

> There are two strongholds in Saxony, whose names I've forgotten, that are quite close to each other. Toward the middle of the night, the watchmen of both castles saw in reality and not in imagination a man emerge from the wall of the first fortress and cross the field separating the two edifices. His entire body was burning like a torch or some incandescent mass. He vanished near the other castle. This apparition reappeared two or three times.[62]

The same phenomenon was noted in the year 1125 in the *Chronicle of Brunswick*. In the nineteenth century, Jacob Grimm collected an oral tradition in Low German that tells the same story while embellishing it: the revenant's ribs can be counted, and he is carrying a boundary marker on his back.[63] The ghost is therefore being punished in the modern era for having moved the boundary marker of a field—for having illegally appropriated a piece of land.

The Dead Woman's Hair

Among the many stories about apparitions left us by Caesarius of Heisterbach, one depicts a revenant that is not a ghost but a creature of flesh and blood. This is an extremely rare incident in medieval Germany and testifies to the same worldview found in Iceland.

On her deathbed, the mistress of a priest asked that a solid pair of shoes be made and buried with her. "They will be useful to me," she said. Her last request was granted.

The following night under the light of the moon, a knight accompanied by his squire was traveling along the road when he heard a woman lamenting. Both men wondered what this was all about when they saw her running toward them crying, "Help me!" The knight alit from his horse, drew a circle around him with his sword, and bade the woman enter it. She was wearing only a shirt and a pair of shoes. Then arose the sound of barking and the sounding of horns, and the woman began trembling. The knight, having grasped the reason for this hunt, entrusted his squire with his horse and wrapped the woman's hair around his arm while holding his sword in his right hand. When the infernal hunter approached, the woman shrieked, "Let me go," but the knight held onto her with all his might. She managed to free herself, leaving behind her hair, and she tried to flee, but the demon caught her, threw her on his horse, and rode off with his prey.

The next morning, the knight reached the village, told people what had happened, and showed them the hair. Becauses no one wished to believe his story, the grave was opened: the dead woman no longer had her hair. All this took place in the archbishopric of Mainz.[64]

The Christian veneer of this tale is quite thin and covers a reality: In the middle of the thirteenth century, Germans believed that revenants had a body. In the nineteenth century this notion was still deeply rooted in German lands, whereas at this same time Icelanders recounted experiences with only incorporeal phantoms. There is an odd reversal of traditions here. In the Middle Ages, Norse revenants were living corpses while in Germany they were more often ectoplasms. Conversely, in the nineteenth century, specters had been completely Christianized in Iceland[65] and pagan traditions survived in the land on the eastern side of the Rhine.

Why did the dead woman ask for solid shoes? We find here an echo of the Hel Shoes (Helskór) that the ancient Scandinavians placed on the feet of the dead so that they could more easily make their way to the otherworld. Two testimonies prove that this belief is quite Germanic: During a still-recent era the last honors paid to the dead were called, in the Henneberg district (Germany), the Shoe of the Dead (Totenschuh), yet the ceremony does not feature any such accessory. In Yorkshire, England, there was a nineteenth-century saying that a person should at least once in his or her life give a good pair of shoes to a poor man because, after death, people will have to cross over a moor filled with rocks and brambles. Before entering this moor, the dead meet an old man who offers them a pair of shoes, the same that were donated to the poor. Everyone knows the old proverb "He who gives to the poor, gives to God."

The White Lady of Stammheim

Caesarius of Heisterbach provides a classic ghost story here. White ladies are still well known even today,[66] and in Fontenay-sous-Bois, near Paris, there is even a street named after them. These banshees, as they are commonly called in England and Ireland, are always a herald of death.

There once lived two knights, Gunther and Hugo, in the village of Stammheim, in the bishopric of Cologne. One night, while Gunther was traveling, one of the serving women brought her children into the courtyard to attend to their natural needs before going to bed. While she was waiting, she spotted the shape of a woman clad in white and with a pale face looking at them from the other side of the hedge. Without saying a word, the apparition drew near to Hugo's home, stared at it from the other side of the hedge, then returned to the cemetery whence she came. A short while later, Gunther's eldest son fell ill and said: "In seven days I shall die; seven days after that, my sister Dirina shall follow me." This is exactly what happened. After the deaths of their children, their mother and the serving woman both died, and during that same period the knight Hugo and his son also perished.[67]

There is one important detail here: the white lady never crosses the hedge, which, as we know today, was regarded by the ancient Germans as a border that provided protection from witches and evil spells, and was under the protection of a spirit of whom all we know is the Latin name, Dusius. This figure from popular mythology became a female demon under the influence of Christianity and also gave a name to the Germanic witch, who in Old High German was Hagazussa and in Norse, Tunridr, meaning "hedge rider."[68]

The Necromancer's Punishment

Between 1180 and 1200, an anonymous cleric wrote an exemplum in Latin that was given the name of *Relation of Reun* (Reuner Relation), based on the manuscript discovered in Rein, near Graz (Styria). The story was translated into German between 1200 and 1250. The text is interesting for its explanation of the incandescent phenomenon that accompanies some ghosts.

Two clerics studying in a monastic school left it to lead a dissolute life and to dedicate themselves to necromancy. Death caught one of them by surprise, and he died unshriven, despite the recommendations of his friend. Yet he promised to return thirty days after his death to a mountain he selected, in order to tell his fellow cleric what fate he had experienced in the beyond. On the date indicated, the surviving friend went to the mountain and met the deceased, who was wrapped in a cloak and surrounded by demons. The dead man stuck his hand out from beneath the cloak: it was burning, and fiery drops were falling from it. "I am burning in this way both inside and out," he told his friend, "and I will thus burn for eternity." The damned soul advised his friend to make penitence to escape this terrible punishment.[69]

According to the Christian interpretation, these men on fire are the guests of hell, and the motif experiences great success in the literature of visions and in the exempla. How indeed could anyone refuse to mend his ways on discovering what dreadful torments were awaiting after death?

The Cursed Hunter

Michel Beheim, born around 1416–21 and murdered 1474–78, has left us a poem illustrating the danger of thoughtless speech as well as the warning given by the Bible: "Thy shalt not take the Lord's name in vain."

Count Eberhard von Wurttemberg left one day by himself to go hunting in the forest. He heard a huge commotion and spied an alarming creature pursuing a stag. He got down from his horse and, terrified, took refuge in a grove, asking the apparition if it intended him harm. "No," it replied, "I am a man like you, and once I was a lord. I loved hunting with a passion and one day asked God to allow me to keep hunting until Judgment Day. Unfortunately, my wish was granted, and it has already been five hundred years now that I have been pursuing this single stag." Count Eberhard then said: "Show me your face so that I might possibly recognize you." The other obeyed. His face was hardly any bigger than a fist and was wrinkled and dried like a dead leaf. The dead man ran off in pursuit of the stag.[70]

The Procession of the Damned

An odd, anonymous tale in Middle High German that cannot be dated with any precision—all we know is that it came into existence between

1198 and 1393—blends information from a variety of sources and features dead people who are only appearances or images, a theme that can be found in France in the *Lai de Trot.** The central detail of the account is that of the dead individual who needs the living in order to find rest.

In Swabia there once lived a count. In his service was the knight Ulrich, a mighty hunter before the Lord. One fine morning, when the sun was shining, Ulrich left to enjoy his favorite pastime but did not flush out any game that entire day. On his way back to the castle, he became lost. He then saw a couple on horseback coming toward him. He greeted them and got no response. Next to appear were five hundred men and an equal number of women who behaved the same way. Behind them was a woman riding by herself. He greeted her, and she returned his greeting and even answered his questions. "We are the dead," she told him. When he confessed his surprise at hearing this from her corporeal lips, she added: "My body has been dead for thirty years. It has rotted, and what you see is naught but a reflection." She then explained how she had cheated on her husband with the Lord of Schenkenberg, Ulrich's master, and had died without making penitence. Ulrich decided to accompany her. She warned him: "Touch nothing that anyone tries to give you." They arrived at a castle, and the couples sat down on the lawn in front of it and were served a meal. Forgetting the advice of the lady, Ulrich grabbed a grilled fish, and four of his fingers caught on fire. The lady seized a knife and cut the sign of the

---

*E. Margaret Grimes, ed., *Romanic Review* 26 (1935), 313–21. The text says this: a Breton knight named Lorois de Morois sets off alone one day listening to the song of a nightingale. In the edge of a forest he encounters a group of noble ladies accompanied by gentlemen. The couples hug and kiss. Hardly over his surprise, Lorois spots a second group indulging in the same activities. Suddenly, he hears a burst of moaning, and out of the forest emerge a hundred wretched, thin ladies clad in rags, soon followed by an equal number of knights in a pitiable state. Lorois asks one lady what this means. The happy couples are those who know how to love truly whilst still alive; the others were too proud, *ne ainc ne daignierent amer.*

cross in his skin, and the blood extinguished the flames. A tourney took place after the feasting, followed by dancing. Ulrich took the lady's hand and fell down as if dead. She dug up a root, put it in his mouth, and restored him to life. As the moment for the ghosts to disappear became imminent, the lady charged Ulrich with a message for Count von Schrenkenberg: he must make penitence. Ulrich returned to the count's castle.[71]

In Christianized stories, the foods from the otherworld are always diabolical. In an exemplum by Caesarius of Heisterbach, a dead knight ties some fish he has brought for his son to the door of his house. At dawn, his son finds instead of fish, toads and snakes, "infernal foods cooked over sulfurous fires."[72] We should also note that the dead in this text lead a life corresponding to that of courtly society and that their diabolical nature is visible only in their food.

Willekin and the Ghost

A short story from the thirteenth century entitled *Knightly Loyalty* (Rittertreue) provides a finished form of the legend of the grateful dead.[73] The dead individual of course appears in an ectoplasmic shape, but the text shows how the importance of the sepulcher persisted and is reminiscent of what we know about Roman beliefs. We should also recall the words of St. Augustine: "Doing good for the dead is very useful."

Count Willekin von Montabur came to an inn one day and learned that a knight had died there but a short while before. Because the knight had not paid his bill, the innkeeper had the corpse thrown under a pile of manure. Willekin paid off the dead man's debt and obtained a decent burial for him. Seeking a good horse to take part in a tourney whose prize was the hand of a noble lady, Willekin saw a man in the street astride a magnificent charger. He addressed him, offering him money in exchange for the horse. The other turned down the sum and surrendered his mount in return for half the prize of the tourney.

Willekin was victorious and took the prize, thus the wedding occurred. The next day, when he shut the door of the nuptial chamber, the knight with whom he had concluded the bargain arrived, demanding his half. The count offered him money and goods, but in vain. In order not to break his oath, he left the room. To his great surprise, his interlocutor followed him and declared: "I am the dead man whose body you redeemed and to whom you provided a sepulcher; I wanted to test your loyalty." Not daring to rejoice, Willekin sought tangible proof of what he was hearing. He stuck out his hand and encountered nothing but air. The dead man thanked him again for his good deed and vanished, renouncing the price of the horse.[74]

Other examples present only slight variations on a minuscule number of themes forming a cycle and repeating the same thing: sinners are punished; if they were not too evil in life, they can be saved, otherwise they will burn in hell. We are a long way from the Norse revenants. The ambience is completely different, which stems from the fact that these stories are not as connected to reality as in the Scandinavian texts in which the revenants are attached to the life of a specific family living in a well-defined domain. In northern Europe, they are not living outside time and space. We can locate their appearances on a map. We learn the names of witnesses and how the facts unfold. We are not facing ghosts who have escaped from purgatory or hell but rather dead people about whom we know almost everything.

SIX

The Name of the Revenants

There are a number of old beliefs, which we know only from the writings of a remote past, that remain quite obscure. Language is a living organism and is ceaselessly evolving, as are ideas. Even if the vocabulary retains the testimony of ancient concepts, the copyists borrow it without always grasping its meaning because it no longer corresponds to any reality and no longer has any contemporary relevance. Because of this, terms become distorted to the point of becoming unrecognizable, and when they aren't, we still do not always understand them because they no longer possess their original meanings.

A lexical study of ghosts and revenants is therefore based on different works of unequal value: the Norse stories are rich with data of all kinds, the English and German literature is quite poor in information, and these regions do not seem to have promoted creating stories of this kind. On the other hand, during this same era, the glosses—the marginal or interlinear commentary of passages from Latin, classical, and medieval works—casts light in the vernacular tongue on what was thought of notions whose roots often lay in classical antiquity. These glosses are even sometimes arranged as lexicons for the purpose of allowing clerics and other educated individuals to use ancient works for teaching and to facilitate reading and possibly translation. Therefore, these glosses have preserved many local traditions reflected by the words, which are marked by the personality and knowledge of their author as well as by his ethnic origin. For instance, a Bavarian from the early Middle Ages is very different from a Saxon or a Friesian of the same era.

Here we are going to begin our exploration with sometimes literal inscriptions that often represent an implicit commentary revealing, through the meaning of the words or expressions used, the contemporary mind-set of the author and his fellow countrymen. We will then examine the infinitely richer but much less problematic Nordic region, in which folk traditions rise above the clerical science of the time.

We find in the *Summarium Heinrici*[1]—a work of the early twelfth century providing High German translations of Latin terms drawn from Isidore of Seville's *Etymology*—an odd analysis of *mania*, "specter," a rare word that is known only because of a play by Novus (first century) entitled *The Specter Doctor* (*Mania medica*). The *Summarium's* author in fact writes: "Revenant, or, in other words, insane person" (*mania i. insanie*). The observation is initially disconcerting and merits analysis. According to Varrius Flaccus (first century), mania would be the mother or grandmother of the larvae, a generic name for evil dead and revenants. The Latin glosses from antiquity define the plural *maniae* as "deformed persons, terrifying spirits." Incorporated into *larva*—Martianus Capella writes *larvae ac maniae*—the term did not completely vanish and crops up again with A. Cornelius Celsus,[2] a doctor who was a contemporary of Tiberius, but the word was used less and less frequently over time. From this particular scholar we learn that *insania* designates mental illnesses in general. The ancients regarded it in fact as a punishment from the gods, and it was believed that the lunatic was, most often, possessed by an invisible force—in this instance, a larva. Isidore of Seville employs the adjective *larvaticus* to designate this kind of possession (*Etymology* IV, 7, 5), but in the Middle Ages, the gods and their henchmen became demons, and madness was considered primarily to be the work of an incubus or succubus. The gloss given by the *Summarium* is thus perfectly exact. The absence of a German translation shows, in any case, that the concept did not exist in the region where the glossologist performed his duties. We will also note the transition from possession by a dead person to possession by a diabolical spirit.

There was another name in Rome to designate ghosts: *monstrum,* whose diminutive form, *mostella,* appears in the title of a play by Plautus, who died in 184 BCE, *Mostellaria,* or *The Comedy of the Ghost.* The meaning of *monstra* is very unclear. Medieval etymologists compared it to the verb *monere,* "to warn," and to *monstrum,* "preceding sign of a deadly event." In the fourth century, Palladius, whose treatise on agriculture was renowned throughout the medieval West, offers "harmful spirits" as a synonym for *monstra* and states explicitly that farmers dreaded the harmful influence of the *monstra* on harvest and domestic animals.[3]

There are many glosses concerning the Latin lemma. Around the eight and ninth centuries, a noun appeared in High German in which the notion of appearance is predominant. This word is *scinleigh,* "apparition." The notion of trickery began to spread in the ninth century with the word *trugnisse,* whose root is *trug-,* "to trick," used to translate *monstra.* The derivatives of the lexemes *trug-* and *scin-* were in competition, but the first prevailed over the second.[4] From this point, revenants became no more than illusions, vain images, and reflections. Language followed the historical evolution exactly. The church attacked the belief in revenants and the worship of the dead—which were too pagan for its taste—and used instead the *De cura pro mortuis gerenda* written by St. Augustine around 421–24 and the *Dialogi* of Gregory the Great (died in 604) to aid in the relegating of phantoms to the realm of the imagination (*phantasia*).[5]

Crossing over to the English side of the Channel we find the same evolution, but here the notion of phantasmagoria and magic predominated. Old English translated *scinlace* into *fantasma*—meaning "phantom, false dream, diabolical vision"—and *necromantia* and *praestigia,* or "magic." Starting from the eleventh century, the idea of sorcery (*wiccecraefte*)[6] was added to this notion. The equivalence of *scinlace* and *necromantia* clearly shows that with the use of these words, we are definitely in the realm of revenants.

If we harbor any doubts about the testimony provided by the glosses, there are several ancient translations of texts from antiquity that confirm such testimonies. The translation of the *Medicina de quadrupedibus* by Sextus Placitus provides the manufacture of a remedy (philter) to heal "possessed" individuals. In the text, "possessed" is *scinseoc,* meaning "made ill by apparitions, ghosts."[7] The same collection draws a connection between the mute disease, or epilepsy (*morbus caducus*) and ghosts (scinlace).[8]

The translations of *monstrum* in two Germanic languages shows how a gradual shift occurred from reality to dream, but other High German glosses translate *monstrum* as *egisia,* meaning "terror, horror," depicting the emotions inspired by revenants.

If we place our faith in Ovid and Apuleius, *lemures* (lemurs) first and foremost designated the dead in general before becoming synonymous with larvae and being applied to the evil dead who came back to plague the living. Horace writes: "Can you laugh at dreams (*somnia*), magic terrors (*terrores magicos*), miracles (*miracula*), witches (*sagas*), revenants (*nocturnes lemures*) . . ."[9]

At the beginning of the eleventh century, no corresponding term existed in German, and the *Summarium Henrici* was content with the following definition: "*Lemures:* night demons; spirits in dead bodies."[10]

For the Romans, *larvae* applied to the souls of the dead that found no rest. St. Augustine regarded them as harmful demons "created by men" (*ex hominibus factos*). The term was the subject of numerous glosses, which implies that it definitely corresponded to a Germanic reality. We first find *sceini,* whose meaning is like that of *simulachrum*—"image, likeness, appearance"—then *sceme,* which survives in modern German in the form of *Schemen,* meaning "shade" or "phantom."[11]

More interesting is *egisgrimolt,* which is *egisgrima* in Old English, used to translate *larva* and *masca,* meaning "witch." This is a compound word whose determiner translates fright (*egis*) and whose determinatum translates the notion of "mask, face, helmet."[12] In Norse poetry, *grima* is also a metaphor for "night." *Egisgrimolt* and *egisgrima* both can be translated as "terrifying apparition." If we compare *grimolt* and *grima* to the modern English word *grime,* meaning "soot," and the Middle Low German *grimet,* "striped in black," the appearance of the figure hidden behind this word brings to mind what Tacitus said about the Germanic tribe the Harii: these people painted their bodies black and carried black shields to terrify their enemies by making them believe they were an army of the dead.[13]

Revenants were gradually repressed into the realm of witchcraft. A gloss from the eleventh century east of the Rhine provides the following commentary: "We call them larvae those shades or those demons created by men."* The proposed translation of larvae is *dalamascha,* in which we can find *masca,* "witch." *Dala*—also found as *cala* and even *tala*—has thus far resisted all elucidation, and any proposed interpretations should be taken with greater caution.

Numerous glosses pose a fascinating problem: *Screzza* and its variations are translations for *larvae.* Etymology is of no help, but the Latin lemma shed light on the idea behind the German word. *Screzza (scrate, scrato)* can also be used to translate *ephialte,* "the nightmare," *nebulo,* "the cloud," *praestigiator,* "the mage, the wizard," and *incubus,* "the nocturnal demon."† We are in the domain of the demonic deceptive image, but other Latin words indicate that two opinions collide here—that of the populace and that of the clerics. *Scrat* is the "evil spirit" (*malus genius*), "terror," "larva," "revenant," or "monster"—the giant (*gigas*).[14]

All these definitions are correct. *Malus genius* refers to a tutelary spirit, *landvaettr* in Norse. It so happens that Germanic dead could be either good spirits, if they died normally, or evil spirits, if their deaths

---

*Let me point out that there is a *gedwimor* in Old English that designates ghosts; the glosses use it for the Latin lemma *fantasma, fantasia, nebulo, necromantia.*
†Steinmeyer and Sievers, *Die althochdeutschen Glossen,* vol. 3, 317, 4. We even have *schrat = faunus* (vol. 2, 678, 45). Excellent examples of the incorporation of beings from German folk mythology into Roman spirits can be found in the *Gesta Danorum* (II) in which Saxo cites pell-mell satyrs, fauns, larvae, fantua, and so forth.

were bizarre or if they came back from death. As far as the church was concerned, these spirits could be only diabolical. Terror and larva posed no problem. *Monstrum* and *gigas* indicated that the dead or the revenants were larger than nature, which was correct, as we shall see later, and that they herald an event, often dire, which was true—for the return of a dead person was followed by another death on more than one occasion.

If we compare the Old High German *scrat* to the Finnish *kratti,* "guardian spirit of a treasure" (*genus thesauri*), knowing that funeral mounds often contained riches, we have an additional element indicating the existence of a link between *scrat* and the revenants because it was said that the good spirits—the good ancestors—inhabited the rocks and stones, the mounds and hillocks. The same holds true for the malefic spirits, but they were then assimilated into dwarves (*dvergar, zwerge*), whereas the good spirits were incorporated into the alfes (*álfar*). King Olaf, son of Gudröd, was nicknamed the Alfe [elf] of Geirstad after his death.

Though the clerics of the Middle Ages were completely familiar with the Latin terminology applying to revenants and ghosts, it is curious to note that they provided no equivalent for *umbra* and *animus*. They did define these terms, however. Around 1050, Papias writes: "*umbra*— souls, likenesses, images, dreams," and William Durand (1237–96) uses *animus* when reporting a superstition: "They think though that spirits wander around graves, those who we call 'shades,' can wreak havoc."[15] On the other hand, the synonym for *necromanticus* is *umbrarius*. The word "umbrarius" appears in 643 in the collection of laws known as *Edictum Rothari* (chapter 108).[16] Even in the Middle Ages, *umbra* covered a category of the dead well concealed by the Christian interpretation—exactly the same categories that concern us here.

In Old High German and in Old English, *geist* and *gaest* did not designate a revenant as *geist* and *ghost* do today, and *scato,* "the shadow," did not apply to phantoms. We can deduce from this that revenants were not evanescent: they were not images or mists, but flesh and blood individuals, which is confirmed by the Norse literature and the rare texts from other Germanic countries.

If we turn to more recent terms—Middle High German *gespenst* and *gespüc*—we have proof that the apparitions of the dead, and postmortem manifestations in general, were contained within the diabolical dream as well as the Latin *fantasma*, which has given us *phantom*. The church therefore managed to adulterate totally the belief in revenants, and these two Middle High German names still have a demonic nuance. *Gespenst*—formed from the word *spanan*, "to suggest"—implies the notion of illusion. *Gespüc*, formed from the Low German *spok*, designates for the preacher Berthold de Ratisbonne (1220–1272) "all those who believe in magic."* Today, the masculine noun *Spuk* means "phantom" or "apparition."

Let's now examine the area of ancient Scandinavian or Norse languages. A large number of tales in these tongues speak of revenants and ghosts and depict their activities, and it is relatively easy to find the words that characterize them. The rarest of them all is *flyka*, mentioned in a single text, the *Saga of Grettir the Strong* (chapter 32). A. Johannesson ties it to the family of *fjós*, "stable," and J. de Vries attaches it to *fljúga*, "to flee."[17] Both interpretations are admissible but not very satisfying. Yet there is an undeniable connection between revenants and livestock—so if forced to pick an association, I would choose Johannesson's.

The second noun, *vafa* or *vofa*, seems to indicate the traveling of the ghost. We can in fact compare these words to the verbs *vafa*, "to balance or oscillate," and *vafla*, "vacillate, wander," or even *vafra*, "to move in all directions." We cannot doubt the antiquity of its accepted usage, "phantom, revenant," because the Middle High German *waberen*—*wafeln* today—means "to haunt."

The most widespread lexeme and undoubtedly the oldest is *draugr* (plural *draugar*), which reflects the Indo-European root *dhreugh*, "to

---

Gespüc designates the seers (*wdrsagen*), prophetesses (*wârsagerinne*), potion makers (*lüppelerinne* = *witches*), and the women who go out in the night (*nahtfrouwen*).

harm, to deceive." It appears first of all in the *Poetic Edda* in which the compound word *draughús,* "the house of the revenant," designates a funeral cairn. *Draugr* also means "dead person" but only seems to mean a certain kind of dead equivalent to the Latin *larva.*

Another word frequently noted is *aptrangr,* from *ganga,* "to go," and *aptr,* "after," and therefore "to come back." We can find this same meaning in *ganga vidara* or even *ganga* by itself. We can deduce from this that wandering, movement, and tribulations are characteristic of phantoms and revenants.

The expression "not to rest in peace" (*liggja eigi kyrr*) and the verb *reimast,* "to haunt, to be haunted,"* from the Indo-European root *erie,* "to rise," translates the idea that the dead person returns because he still has a task to fulfill. He gets up then, unable to rest, and attends to business known only to himself—business that is malefic in the majority of instances. If we add to these pieces of information the nickname of the god Odin—*draugadrottinn,* "the master or the lord of revenants"—we can see that the belief was deeply rooted in the mind-set of the ancient Scandinavians.

This intentionally oversimplified linguistic approach is necessary because, by adding together these various pieces of information, we can see that the revenants become more formed. They are large, alarming, sometimes black in color, and often harmful. They inhabit the mounds and tumuli, and, unable to find peace there, thus return. They are also spirits of a kind that guards treasures. Little by little, they were destined to become fantasies, illusions, demons—mixed higgledy-piggledy with all the beings that emerged from allegedly pagan beliefs.

Reimast appears in the very common expression *reimt thykkir thar vera,* "there are ghosts." We should note that the verb *rida,* "to ride," is also used to indicate a haunting, as in the *Eyrbyggja Saga* (chapter 34). In other cases, it expresses, as a compound word, possession by a spirit or a dead person, *trollrida.*

SEVEN

Questions and Answers

The texts I've chosen, with the support of additional works, should make it possible to respond to an initial group of questions that make up one stage of our investigation. We can ask ourselves who comes back and for what reasons. As it turns out, we can pinpoint the time and the place of returns, and finally examine the methods used to get rid of revenants.

Who Comes Back?

The question is an obvious one, for not all the dead became revenants. The number of people who have drowned or are murdered and those who are victims of accidents or illness is quite high in the sagas. But not all the dead cry out for vengeance, and more than one adapt to the cold of the grave quite nicely. Could certain individuals have been pre-destined to become revenants after their death? Analysis of the textual evidence suggests this; there is indeed a link between the nature of the deceased and haunting.

Men of a difficult nature—which is in no way pejorative in the Scandinavian north—disagreeable, taciturn, quarrelsome, or malicious individuals, were difficult for the family or clan to accept. They remained on the margins of social life because once they start mixing in, all sorts of problems arose. Thorolf Twist-Foot is an excellent example: He begins his life in Iceland in a duel in which he kills Ulfar so he can take owner-ship of Ulfar's lands. He then breaks with his son, despoils some indi-viduals and starts quarrels with others, and even goes so far as to employ a hired killer to get rid of people who irk him. The *Eyrbyggja Saga* des-ignates him as "unjust," "petty," and "irritable." Thormod and Glam also are men who are hard to get along with—and the same holds true for many revenants. They were feared when they were alive and are dreaded after their deaths. The transformation of these individuals into ill-intentioned revenants is therefore explained by the feelings they inspired. Their return was logical: their character, in some cases their wickedness, prevented them from resting in peace because they had no grounds for being satisfied with their deaths. Revenants teach us that eternal peace is not given to men who, like it or not, did not integrate into the com-munity of the living. They were equally incapable of integrating into that of the departed. Knowing that sin excluded the human being from the Christian community, it is easy to see how the church was able to twist to its own advantage the belief in revenants and ghosts.

Yet we can separate the character of the departed from the reasons for their return. Let's take a look.

Why Do Some Come Back?

The reasons for postmortem manifestations and apparitions are rarely put forward, but they can be deduced from their context. Most often the dead were pursuing a desire for vengeance: Klaufi persecutes Yngvild, who played an active role in his murder, and because Gris and Ljotolf decapitate him, he visits his cousin Karl to prompt him to obtain rep-arations for this crime. In the *Laxdaela Saga* (chapter 38), Hallbjörn Slikisteinsauga entices Thorkel to a secluded location and then pounces on him to kill him. Thorkel is one of those responsible for Hallbjörn's execution. In the *Saga of Halfdan Eysteinsson*, the giant Kol and his daughter Gullkula assault their murderer at night.[1] Thormod (the *Saga of Havard of Ice Fjord*) returns to stretch out in his own bed as an act of revenge against the clan that never accepted him. Violent death is not the sole cause for hauntings, and Thorolf Twist-Foot, who dies bizarrely in his high seat, is proof: he returns to pester, molest, and slay the inhabitants of the region with which he was endlessly quarreling in life.

Vengeance is undoubtedly the oldest idea that props up stories about revenants. Cicero recounts a tale about a specter who denounces his murderer, and Titus-Livy tells of a ghost who demands punishment for the person guilty of his death.[2] In the legend of Sigurd, also known as Siegfried, Brunhild lets it be known that she has no desire to survive the one she loves. Gunnar tries to dissuade her and calls Högni (Hagen) for help, asking him to prevent this suicide, "the fatal journey of the woman before her evil hour has come upon her."[3]

The words of Gunnar refer implicitly to the belief in a possible posthumous vengeance, an idea we find among other Indo-Germanic peoples, particularly in Rome, where an individual may have committed suicide with the idea of becoming a lemure and punishing his enemies:[4] his creditors. The idea was rooted deeply in people's minds: the departed exacted revenge, either personally or through an intermediary. In *Hamlet,* the hero's father appears to demand the punishment of his murderers.[5] The theme is a frequent staple in folktales and has been responsible for many fine narratives, such as *The Singing Bone:* "A shepherd found a bone in a field and carved it into a flute; when he sought to draw a sound from it, the instrument began speaking and denounced the murderer of the bone's owner."

The second reason for hauntings was the announcement of death: the revenant played the role of messenger, indicating an imminent death or news of a death that had already occurred.

To see the deceased is often synonymous with the final journey. In the *Saga of the Sworn Brothers* (chapter 19), Karl and Steinholf think—note the narrator's prudence—they see men coming from the west across a prairie. They recognize them as Thorgeir Havarsson and the eight men of his crew, all covered with blood, who eventually come to a brook and vanish. Shortly after this, Eyjolf and Thorgeir Measureless kill each other. In the *Saga of Viga-Glum*, Una spies dead people going to meet a bard, who is slain by the men of Sigfus a short time later.[6] The most beautiful scene is no doubt the one told in the *Laxdaela Saga* (chapter 76): Thorskel and his crew are drowned in a shipwreck in Large Fjord near Bear Island.

> And the very evening of the day Thorskel drowned, it happened that in Helgafell, Gudrun was going to the church at the time all were going to bed. As she was crossing through the cemetery gate, she saw a revenant rise up before her. This revenant bowed and said: "I have big news, Gudrun." She responded: "Shut up, wretch."
>
> Gudrun continued on her way to the church as she had planned and when she got there, she thought she could see that Thorskel and his crew had returned home. She saw that their clothes were dripping wet with seawater. Gudrun did not speak to them and entered the church. . . . She then returned to the great hall, thinking that Thorskel and his companions would have gone there, but when she arrived no one was there.

Shortly afterward, Gudrun gets news of the shipwreck.

Revenants (such as Gunnlaug or Blundketil) were also capable of letting their deaths be known in dreams or even in broad daylight (like Thorkel), or they (like Klaufi) might have designated those who were slated to join them. Here we find the notion of the white lady—but there is a notable difference between the white female phantoms and the Norse dead who were heralds of death. The first were anonymous whereas the latter were almost always recognizable. Karl identifies Klaufi immediately when he thinks he sees him traveling through the sky on a horse that pulls a sled.

The dead could appear for other reasons. One of these is illness, as in the story of Thorgil's sojourn in Greenland (the *Saga of the People of Floi*) or in the story about the shepherd and Thorir Wooden-Leg (*Eyrbyggja Saga*). On examination, we can see that dream ghosts existed for a large variety of reasons: the deceased threatened, advised, requested, predicted, and thanked—in short, they interfered in the lives of human beings and did not abandon playing a role in them. For evidence of this, we can refer to the story of Thorodd and Thorgunna (chapter 5of this book).

At What Time Do These Events Take Place?

All the witnesses were in agreement on one point: revenants were winter guests. "With the coming of winter," says the *Saga of the Faröemen* (chapter 34) "many revenants appeared." Their manifestations generally began around December, were the most numerous around the solstice, and decreased in number in March (though they didn't stop completely). The narrators pepper their stories with explicit observations: "It was shortly before Christmas," the *Iceland Annals* says, and "the night of Christmas," the *Saga of the People of Floi* reports.* For the Germans, Jól, and more generally speaking, the cold season, were connected to the memory of the dead. The ancestors were honored then, sacrifices were made—Jól's other name is "the sacrifice to the alfes" (*álfablót*), when people slew a boar, which was the sacred animal of the god Freyr, who embodied the third function (fertility and fecundity). This was a family feast, a commemoration of the dead, and *The Words of Harald* indicates that the Jól table was set for invisible guests, the departed, the gods, or their hypostasis.[7] The feast was accompanied by games, which were maintained until a recent era in all Germanic countries. The ancient *Laws* of the Gulathing (chapter 7) say the reason for the festival was to welcome "a fertile year and peace" (*til árs ok fridar*). Jól was also the feast of the god Odin, one of whose names was "The Master of Jól" (Jólnir), which only reinforced the ties between Jól and

---

*Flóamanna Saga, chapter 22: *lidr nú vetrinn ok dregr at Jólum.* In *Grettir's Saga* (chapter 33), it is twice noted: "As the days grew longer, the incidences of haunting diminished"; "and when spring returned and the days grew longer, the hauntings grew less."

the dead, for Odin was, as we have seen, one of the gods of the dead and revenants. It was therefore normal for hauntings to increase at this time of year, especially during the cycle of the Twelve Days (Christmas, New Year's Day, Epiphany) during which, in France for example,[8] people witnessed the passage of the Infernal Hunt. In Scandinavia, bands of the dead flew through the skies, sneaking food from the living.

Yet revenants also manifested at other times of the year, but especially when darkness ruled. Night was their domain. "No one could stay outside in peace," says the *Eyrbyggja Saga* (chapter 34), "once the sun had set." When Thorkel meets the specter of Hallbjörn Slikisteinsauga, "it was after sunset when the moon was shining." Revenants could be seen during daylight hours as well, but they were rarely active because natural and artificial light stole their strength. A poem from the *Edda* expresses it quite well: "Do not be so mad as to venturing alone, daughter of the Skjoldungs, into the dwelling of ghosts; these enemies are much more powerful at night than when the light of day dawns."[9]

For this reason, revenants were always trying to lure outside—far from the light that gleamed fitfully in the common room—those they wished to hurt.

Where Do Revenants Manifest?

Revenants were not great travelers: They remained attached to their homes and manifested on their lands—sometimes, when they were particularly wicked, making raids on their neighbors, as in the case of Thorolf Twist-Foot or Klaufi. They differed in this way from the ghosts and doubles studied by Emmanuel Le Roy Ladurie, who "stroll in this mountainous no man's land located beyond the strictly defined territory of the village. . . . Doubles are thus also driven toward the infertile and hilly *outfield,* with the bodies of men being transformed into quite simply good nourishing earth inside the boundaries of the *infield.** The rea-

---

*Emmanuel LeRoy, *Montaillou, village Occitan* (Paris: Gaillimard, 1976), 590ff. In Iceland, the body is transported to the outfield only when there is a haunting. [*Outfield* and *infield* are written in English in the original French text. —*Trans.*]

sons for such a discrepancy give us good grounds for question.

Among the Germans, the home was never built in a random fashion. The *Book of Settlements* informs us of several rites for settlement and taking possession of a piece of ground, which conferred a sacred character upon the farm and the domain. Ingolf tosses overboard the posts of his high seat and declares he will live where they first come ashore. When Thorolf Mostrarskegg enters Large Fjord, he does the same; the image of Thor has been carved upon the posts, so it is therefore left to the deity to designate the place where the house will be built.[10] The god Freyr steals Ingimund's amulet and hides it in Iceland. A seer tells Ingimund that he will find it by digging at the spot where, after having disembarked, he will set the posts of his high seat.[11]

The dead, too, could decide on the precise location for the living to settle: before dying on the boat bringing him to Iceland with his people, Evening Wolf (Kveld-Ulfr) asks that his coffin be thrown into the sea, and adds that his son, Skallagrim, should settle close to the spot where his body touches land.[12] The living and the dead were inseparable and met each other in the family home. If the deceased was a stranger, such as Glam (the *Saga of Grettir the Strong*), he haunted the spot where he died. Both literally and figuratively, death affixed the man to the earth in some way.

Other acts of a magical and religious nature accompanied the formation of a domain. Taking possession of the land was performed by planting into the ground a staff, sometimes freshly stripped of its bark, establishing the area's boundaries by a day's walk or by firing a flaming arrow above the territory to be appropriated.[13] When Önund proceeded in this fashion, the bishop Sturla wrote, "He consecrated (*helgadi*) the land."[14] The verb *helga,* "to consecrate, sanctify, legitimate," formed from the root *hail-*, very strongly reflects the notion of immanent powers. Knowing that the home and domain formed a sacred space allows us to grasp more easily one motif of the sagas: When two brothers share ownership of a domain and then separate, one takes the furnishings and transportable goods and the other keeps the house and land.

It is not shared, and the domain is called *ódal,* "that which cannot be cut." The *ódal* is the patrimonial land, the hereditary legacy.

Therefore, the revenant did not become at all detached from the family seat, and this is noted in a thousand different ways in the sagas. "Thorkel was buried beneath a cairn in Hvalseyjarfjord field and returned constantly to haunt his house," says one.[15] "It was discovered that someone was haunting the common room," tells another.* Hrapp wishes to be buried inside his house, and Odd declares: "I want to be buried in Skaneyjarfjall; from there I will be able to see the entire region."[16] Men therefore chose their final home on their lands, a motif that opens a very large perspective on the transformation of the good dead into tutelary genies (Landvaettir).

It can easily be seen to what extent revenants formed a part of daily reality. Their actions fitted within a given civilization, with all it contained.† Belief in revenants was not simply superstition but truly notion tied closely to the worship of the dead and the family, whose importance we cannot underestimate. While a revenant may have been at odds with his wife—there is even a ghost who forbids his wife to remarry‡—it was rare for one to attack directly the members of his family. In the *Eyrbyggja Saga* (chapter 34), we read this instructive remark: "Wherever Arnkel and his crew went, no one suffered any harm," and later (chapter 63): "Thorolf began reappearing once Arnkel died." The wicked cripple, however, has broken relations with his son.

When preventive measures—closing the eyes, stuffing the nostrils

---

Eyrbyggja Saga, chapter 34. Its scribe wrote that an individual "rode the common room" (*at opt var ridit skálanum*).

†See, for example, the *Saga of Saint Olaf* (chapter 85): Thormod left the field of battle, transfixed by an arrow. He met a woman carrying firewood. On seeing him, she dropped her load and screamed: "The dead are walking" (*dauda menn ganga*), but Thormod reassured her.

‡See Gervase of Tilbury, *Otia imperialia* III, 99: *De mortuo qui occidit uxorem quondam suam.* (William of Moustiers made his wife swear an oath never to remarry. She did not keep her promise, and the deceased came back and slew her with a mortar. Another ghost story can be found in *Otia iperialia* III, 103: *De mortuo qui apparet virgini, mira dicit et anunciat.*

and the mouth, removing the corpse from his home through a hole in the wall—proved to have no effect, the only remaining recourse for the living was the use of force. The texts provide a complete scale of methods going from the gentlest to the most brutal.

The simplest method was to scare away the revenant with a show of open hostility. He was made to feel unwanted, especially by the living giving him a sound thrashing. Thorkel beats Hallbjörn Sliksteinsauga, who gets away from him, and the saga says: "Henceforth he caused no more wrong." Olaf gives Thormod the same treatment, but without much result. As we have seen, the most common measure for ridding the living of a revenant was decapitation, followed occasionally by cremation. Decapitation brings the archaeological findings to mind and underscores a notion shared by many peoples: the head was believed to be the seat of action. But here again the dead escaped certain natural laws and could wander without their heads. In Lower Saxony during the nineteenth century, an acephalic individual traveled on the road connecting Wellen to Robensleben. He did no harm, but a detour was installed as a precautionary measure. A headless horse also appeared on the border separating Bavaria from Czechoslovakia.[17]

It was therefore necessary to vanquish revenants at one time. The sagas differ markedly on this point from the exempla, but some of them

Mutilation of the corpse was a postmortem punishment: the dead individual would have a miserable life in the beyond. (Poetic and Philosophical Codex, *Folio No. 2, Stuttgart, folio 12 v°)*

attest to a gradual contamination: The sound of church bells causes the ghost attacking Thorstein to flee.[18] A cross prevents Agdi from entering a house, and another planted in front of his cairn condemns him to stay in his tumulus.[19] Christianity was the great enemy of revenants.

> Kodran, the father of Thorvald, did not accept the new religion preached by the bishop. He explained that he had a spirit familiar, a man with the gift of second sight (*spámadr*). He lived in a rock, and he took care of Kodran and his livestock. The bishop sprinkled the rock with holy water. The spámadr appeared to Kodran in a dream to reproach him. He and his children had been burned by the holy water. The bishop continued his persecution, but the spámadr appeared a second time in a pitiable state, then came again, one last time, to bid farewell to Kodran.[20]

Didn't the new faith prompt the flight of the rural spirits and the dead? In the *Book of Flat Island,* Thorhold sees the mounds opened and the creatures living in them flee.[21] When King Olaf spends the night in a haunted hut, he prays and hears echoing that shrieks: "King Olaf's prayers burned me so that I could no longer stay in my house. I had to flee and never return."[22] The text says the spot was haunted by trolls and evil spirits (*trollagange oc maeinvetta*).

No text better confirms the role of the church than the *Vita* of Bishop Gudmund Arason (1203–1237): Gudmund orders a cross carved on the small bell of a haunted stable. He plants crosses at the spot where the strange Selkolla—literally, Seal Head—made her appearances. This is a feminine being that is an evil spirit, a witch, and a revenant. She bears the label *flagö,* causes bizarre manifestations, and sinks in and out of the earth on various occasions. The cleric who tells tales of her exploits equates her with the devil.[23]

Couldn't the light that often sent ghosts and revenants fleeing also be a symbol of the new religion attempting to wrest man from the dark shadows of paganism?

PART THREE

EIGHT

Revenants, Death, and the Beyond

Revenants are irritating beings; they escape all logic and transgress natural laws because they do not continue on sensibly to the next world, they do not decay, and they continue to meddle in people's lives. They offer a challenge to the wise division of the world between the kingdom of the dead and the universe of the living. They open a third way with respect to beyond the grave. In short, they cause trouble and create a shock within a Christianized society that has installed a simple redemptive and punitive scheme with three sides: hell, purgatory, and heaven. If the church put revenants in their index, at least those from whom they could not gain anything, it was clearly because these revenants had no place in the dogma. But wouldn't pagans have looked on revenants in much the same way? They also held notions about heaven and hell. As it happens, revenants go to neither of these two worlds, and they do not move on into the beyond, which is cause for questions. When confronted with the obvious contradiction between the simultaneous existence of specters and an empire of the dead, how was death to be understood?

Beyond the Grave

Ancient Norse texts spoke of three kingdoms of the dead: that of Ran, the sea goddess with the evocative name meaning "theft" or "pillage," about whom we know almost nothing;[1] that of Hel, goddess of the infernal regions; and that of Odin, Valhöll (Richard Wagner's Valhalla)—in other words, "the Paradise of warriors."

Hel—etymologically speaking, the "dissembler"—was the daughter of the wicked Loki. Her mother was the giantess Troublemaker (Angrboda), and her brothers were the wolf Fenris, who purses the sun tirelessly in an attempt to swallow it, and the Midgard Serpent, keeper of the aquatic depths. Hel was half black and half blue and ruled over an empire located in the north of the world. In this regard, it should be noted that tombstones were being oriented toward the north as early as the Stone Age. This northern empire bore a variety of poetic names: the Dark Plains of the Field of Shadows (Nidavellir), Shore or World of Cadavers (Nástrandir, Násheimir), and the World of Mists (Nifhel). Hel was surrounded by burning rivers named Din-of-Combat (Valglaumr) and Tumultuous (Gjöll). Coming from the east was the river Peril (Slidr), which transported weapons, and the same was true for the river Swarming-with-Spears (Geirvimul). In order to cross them, the deceased traveled on Gjallarbru, the large, gold-covered bridge spanning the Tumultuous River. This bridge was guarded by the virgin Modgud, and tethered at one end was a dog whose chest was dripping with blood. The kingdom of shadows was closed with a portcullis or grill (Helgrind, Valgrind) that would open only for the dead. Let's accompany Odin's son, Hermod, for a moment, when he goes to offer a ransom to the goddess Hel to release Baldr, slain by the blind Höd.

> But about Hermod, the following is told. For nine nights he rode through valleys so deep and dark that he saw nothing before he reached the river Gjöll and rode onto the Gjöll bridge. The bridge was roofed with shining gold, and the maiden guarding it was named

Modgud. She asked Hermod about his name and family and said that the previous day five troops of dead men had ridden across the bridge, "yet the bridge echoed more under you alone, and you lack the color of the dead. Why do you ride here on the Road to Hel?"

He answered, saying, "I ride to Hel in search of Baldr. But have you seen anything of Baldr on the Hel Road?"

She replied that Baldr had ridden across Gjöll Bridge "and down and north lies the Road to Hel."

Hermod rode on until he came to the Gates of Hel. He dismounted from his horse and tightened the girth. Then he remounted and spurred the horse, which sprang forward, jumping with such force that it cleared the top of the gate without even coming near it. Then Hermod rode up to the hall. He dismounted and went inside. He saw that his brother Baldr was sitting in the seat of honor.[2]

As with most peoples, the empire of the dead is underground. If we refer to the *Words of Vafthrudnir,* it seems to consist of several dwellings. In this poem from the *Edda,* the giant Vafthrudnir questioned by Odin declares: "Nine worlds have I traveled through to come down here to Nifhel. This is where men die."[3] But in this space there is one spot worse than the rest, and *The Seeress's Prophecy* describe it this way:

> *A hall she saw standing far from the sun*
> *On Naströnd whose doors look north;*
> *Poison drops fall through its roof-vents,*
> *And this hall is woven from snakes' spines.*
> *There she saw wading through thickened rivers*
> *Men who swore false oaths and criminal beserkers,*
> *And those who seduced the women of other men.*
> *There, Nidhog sucks the corpses of the departed;*
> *A wolf tears at the bodies of men.*[4]

This is therefore the abode of those who break the moral laws of the Scandinavians. We can see a possible Christian influence in this Strand of Corpses (Naströnd). We should note that the great crime for Germanic peoples was oathbreaking.* It is therefore quite possible that this abominable crime prompted men to reserve a special treatment for those responsible for such crimes. This interpretation is reinforced by the mention of criminal wolves, which means the authors of shameful crimes (*mórd*) and not just simple homicides.

In Hel, the dead lead miserable lives, and the seeress that the god Odin awakens through necromancy says: "Who is this man, a stranger to me who prompted my perilous journey? I have been drowned in snow, battered by the rain, and awash in the dew. Dead I have long been."[5] The same poem sees Hel as a tall building containing many doors, and, oddly, the seeress is buried while Baldr lives in a house. These various notions of the World of Mists are not necessarily conflicting: Baldr is a demigod and cannot be treated like a common mortal; he, with his wife, Nanna Nepsdottir, who does not outlive him, is the guest of Hel. In contrast to the seeress from *Baldr's Dream,* Hermod's brother seems actually to be alive inasmuch as he can return to the world of the living, which accepts the condition laid down by Hel: "If all things in the world, alive or dead, weep for him, then he will be allowed to return to Aesir. If anyone speaks against him or refuses to cry, then he will remain with Hel."[6] Yet Loki, who is responsible for Baldr's death, shows no regret, and Hel keeps her prey.

The story of Baldr casts an initial light upon the notion of death: it is in fact a timeless retirement.

Hel's kingdom seems to have been reserved for the common dead, especially those who were not slain by handheld weapons. Valhöll, however, welcomed the valiant. Originally located beneath the earth, the "Hall of Warriors fallen in battle" was transported close to Asgard, the abode of the gods, and according to the *Sayings of Grimnir,* it occupied the fifth heavenly dwelling place, the World of Joy (Gladsheimr).[7] There,

---

*The principal German myths teach us that a broken oath or betrayal is the cause of all catastrophes, see R. Boyer, *Les Religions de l'Europe du Nord,* 37.

every day, Odin chose the warriors who died in combat and shared them with Frigg (Freyja). It was believed that Valhöll had the Unique Warriors (Einherjar), the elite. It is easy to understand why the Germans dreaded to die bedridden; if they were at risk of this, they asked those close to them to mark their bodies with spears. In the *Saga of Ynglingar* (chapter 9) Snorri Sturluson says that the god Odin, seen here from a euhemeristic perspective, proceeded in this way, but it is surprising to see Njörd, a god of the third function, demanding to be marked with this martial sign.

We are better informed about Valhöll than we are about Hel, undoubtedly because people preferred to envision heaven rather than hell. Valhöll was a large, easily recognized hall. The rafters of the building were made of spears, it was covered with shields, and coats of mail were strewn across the benches. A wolf was hanging west of the doors, an eagle soared above the building, and the goat Heidrun, from whose udder flowed mead, could be spotted atop the roof. Odin did not live there. He resided in the Hall of the Slain (Valaskjalf) or the Sunken Halls (Sokkvabekk),* where he drank with Saga, a hypostasis of the goddess Frigg.

Valhöll contained 540 doors. From each there emerged simultaneously 800 warriors who spent their days fighting one another, but the dead and wounded found their lives and health restored every evening. They then dined together, eating the flesh of the wild boar Saehrimnir, which always grew back, and drinking the mead served them by the Valkyries. This would continue until the Twilight of the Powers (Ragnarök), which Wagner immortalized under the name of Twilight of the Gods. At this time, three cocks would crow in Hel; the wolf Fenris would become free; the earth would convulse; Yggdrasil the World Tree would tremble; the sun and moon would vanish; the stars would go out; the Midgard Serpent would leave the sea; the giants would set sail on Naglfar; Surt, the fire giant, would advance by rainbow; and, at the sides of the gods, the Unique Warriors would engage

---

*Fourth celestial dwelling whose name is formed from the verb *søkkva*, "to sink, to flow."

in their ultimate battle, a combat that would culminate with the con-
flagration of the world.

Opposing this mythical vision of an organized beyond, the sagas
suggest something entirely different: another world that is the grave
beneath the mound—or, in an expanded and extrapolated vision of the
tumulus, the mountain.

The *Book of Settlements* notes on more than one occasion the
connections between the mountain and the beyond. When Thorolf
Monstrarskegg moves to Iceland, he settles in Hofstad, not far from the
sacred mountain (Helgafell), because "he believed that he would enter
it when he died as would all his relatives living on the cape,"[8] the Cape
of Thor. When Thorstein Cod-Catcher perishes off Höskuld Island, a
shepherd sees the north side of the sacred mountain open and a rousing
welcome given to the dead man. *Njal's Saga* (chapter 14) relates this:

> News came from up north in Bjarnar Fjord that Svan had rowed
> out to fish in the spring and a great storm had come on them from
> the east. It drove them into Veidilausa Bay and they were lost there.
> Fishermen who were at Kaldback thought they saw Svan enter the
> mountain Kaldbakshorn and get a warm welcome there. Some
> denied this and said that there was nothing to it. Everyone was cer-
> tain, however, that he was never found, alive or dead.[9]

On each occasion, the dead individual joins other dead who stay
in the mountain, hence their name Inhabitants of the Mountain
(Bergbúi). Thorstein Cod-Catcher is invited to sit in the seat of honor
facing his father—which is how the family is reformed in the beyond.
Inside the mountain there are fires, the clinking of ale horns, and the
sound of shouting. In these narratives the otherworld seems to be a
perfect reflection of our own.

We should not be surprised that the mountain was regarded as an
empire of the dead. Many medieval legends reflect this idea in a variety of ways. One tale involves the Glass Mountain[10] where fairies pull

their lovers. There are also the stories devoted to Frederick Barbarossa and King Arthur and King Valdemar in which these great figures, the last resorts for their people in calamities and invasions yet to come, are asleep inside a mountain. Folktales also contain an echo of this belief: with his enchanted music, the Pied Piper of Hamelin draws the children with him into a mountain, where they vanish forever.

The mountain deserves more than a simple mention.[11] An intermediary world between men and gods, its head is neighbor to heaven and its base touches the empire of the dead. It therefore possesses an undeniably sacred character, which is explained first and foremost by the fact that it is the home of the gods, the meeting place of supernatural beings. This has been true since the Babylonian epic of Gilgamesh, the text for which was discovered in the library of Assurbanipal (668–29 BCE) and in which the deities hold counsel at the top of the Mountain of Cedars. And doesn't Greek mythology make Olympus the abode of the gods?

Higher beings gladly frequent mountains: Mount Helicon welcomes the muses of Boetia, it is here that the Hippocrene spring gushes forth under the hoof of Pegasus, and it is here where Crotos, the son of Pan, lives as well as Eupheme, the wet nurse of the muses. Mount Pelion houses the union of Cronos and Phylira; Sylee and Dycaeos, the son of Poseidon, live there.

Germanic mythology offers similar details: the seat of the god Heimdall is on Mount Heaven (Himinbjörg) and the sides of Clashing Mountain (Hnitbjörg), reminiscent of the Greek Symplegades, provide shelter for Gunnlöd, the guardian of the sacred hives in which the blood of Kvasir is preserved by blending it with honey—and this marvelous beverage transforms into a poet everyone who tastes it.

Starting in the twelfth century, because of its pagan character, the mountain became the abode of fairies and demons, and later it became the site where witches held their Sabbaths. It was therefore an intermediary world between man and the immanent powers, between the gods and their secularized or demonized forms. It was the meeting place for the sacred and the human. It is worth noting that pagans built temples to their gods on mountains and the Christians built chapels to the saints or the Virgin on mountains. Moses received the tablets of the Commandments there, witches coupled with demons there, and it is where the fairies had their fountains of youth. The mountain is ambivalent and its dual nature, when all is said and done, is normal because it takes part in two different worlds and forms their border. A place of punishment (Prometheus) and reconciliation, the home of earthly paradise and hell, it separates gods and men, Christians and the Antichrist, good and evil. It is here where two diametrically opposing worlds face one another and attempt to communicate by means of heroes and the chosen ones, perhaps even by means of the dead.

Coexistence of Two Visions

The mythical world is opposed to another world: the grave is opposed to the mountain. There lies a collision of folk opinion with scholarly concept. The first wears away gradually in the presence of the second with the usury of time, historical evolution, and Christianization. Formerly, heroes found a place in Valhöll and the other dead found a home in Hel or with Ran but—it is noteworthy—they could come back, which means that the notion of another mythological world had undoubtedly erased the original, pragmatic representation of a home escaping all reasoned reconstruction of an empire of the dead.

A beautiful poem from the *Edda,* the *Song of Helgi, Murderer of King Hundingm,* suggests these conclusions.[12] After his death Helgi is buried beneath a cairn "and when he arrived at Valhöll, Odin offered to let him rule over all things with him." The anonymous poet expressly says that the hero wins his way into the warrior's Paradise, but immediately afterward, the poet shows Helgi returning to his mound: "One evening Sigrun's maid went past Helgi's mound and saw Helgi riding into the mound with a large number of men." She asked herself if she was dreaming. Helgi told her she was not delirious and asked her to warn Sigrun of his return.

The mound has opened up,
Helgi has come.

Sigrun comes, enters the mound, and speaks with her dead husband. She prepares a bed because she wants to sleep in Helgi's arms, and the hero allows his joy to burst forth:

"*I declare that presently*
I am lacking for nothing
Neither late in the evening nor in the early
    morning
In Sevafjöll,
Because it is in the arms of a dead man
That you sleep
White lady, in the mound,
Hogni's daughter
And you are alive."

The text seems to imply that Helgi splits his posthumous life between his mound and Valhöll, but love demands decision, and the hero chooses the grave so that he can meet Sigrun there. The syntax of the poem leaves no doubt about this: Helgi clearly visits Odin:

Er hann kom til Valhallar,
(he comes to Valhöll)
Helgi reid til haugsins,
(he rides into the mound)

The preposition *til,* which governs the genitive, expresses the objective—Helgi therefore is clearly moving from one world to another.

Beyond the simultaneous presence of two opposing notions of the otherworld, *The Song of Helgi,* leaves us free to choose what we want, to choose our afterlife.

Death

Based on the evidence provided by Scandinavian writings, the Germans conceived a dynamic cosmogony: a perpetual motion animated the world, pulling men and things; everything fit inside a perfect circle encompassing the visible and the invisible; human beings and gods; the real and the possible; past, present, and future. Is it by chance that the three Norns, the Nordic Parquae, were named Past, Present, and Future?* A permanent circulation was at work connecting one world to the next, and there were no definite borders between life and death.

A tight-knit framework of relationships was believed to join us to the cosmos. The idea is an old one, and Gregory the Great—who died on March 11, 604—expressed it well by comparing the human being to stones, trees, and animals.[13] But it is undoubtedly an eleventh-century German poem entitled *Theological Summa* that has best translated these relations: the earth is our flesh, the dew our sweat, the stones our bones, the plants our veins, the grass our hair, the sea our blood, the clouds our mind, and the sun our eyes.[14] This Christian philosophy is not that far from Norse cosmogony. The earth was created out of the body of the primordial giant Ymir.

> *From Ymir's flesh the earth was shaped,*
> *and the mountains from his bones,*
> *the sky from the skull of the frost-cold giant,*
> *and the sea from his blood.*[15]

It was thought that Death is connected to us and rarely surprises us if we know how to interpret its precursory signs: the person whose shadow was headless on Christmas Eve would die the following year; if a candle went out by itself in the house, if a nail was bent when being hammered into the coffin, if the gravedigger's spade gave off a humming noise, or if the board used to carry a dead man fell over,[16] the

---

*Urd, Verdandi, and Skuld.

Grim Reaper was not far away and had already picked the next victim of his scythe.

The individuals soon to be carried off by death even had a singular appearance easily recognizable to people of the Middle Ages. It is expressed by the adjective *feigr,* "destined to die soon," or *feigi (moriturus)* in Old High German. The *Book of Settlements* indicates clearly that even animals bear this sign. Thorstein Red Nose "saw in autumn, no matter how many sheep were in his flock, which ones were going to die."

Thorstein feels the approach of death, although he is unsure if it will strike him or his flock: "Slaughter hence the sheep you want," he declares during the final autumn of his life, "at present I am destined to die, me or all my sheep, unless it is all of us." Sturla then finishes his story with the following observation: "The same night he died, all his sheep fell into the river."[17] Death therefore has more than one way to announce its arrival, such as the visit from a dead person, a dream, or a premonition. We shall have opportunity to discover yet more.

The human being formed part of the cosmos as a living entity capable of experiencing death. Various superstitions collected in the Germanic countries leave no doubt about this. When a person died, the vinegar needed to be stirred to prevent it from turning, the wine barrels needed to be moved to prevent the formation of lees, the bird cage required changing to a new location, the yoke on the livestock had to be changed, the beehives required moving; the seed in the attic needed to be turned so that it wouldn't fail to germinate, and everyone who was sleeping—especially children and livestock—had to be awakened. More is required when it was the master of the house who died. His decease was announced to the horses, bees,* and other animals by clinking a ring of keys.† Otherwise, the beasts would die and the bees would fly away. It also had to be announced to the fruit trees; oth-

---

*Bees have an odd connection with death. See the *Georgics* (IV, 317*ff.*), where Virgil tells how Orpheus, turned into a larva, kills the bees of Aristeus, an indirect cause of the death of Eurydice.

†A gesture strangely reminiscent of that of the *pater familias* during the Roman *Lemuria.* Did this involve prevention of the possession of livestock?

erwise they would wither. Death was contagious, and if precautionary measures were not taken, it threatened all life-forms. This was why a funeral procession was never to cross through a field, even a fallow one; and it was why the wicked dead were carried into infertile grounds. (It was common knowledge that lightning struck for three years on the border of a field or forest in which a suicide was interred.)

The bonds joining man to the universe of course extended to the family, both to ancestors and to children not yet born. The belief in an inextinguishable vital principle ensured that nothing perished in an irreversible fashion, which explains Norse ethics: death was but one stage of a cycle, the return to the immanent or transcendent world and the return to the sacred. "Retirement to the kingdom of the dead," Régis Boyer notes judiciously, "is not actually timeless as much as it is irrelevant to the present time. It is capable of opening at any moment to create a path for returns."[18] In this mental universe, which could be difficult to grasp by minds permeated by Roman and Christian culture, "the dead individual is not really dead. He has returned to one of the states of the cycle, but remains active in the form of landvaettr"[19]—that is, tutelary spirit (genius loci). Revenants were no cause for surprise to the Germanic peoples; they fit perfectly within their mind-sets, their place has not been usurped, and we cannot dismiss these stories as "old wives' tales."* The roots of the belief are too deep.

The dead are also alive, as we saw in the story about Grettir's descent into Kar's tumulus. Archaeological discoveries have allowed us to realize that in the otherworld, the dead lead an existence similar to their lives on earth; the sagas suggest that they find their relatives again in a somewhere else haloed by an ambiguous mystery. Let's revisit these points in greater detail.

In the Icelandic sagas there is not a hint of pagan heavens or hells, but there are mounds and mountains. These are where posthumous life takes place as if it truly is a real life. The dead man Brynjar invites

---

*"It's an old wives' tale," says the scribe of the second *Song of Helgi* about the reincarnation of the hero and Sigrun.

Thorstein Uxafot to follow him into his mound. What Thorstein finds there is a large hall bordered by seats on each side in which two groups of twelve men are sitting facing each other. Those on one side are clad in black and are hideous; the others are wearing red and are pleasing to look upon. Oddly, Brynjar's brother, the leader of the men in black, demands tribute from Thorstein, who refuses. A battle then breaks out, with the men in red supporting Thorstein; all the dead strike blows against each other without any effect; the only strokes of any consequence are those delivered by Thorstein.[20] Another saga offers an analogous story: a hero, also named Thorstein, assists a dead man, Gudmund, against the diabolical Agni, with whom he shares his cairn.[21] When Gest enters the tomb of the Viking Raknar, he finds Raknar sitting on a throne in the front of a large boat occupied by four hundred men. He decapitates them and, in an interesting detail, his sword makes the same sound it would make if striking the water. He then takes possession of the Viking's sword. Raknar then hurls himself on him, and all the decapitated men rise back up and rush the intruder, who is saved only by the arrival of King Olaf's ghost.[22] Death does not put an end to bellicose enthusiasms—the dead remain identical to what they were when still alive.

Finally, the grave is considered a dwelling like any other, an imposed retirement where the departed lead a life that is sometimes far from being hermitlike. In the *Saga of Hromund, Son of Grip,* we make the acquaintance of a dead man named Thrain, who prepares a meal for himself. Having a problem accepting this, the narrator takes the precaution of saying that he entered his mound alive,[23] but the explanation is the work of a man denying the obvious. We find this style of narration in the story of King Herlaug, who goes to his mound with twelve men. This discomfort of the storyteller is valuable because it transports us into the real instead of fiction.

The moment has come to introduce an extraordinary story of the living dead, which makes it easier to understand how belief in vampires was born.

Asmund and Aran were sworn brothers, and they had also sworn the following oath: whoever outlived the other would build his brother a funeral cairn, place him inside with all his material goods, and spend the first three nights with him. Looming in the background was the notion of the rite of passage in which the living take part.

After Aran's death, Asmund had the funereal chamber dug and erected a mound above it. He placed his friend inside along with his saddled and bridled horse—as if the deceased needed it to undertake his final journey—and added his weapons, his falcon, and his hound. He entered the mound himself to fulfill his vow, and the mound was sealed behind him.

Aran got up the first night and killed and ate the falcon and the hound; on the second night he killed the horse, tearing it to pieces and devouring it with such ardor that blood dripped from his jaws. He even invited Asmund to share this bloody repast. On the third night, Asmund was dozing when Aran hurled himself upon him, tearing off one of his ears. Asmund drew his sword, sent the dead man's head flying, then reduced the body to ashes. He was then released from the mound in which he had been sealed.[24]

Saxo Grammaticus recounts this story in the fifth book of his *Gesta Danorum,* but the saga, although more recent, has better preserved two features: the funerary gift—the dead man's share—and the length of the sojourn. For Saxo, Asmundus seems to have remained in the tumulus for more than three days. Without spelling it out, the text suggests an explanation for vampirism. The dead are hungry and have to go out in search of food. In many folk beliefs, this food would be blood, but in Romania for example, it is still said that vampires, known there as *strigoi,* eat the hearts of men and animals.[25] In the eighth century, this act was attributed to witches (*strigae*), mainly by the *Capitulatio de partibus Saxoniae* and the *Lex salica,* in an edition from around 800. Between 600 and 643, two other texts of the law—the *Pactus Alamannorum* and the *Edictum Rothari*—refer to a superstition according to which witches eat people from the inside.[26] Witches, however, maintained tight relations with the dead and revenants, if only by virtue of necromancy, and the contamination was explained by a transfer of malefic powers. But let's return to the departed.

What is it that in the end distinguishes a dead person from a living one? These are distinguishing features: the sword stuck in his chest,[27] the blood covering him, the flames surrounding him, his drenched clothing, but when he has not died violently the dead individual is harder to recognize because he behaves like a living man. This is how King Beli could ask that his mound be placed not too far from that of Thorstein. "We could talk," he says.[28] Isn't this an argument in favor of the life of the dead? Gest asks to be buried close to Osvif and states: "We could talk, if it is permitted."[29]

This is a strange restriction, for it implies that the dead individual is still subject to fate, thus that death is not an ending—*letum non omnia finit,* Sextus Propertius noted—and does not stop the cycle because, in theory, only the living are the hostages of the Norns. It so happens that here the sinister spinners, the weavers who use men's heads instead of weights, human viscera for warp and woof, a sword for a comb, and an arrow for a spindle,[30] never lose hold of their prey. The mound is no refuge against their power that extends beyond the grave. Another saga confirms this point. The deceased Hreggvid informs Hrolf: "Destiny has given me the power to thrice quit my grave, from which I shall not be able to leave again once it has been resealed." *That hefir mér skapat verity, at ek skal mega fara thrjá tíma ór haugi mínum, ok tharf eigi aftr at brygjast utan í sidasta sinn.*[31] The verb *skapa,* "fashion, create," carries the idea of irrevocable destiny without any human participation.

What a splendid scene when Hreggvid leaves his tomb for the final time and proclaims joyously three strophes, each of which begins: "Rejoice, Hreggvid!"[32] His murderer, Grim, is dead and Hrolf is going to marry Ingigerd, the daughter of the mound's inhabitant. Is this the joy of a dead or living man? The distinction blurs and disturbs us because the life of a dead man is hard to accept, even when the deceased reveals, as Thrain did before being "killed" once and for all by Hromund: "I have long lived in my mound."[33] Finally, what should we think of the following anecdote? The storm is raging and Fridthjof's boat is in great peril. The hero shares his gold with his crew, saying: "Now we know we shall be going to Ran's; we should have gold."[34]

Life is tough and tenacious and never abandons the deceased completely, and this belief was just as tenacious. Even in the nineteenth century, Swedish peasants placed the pipe and knife of the deceased— and sometimes even a flask of brandy—in the coffin with him.* In Germany, once when a shepherd was being carried to his final dwelling, a storm forced the two pallbearers to seek shelter beneath a tree. One was worried that his harvest was not yet in, whereupon the other reminded him of the shepherd's favorite words. A voice then emerged from the coffin: "He is still saying them!"

The dead continued to live beyond the tomb in folk belief,[†] and I have discovered a strange story that forms in some way the synthesis of what we have learned thus far. Heinrich von Herford (Henry of Erfut), a German Dominican who died October 9, 1370, has written a story in his *Chronicle*[35] in which we again find the mountain as a lair of ghosts and revenants, individuals—Henry avoids using the word *deceased*—

---

*This can be understood as an apotropaic measure: by possessing his familiar or favorite objects, the dead individual had no reason to return. This was something that was still believed in central Europe around 1900. Among certain European peoples, when individuals have forgotten to give a certain object to the deceased, it is placed in the coffin of the next to die with the charge of passing it on to the deceased.

†I have been sticking to Germanic beliefs, but they can be found elsewhere. In Hungary, a table is set for the dead. See Eva Cs. Pócs, "A karásonyí vacsora és a karásonyí asztal hieldelemköre" [The Superstitions on the Christmas Table and Meal], *Néprajzi Közlemények* 10 (1965): 3–323. There also exists a certain ceremony known as the Wedding of the Dead: using the marriage ceremony, an unmarried young male or young girl is buried with an individual playing the role of the fiancée. See A. Szendrey, "A halott lakodalma," *Ethnographia* 52 (1941): 44–53. Tekla Dömötör cites an event that took place around 1900 in a village of western Hungary: the dead individual was seated in a chair and given food and drink, much to the great despair of the pastor who was present. See *Volksglaube und Aberglaube der Ungarn* (Corvina: 1981), 256.

who have the gift of foresight and marvelous (magical?) powers that are externalized here in the form of a meal. I have called this odd passage "The Ghostly Hand."

In 1349, the second year [of the reign] of Charles IV, another ghost (*fantasma*) showed itself in Cyrenbergh (on the Warme), a village of the landgrave of Hesse. It was heard that something remarkable had occurred, though I do not know if it was really merely a fantasy (fantasma). A soft and gracious, small human hand (*manus homi-nus parva*) permitted itself to be seen and touched, and perhaps a thousand people have viewed and felt it. Nothing other than the hand of this individual could be seen or touched, but one could also hear the hoarse voice of a man quite distinctly. Someone asked him who he was, and he answered: "I am truly a man and a Christian like yourself, baptized in the town of Göttingen." "But what is your name?" He responded: "Reyneke." "But are you alone?" He declared: "No, there is a large crowd of us." "And what do you do?" "We eat, drink, marry, have children, arrange the weddings of our daughters, and find wives for our sons. We sow, we reap, and we do everything else that you do." "But where do you live? Is it here?" He answered: "We dwell in Mount Krykenberch (*im Monte Krykenberch*), which is next to the town of Cyrenbergh. Here in town we are each given welcome by that worthy man who is our host." "But don't some of you live in the mountain called Berenberch—in fact Derenberch, and today Dörnberg?" "Yes, many of us do," he answered, "but my family is well-established and benevolent. Those others, to the contrary, are bandits who cause much trouble and invade the surrounding lands." "Can others receive hospitality from this house with you?" "That is something we reject in order not to overburden our host. It is enough that he gives us a gracious welcome. He can receive others though, if he likes, if they are people connected to him by family or marriage. . . ." Reyneke told how his host received the unexpected visit of a relative. He was quite upset by this, for he had nothing to offer the relative to eat. But Reyneke told him: "Do not worry; I will give you enough to fill your needs." Immediately, he prepared a magnificent table loaded with everything necessary—whole-wheat bread, good wine, good beer, boiled and roasted meats, and game—and offered it to his host. He displayed aversion toward his host's mother, a little old lady about whom he said: "She is an evil woman." But he felt otherwise toward the maid of the house, a young girl named Styneken, for whom he cared deeply. It so happened that once Hermann von Scardenbergh, a servant . . . gave a fruit to the young girl. Reyneke rebuked him: "Do not do that again." "But all I did was give her a piece of fruit." "I know that full well," said Reyneke, "but you had other ends in mind." He assured another [man] who was in his good graces that he would soon wed Styneken, and he promised to make him rich.

At this point in our investigation the matter of the soul necessarily comes up, because the most important question has been left hanging: What is it that animated revenants, those living corpses?

NINE

The Soul

The general movement of all the ideas specific to all the Germanic peoples and, even later, to the medieval West, aimed at reintegrating the dead back into the family of the living. From being a source of dread, the dead were now being tamed through the development of ancestor worship and complex funeral practices. In tandem with this evolution was the establishment of the notion of the beyond. Of course, this development did not follow a simple outline or a flawless chronology; overlaps and slippage occurred and various notions coexisted for certain periods of time. The good dead returned to sacred status, became a relay between the living and the gods, and watched over the clan. In compensation, the dead's name was given to a newborn ten days following the infant's birth, an event called "the attachment of the name" (*naf-nfestr*).* This was intended to allow the child to share in the deceased individual's "capacity for luck" (*mátr ok megin*). This is why Karl, fearing he will not return from his fight with Ljotolf, asks his wife, Thorgerd, to give his name to the son she is carrying: "This will bring him luck," he adds.[1] By virtue of the name, the child possessed the qualities of the

---

*The name should be chosen carefully. The son of Helgi Hiörvardsson and Sigrun does not receive one (*ekki nafn festiz vid hann*) because none are suitable. See *Edda, Helgakvida Hiörvardssonar,* prose after strophe 6.

162

deceased. This motif crops up repeatedly in the sagas and even outside the circle of the family. Thorstein fatally wounds Jökull, who asks him not to let his name be lost (*nidri liggja*).[2] We should note that the gift of a patronymic is not always beneficial: "My name is Hrapp the Killer," one individual declares, and at the same time I was granted the name, I received the gift of not being an easy companion."[3]

The name therefore transports something, and if we refer to Norwegian traditions, the *nafnfestr* was important because an illness known as *elsk* would strike a child who had not been given the name of a recently departed ancestor.[4] Researchers have long noted that such a custom is evidence of a belief in the transmigration of souls, already mentioned in the *Poetic Edda:* "Once upon a time," we are told by the poet to whom we owe the second *Poem of Helgi,* "it was thought that men were reborn. . . . It was said that Helgi and Sigrun lived again."[5]

Was the revenant simply waiting for the moment to live again in another body, preferably in one of his descendants? Would its haunting, so well explained in the Christian texts, be a purification (catharsis)? There is nothing that allows us to state this definitively. The problem posed by the soul thus appears in all its acuteness.

The first pitfall: the Norse *sál* or *sala,* "soul," is borrowed from the Old Saxon *sala* (German, *seele;* English, *soul*). This term did not exist in the Norse language, just as, incidentally, the word *religion* replaced *custum* (*sidr*). Conversely, the Norse language did possess three words that translated the notion of soul (although not completely and without any Christian coloration) in the sense of a spiritual principal: *fylgja, hugr,* and *hamr,*[6] all three of which were used in the sense of fate, therefore testifying to the relation between the visible and the invisible.

Fylgja

The noun *fylgja,* formed from the verb "to follow, to accompany" (*fylgja*), referred in some ways to an individual's double, comparable to the Egyptian Ka and the Greek *eidolon.* It was a kind of guardian angel that took the form of a female entity (*fylgjukona*) or an animal that protected the family or person it had adopted. The *Vatnsdaela Saga* provides a good illustration of this point.

> Groa the witch invited Thorstein to a feast. But three nights before going to her house, he dreamed that the woman serving his family came to him asking him not to go. He replied that he had promised. She said: "That seems imprudent to me and harm shall befall you." This happened for three nights in a row: She came; scolded him, saying it would prove ill for him; and touched his eyes. Thorstein ignored the warning and met his death during the banquet—Groa caused an earthquake that crushed the farm.[7]

Fylgja could thus be translated as "tutelary being" because the evidence shows this entity kept watch over the person it accompanied.

The fylgja often took the form of an animal, and it was the mental state of the individual to whom it appeared, most often in dreams, that determined its shape. Friends generally appear in the form of bears and enemies in the form of wolves. Two examples make this notion easy to grasp.

> At Hoskuldssrdir, Hoskuld woke up early in the night and woke all his household. "I want to tell you what I dreamed," he said. "I saw a big bear go out of the house . . . , and two cubs went with it, and they were fond of the beast. It headed toward Hrutsstadir and went into the house there. . . . This bear was the personal spirit of none other than Gunnar of Hlidarendi."[8]

In the *Saga of Gisli Surrson*, after Vestein's death the hero reveals two premonitory dreams: "On the first night, this is what I dreamed: a venomous snake left a certain farm and bit Verstein, who succumbed; the second night I dreamed that a wolf came out of the same farm and bit Verstein, who died from it."[9]

The tutelary spirits (*fylgjur,* plural of *fylgja*) appeared especially during the hours that humans slept and were connected to slumber. In fact, the sagas make use of one motif far too frequently for it not to be highly significant. Torpor abruptly takes possession of the individual whose tutelary spirit escapes him or of an individual who is attacked by the fyljur of others. Here is an illustration of this strange phenomenon: "While Svenn was heading to meet the enemy with his men, he was attacked by a fit of yawning and said outright: 'Here are the tutelary spirits of Isvif attacking us.'"[10]

Thus the living received visits in dream from these spirits that took on the appearance of animals or women.

Thorstein revealed that in a dream he had seen a swan perched on the roof of his house that was joined by an eagle with black eyes and claws of iron. The two birds spoke together and another eagle landed next to the swan and began wooing her, which greatly displeased the first eagle. The two eagles then fought each other to death. This saddened the swan greatly, but another bird arrived from the south and, shortly after, left with the swan. The Norwegian to whom Thorstein told his dream did not hesitate a moment in saying: "These birds are the tutelary spirits of men."[11]

Identifying these spirits was not always easy. In the *Laxdaela Saga,* an odd figure comes into the story—one who could well be one of these spirits.

A woman visited An the Black in one of his dreams; she was holding a knife and a jug; she opened the sleeper's stomach taking out his intestines and replacing them with brushwood. In a battle that took place a short while later, An was mistaken for dead. The next night, during the vigil held over his body, he got back up and said: "In God's name, do not be scared of me because I am alive and was completely aware until I lost consciousness. I then dreamed of this same woman and it seemed to me that she took the brushwood from my body and replaced it with my entrails, and this change did me much good."[12]

We can now advance this hypothsis: the substitution no doubt prevented the blows that struck An from being fatal.

The primary function of the fylgja was in fact protection, and its second duty was prediction. In the saga bearing his name, Gisli Sursson is visited by two women in a dream. One of them, who is friendly, predicts good fortune for him, the other predicts disasters, and he learns he has but two years left to live. These apparitions become ever more frequent, and one day the friendly woman appears on a gray horse—a revealing detail—and invites Gisli to follow her. She then shows him the place to which he will go after his death. She appears one more time to attach a bloody cap on his head, splashing and spattering him with blood. A short time after this last dream, Gisli is killed.[13]

When the fylgja appeared elsewhere then in a dream—that is, when it showed itself to someone while he was awake—it meant an imminent death. While Thorgils is on his way to an assembly, he sees his tutelary spirit, who seems to be on its way back. During this meeting, Audgisl kills Thorgils.[14] *Njal's Saga* leaves no doubt as to the meaning of such an encounter: Thord sees a blood-covered billy goat, but Njal sees nothing and says: "You must be doomed to die soon, and it is your personal spirit you must be seeing."[15] It is at this juncture that Hallgerd murders Thord.

It was not rare for the fylgja to bid farewell to its protégé whose death was near. In the *Dream of Thorstein Son of Sidu-Hall*, the hero is visited during three consecutive nights by three women, one of whom asks him: "To whom should we turn after your death?" Thorstein answers: "My son." "We shall not stay with him long," the woman says, thereby announcing this son has not long left to live.[16] This is an interesting anecdote because it reveals that a man could have several tutelary spirits. Next is the *Saga of Hallfred Troublesome Skald*, which gives us a splendid example of how the tutelary spirit follows one family.

Then they saw a woman following the ship. She was tall and dressed in a mail-coat. She walked on the waves as if on land. Hallfred looked and saw that it was his fetch [fylgja].

Hallfred said, "I declare myself finally parted from you."

She said, "Will you take me on, Thorvald?"

He said he would not.

Then the boy Hallfred said, "I'll take you on."[17]

All these examples suggest that human beings have corresponding selves, perhaps doubles, in the otherworld and that communication is possible because there is really no real border between that world and this. "The living body," says Régis Boyer, "would be only the material, visible intervention of a reality whose true essence would be in the kingdom of the dead, and which helps and follows each individual. The soul, here, would be a reflection."[18] This is one more proof that we take part as a microcosm in the life of the macrocosm, the world of the spirits, the dead, and the ancestors, because the fylgja does not vanish with the disappearance of the one to whom it is attached and does not die out with a family. We can easily see that a lucky fate—or simply fate itself—is expressed in the term *tutelary woman* (*fulgjukona*). This spirit, which was one of the forms of the soul for the ancient Scandinavians, was independent of the human being even though it incarnated inside the human being. It was an emanation of the otherworld, hence its function as white lady and fate that was inseparably linked to the mind-set of the people of this time. By no means is this simply a literary fiction.

Hugr

Hugr, "spirit, mood, thought," more or less corresponds to the Latin *spiritus* or to *animus*. If we take as our base a metaphor from scaldic poetry where it is rendered as "the wind of the female magicians" (*trollkvena vindr*), it could be the breath. It is first and foremost an active force, an idea expressed in the compound word meaning "spirit of battle"—*víghugr,* for example a spirit that determines personality. It seems to have had its own life in a semantic study of the expressions in which it appears. "As my *hugr* tells me" is used when having a presentiment. "Making his *hugr* race toward an individual" expresses the affection a person holds for another. Desiring a woman is rendered by a man as "placing his *hugr* on a woman," and thinking is expressed as "making his *hugr* run."[19] All these expressions carry a dynamic idea of a force that incarnates within an individual, and, going further, the independence of this force. "We could say that it was an arrangement, a means, a tool that the owner could use as he pleases," notes R. Boyer. "In other words, we have the impression that it involves an element that was outside the human being and which the human being considered with detachment."[20]

The hugr could get away and take on shape, then achieve its owner's desires, as we can seen in the following story. "A farmer had to take in his harvest but his horse was in the high mountain pastures. He wanted to go fetch the animal but could not abandon his hay. At that moment, the men who were in the high pastures heard something moving outside the door, but they did not see anyone."

Jan de Vries, who tells this anecdote, concludes: "His *hugr* had therefore gone to the place where the object of his desire was located."[21]

This is obvious in a number of cases. In the *Saga of the Sworn Brothers,* King Olaf appears to Grim in a dream:

Are you sleeping?
    No, but who are you?
    I am King Olaf Haraldsson and this is what brings me: I wish for you to seek out my vassal, the poet Thormod, and help him to get off the reef on which he has found refuge.[22]

Alarmed at Thormod's fate, King Olaf thus sends his hugr to carry his message.

The *Laxdaela Saga* offers us a strange story that seems to bring onto the stage the hugr of a dead woman, the mother of the dappled gray ox named Harri whom Olaf had recently killed because he was too old.

The following night Olaf dreamed that a woman came to him; she was large and angry. She spoke: "Are you sleeping?" He replied that he was asleep. The woman said: "You are sleeping but you shall see everything befall as if you were awake. You had my son slain and sent him to me in a miserable state. This is why I am cursing you so that you, too, shall see a son lying in his own blood, and I shall choose the one that you would least like to lose."[23]

This odd passage bordering on the unintelligible lets us know that Harri's mother comes from the otherworld and that the ox was only the shape of a human being. It is certain that one part of the oneiric apparitions is due to manifestations of the hugr, with the fylgja and the dead representing the other parts.

The hugr, that force that leaves and momentarily does what it likes with an individual while he or she is sleeping, can take on a shape (hamr)—another human or animal figure—and act at a distance, show itself to a sleeper, or physically intervene. It is this body with which we are now going to get acquainted.

Hamr

Hamr, whose literal meaning is "the skin," is the expression of an astonishing belief that is deeply rooted in the Norse mentality. In the old texts, it is the inner shape that determines outside appearance. It so happens that a person could have several of these shapes. A person could be described as "having only one hamr" (*eigi einhamr*) or that his hamr "is particularly strong" (*hamrammr, rammaukinn*). Expressed here is the fundamental idea that man is not restricted to his body.

In his *Prose Edda,* Snorri Sturluson writes about the god Odin, whose relationship to the dead is well known: "Odin shifted shape. While his body lay as if dead or sleeping, he was beast or bird, fish or serpent, and traveled in the blink of an eye in remote lands."[24]

Let's keep this information in mind because it represents a veritable comprehensive survey. It refers to the changing of shape, the hamr,* and its departure† when the individual falls asleep, a point that precisely recalls the trance during which the shaman's spirit visits the otherworld and makes contact with the spirits that it interrogates.[25]

Rather than uniquely a Nordic belief, this is a Germanic belief, as shown by Paul the Deacon (ca. 720–783), Lombard historian and Latin language poet.

> One day, while hunting, King Gunthramnus fell asleep at the foot of a tree with his head resting on the knees of a loyal vassal. A small animal emerged from the king's mouth and looked for a way to cross a nearby stream. The vassal used his sword to provide a bridge for it, then watched the animal cross and vanish down a hole in the mountain, to reemerge shortly later and slip back into the king's mouth. When Gunthramnus awoke, he told how he had believed he had, while sleeping, crossed a bridge, entered a mountain, and seen a treasure. The vassal informed him of what he had seen. Gunthramnus saw to the digging open of the area near the hole where the animal had disappeared, and a treasure was found.[26]

For anyone who knows of the inner shape's ability to leave and metamorphose, this is obviously one of its journeys, *hamfor,* or, in other words, "the journey of the hamr," and not simply a legendary motif.

Paul the Deacon recounts another anecdote that goes in the same direction and shows that this operation is not without its dangers.

---

*Locutions: *vixla hömum, skipta hömum;* medial-passive verb *hamask.*
†Compound word *hamhleypa* (*hamr* + verb *hleypa,* "let run").

While Cunibert, king of the Lombards, was deliberating with his high squire on a way to kill Aldo and Grasso, he spotted a fly on the window. He drew his knife to slay it but missed and only cut off one of its feet.

Aldo and Grasso were making their way to the convocation of the king, but on the road they met a lame man who was missing one foot. He warned them that Cunibert wished their deaths. The two men then took refuge in a church. Furious at the sight of their escape, Cunibert promised to spare their lives if they revealed the name of the one who had betrayed him. Aldo and Grasso told of meeting the lame man, and the king realized that the fly whose foot he cut off was an evil spirit.[27]

The final interpretative remark should not come as a surprise: It is a Christian writer who states that all these manifestations could be the work of only the devil. In fact, they are nothing other than the "animal form" of a man.

Norse texts confirm the risks thus incurred. Helgi Hiövardsson slays with a blow from his spear the earl, Franmar, who has taken the form of an eagle: "Jarl Franmar had transformed himself into an eagle."[28] In another poem from the *Edda,* Odin boasts of a terrible charm he knows.

> *If I see witches*
> *Riding through the air,*
> *I cast a spell*
> *So they get lost*
> *Without finding their skin again*
> *Without finding their spirit again.*[29]

But the body from which the inner form detaches itself also is subject to dangers. Here is how the departure of those of three Finnish wizards is told in the *Vatnsdaela Saga:* "Ingimund lost his amulet and asked the Finns to find it: 'This is a dangerous mission . . . but because you press us, we shall certainly try our best. It is now necessary to seal us up all alone inside a house and for no one to utter our names.'"[30]

Failing to respect this kind of interdiction would prevent the hamr from reintegrating into the body it left, which is what the adjective *hamstoli* describes. Literally, it means "deprived of his hamr"—that is, "intense," "furious," or better yet, "beside himself." The *Book of Settlements,* which recounts the same event, specifies that Ingimund sent two Finns, "who had the ability to change shape, all the way to Iceland in search of his amulet."[31] *Ingimundr sendi tha Finna tvá hamforum til Íslands eptir hlut sinum.* The phrase "in a journey of the hamr" (*í hamforum*) leaves no doubt as to how the operation took place: each of the Finns sends his inner form to the island of Thule.

Once more, this motif is not legendary; it corresponded to a belief. In his text of the *Book of Settlements,* Sturla cites several individuals who have this power at their disposal: Vékell, nicknamed "with the very strong inner shape," which can be rendered in French as "loup-garou" or English as "werewolf" (*ennhamrammi*); Odd of Hraunhöfn; Thorain Korni; Olaf Tvennumbruni; and Dufthak.[32] For the last four individuals, Sturla uses the expression: "He had a very great power to change shape" (*hann var hamrammr mjok*). For two other people, Lod and Thorkel, he uses a phrase with the same meaning (*hann var mjok rammaukinn*), which provides additional information: the change of shape was accompanied by an increases of the strength* and vigor of the inner shape.

The sleeping individual could therefore take on another figure that then leads an independent life. I cannot fail to mention here the belief in werewolves that was so widespread in Germanic countries and France. It is too often overlooked that the French people inheirited this legacy of belief from German invaders. In the twelfth century the werewolf phenomenon was no longer understood, and it was believed, like Marie de France in the *Lai du Bisclavret,* that it involved a man who changed

---

Rammaukinn is compounded from *rammar,* "strong," and the verb *auka* (Latin, *augere*), "to increase."

himself into a wolf after being stripped of his clothing and whose human shape could not be restored if his clothes were stolen. The same idea is found in thirteenth-century Scandinavia. In the *Saga of the Volsungs,* lycanthropy is attributed to sorcery and magic on the one hand, and on the other to a wolf pelt that is donned when a person is a man-wolf.[33] In fact, this animal is only one of the appearances the hamr can adopt for wandering as it pleases, and if it gave birth to many legends, it was out of the fear it inspired by decimating flocks and sometimes attacking men.

Two traditions have often been confused, one coming from classical antiquity and vouched for by Herodotus (IV, 105), Pliny the Elder (VIII, 80), Virgil (Bucolica triennio. VIII, 97), Ovid (*Metamorphoses* I, 209 ff), Petronious (*Satyricon,* 62), St. Augustine (*De civitas Dei* XVIII, 17), and Isidore of Seville (*Etymology* XI, 4, 1); and that tradition, which is specifically Germanic. In England, Wulfstan spoke of the werewolf in one of his sermons in 950. In 1014, the laws of Knut the Great and in 1114 the *Quadripartitus,* a collection of laws, cite the belief. Burchard of Worms does the same around the year 1000, and in about 1219, Gervais of Tilbury connected the metamorphosis to phases of the moon, in reference to an English tradition and a testimony concerning Auvergne.[34] Folk beliefs certainly owe their passage into the scholarly literature to the existence of the tradition coming from antiquity, which served as a kind of security deposit.

The *Book of Settlements* brings us several precise bits of data on individuals having several shapes at their disposal, and I must cite the extraordinary battle between Storolf and Dufthak.

Dufthak of Dufthaksholt . . . had a very strong ability to change shape, as did Storolf, son of Hoeng, who lived in Hvall. A quarrel had broken out between them on the subject of some pasturelands. One evening, toward sunset, a man gifted with second sight saw a large bear leaving Hvall and a bull leaving from Dufthaksholt. They met in Storolf's Field and engaged one another furiously in battle, and the bear had the upper hand. The next morning, it was seen that the valley where they met was as if the ground there had been turned over. . . . Both of the men were injured.[35]

It is clear that the protagonists here confront each other in their animal shape, which is strengthened by the indication of the time— "the evening, toward sunset," which brings to mind the French expression *"entre chien et loup"** in which we find the idea of metamorphosis at nightfall. In this passage from the *Book of Sturla,* the shapes (hamr) of the two men are visible only to those possessing second sight, a feature reminiscent of the bloody billy goat that Njal cannot see.

A second example provides an almost too-rational explanation of the way the possession of several shapes reveals itself.

Odd customarily remained close to the fire, where he liked to linger, so he was called Kolbitr (Coal-Biter). Arngeir, his father, and Thorgils, his brother, left their house during a snowstorm to look for their livestock and did not return. Odd went looking for them and found both dead. A white bear had slain them and was in the midst of devouring them when Odd came upon the scene. He killed the bear and brought it back to the house, and it was said he ate the entire animal, declaring that he had avenged his father and brother by killing the bear and then eating it.

Subsequently, Odd became wicked and a hard person to deal with. His power to shapeshift was so strong that one evening he left his home in Hraunhöfn and reached Thjorsardal the following morning—a distance of two hundred fifty miles!—to aid his sister, whom the folk of Thjorsardal wanted to stone to death for sorcery and magic.[36]

Sturla seems to indicate that there is a close connection between ingestion of the bear meat and the discovery and mastery of the hamr's properties, which are revealed by Odd's change of character. Because

_____
*["Between dog and wolf" is a French expression for dusk. —*Trans.*]

the bear had eaten Odd's father and brother, Odd himself became invested with their strength and certainly their vital principle, hence the increase of his inner shape's vigor (*hamrammr*). One final example confirms the hamr's possibilities for action.

> Lodmund possessed the ability to change his shape at its highest degree and was a great wizard (*fjolknnigr*). He threw overboard into the sea the posts of his high seat and declared that he would dwell where they came to shore. . . . He colonized Lodmund Fjord and lived there that winter. He then learned that the posts of his high seat were in the south of that land. He carried all his equipment onto his ship and, once the sail had been raised, lay down and commanded that no one should have the audacity to utter his name—because his inner shape would be leaving him to fulfill his desire. He had not been stretched out long when a huge din erupted. It was then seen that a huge avalanche had fallen on the farm where Lodmund had lived. Lodmund then sat upright and said: "The spell I cast is that no ship that ever ties up here will find a safe and sound berth."[37]

The text does not explain why Lodmund sends his hamr to trigger the avalanche that destroys his former farm. Undoubtedly, it is to prevent anyone else from living in it, as confirmed by the curse he makes. It is also instructive to compare this passage from the *Book of Sturla* to that in the book of Haukr Erlendsson: the expression "he possessed the ability to change his shape at its highest degree" (*hann var ramaukinn*) has vanished and is replaced with "He was well-versed in sorcery" (*var mjok trollaukinn*). The perspective has changed, and Erlendsson attributes Lodmund's power to witchcraft—an art and acquired power—and thereby erases an important testimony of ancient beliefs.

As a reflection accompanying the human being as dynamic principle or as inner shape, the soul (fylgja, hugr, hamr) was considered independent. It followed the individual, lent itself to him for his use, and determined his personality. It was an emanation from the invisible world, which is clearly reflected in the word derived from *hamr* and *hamingja,* corresponding to the Latin *fortuna:* today's *happiness.* It is proof that no border separated the real and the beyond. A power established itself in the human being. The key to the pagan notions appeared to be hugr. The spiritus or *animus*[38] escaped, changed shape, and set off on adventure.

I am thinking here of a phrase that recurs often in the German literature of the Middle Ages when it involves fairies: "Where I wish to be, I am" (*wa ich wil, da bin ich*). These words are spoken by Peter von Staufenberg's lover.[39] In France, in the *Lay of Lanval,* the hero's girlfriend says almost the same thing.

> *quant vus vouldrez a mei parler,*
>
> *ja na savrez cel liu penser*
>
> *u nulls poïst aveir s'amie*
>
> *senz repruece e senz vileinie*
>
> *que jeo ne vus seie en present*
>
> *a faire tut votre talent.*[*40]

Summoned by the thought and desire of Lanval, the fairy can bridge distances instantaneously and appear to her lover—and no one else can see her. Some might object that Marie de France is using Celtic traditions, but in my opinion, this does not exclude a Germanic influence if we are aware of the close ties between the Germans and the Celts until the eleventh century, evidence for which is visible in the history and mythology of the two peoples.[†]

---

*"Whenever you wish to speak with me, you will not be able to think of a place where a man may enjoy his love without reproach or wickedness, that I shall not be there with you to do your bidding" (*The Lais of Marie de France,* trans. Glyn S. Burgess and Keith Busby [London: Penguin Books, 1986]).

†For example, a good fifty of the first colonizers of Iceland were Celts or were from areas under Celtic influence, we are told by the *Landnámabók.* Hence Iceland was certainly a substantial cultural melting pot. Furthermore, the incessant raiding in Ireland by Scandinavians and their settling in the Shetland and the Orkney Isles encouraged exchanges. Another hypothesis is imaginable: there was a common Indo-European base. This remains to be studied.

The Animation of the Corpse

To find out what permitted the cadaver to continue living—to leave the tumulus, to speak, fight, and kill—there are several clues at our disposal that have been gathered over the course of this investigation. The time has come to put them together and interpret them because while it is certainly beneficial to see the reason for these phenomena in the inextinguishable vital principle, this explanation remains unsatisfactory and incomplete—it leaves too many points unexplained.

We should first note that the strengths of the dead were greater than the strengths at their disposal when they were still alive. Remember that when a body was disinterred in order to be destroyed, it was very often "large as an ox," quite heavy, and very difficult to transport. Thorolf Twist-Foot and Glam are two examples. The narrator says that Glam's head is amazingly huge and that the revenant almost touches the tranversal beam of the roof. When a revenant walks on top of a roof, it barely avoids collapsing the structure. When a revenant attacks a man of normal strength, he tears him to pieces, breaking all his bones. Undoubtedly, these displays were beyond his means to achieve when he was still alive. This is something the shepherd Thorgaut, Glam himself, and Grettir's horse all learn at great cost.

Likewise, the mental powers of the walking dead increased. "Hrapp was already terrible when he lived; he was much worse following his death," states the *Laxdaela Saga*. "Soti was a great devil when still alive and this only got worse after he died," states the *Saga of Hörd*.

We also have encountered revenants in animal form, notably when Thorolf Twist-Foot reincarnates in the bull Glaesir; when a seal appears in the burning pit after the death of Thorgunna; and when Hrapp, in the guise of a seal, prevents Thorstein the Black from reaching Hrappstadir. There are other examples: Hreggvid takes the form of a lark to make his way to Earl Thorgny's and do what is necessary to free his daughter; Agnar, the son of Reginmod the Bad, defends his cairn in the form of a dragon, and with the aid of sorcery he kills all those who come seeking to violate his tomb.[41]

When the dead individual was threatened, he attempted, in animal or human form, to forestall the danger, as in the story of Gest.

Gest was on his way to open the cairn of the Viking Raknar in order to take his sword. While he was camping, a dreadful bull emerged and attacked him. Gest grabbed an ax and defended himself, but his blows had no effect—iron could not penetrate the beast's hide. Only the intervention of a churchman present caused the bull to vanish: the priest struck him with a cross, and the animal sank into the ground.[42]

When the revenant was in a disadvantaged position, without leaving a trace, he hastened into the ground from where he came. Hallbjörn "slips between the hands of Thorkel and disappears into the ground."[43] Soti acts in a similar fashion, and in the *Eyrbyggja Saga,* as quoted here in chapter 5: Kjartan strikes the seal, which "sinks back into the ground as if hammered down like a nail."

These amazing disappearances bring to mind those of ectoplasms, but ectoplasms did not exist in northern Europe, inasmuch as specters have bodies, weight, and volume—that is, they are three-dimensional. Their ability to sink back into the ground is logical, after all—otherwise, how would they have emerged from their cairns? Several authors, undoubtedly out of discomfort or perhaps from incomprehension of the phenomenon, claimed that the mounds opened. Others more prudently imagined that it was an illusion: in *Njal's Saga* (chapter 78), Högni and Skarphedinn "have the impression" that Gunnar's mound is open. But this is an erroneous interpretation and testifies to a refusal to accept disturbing evidence: the revenant could melt back into the ground, a phenomenon sometimes explained as magic, which is again only an attempt at a rational explanation.

What accompanied an increase in strength if not the manifestation of the hamr (hamrammr, rammaukinn)? What was capable of taking on animal form? The hamr. What scoffed at distances and obstacles? The hamr.

What therefore animated the living dead (draugr) is his inner shape—which, in fact, seemed to be confusing itself for the cadaver and could no longer separate from it. Here are some facts:

- The revenant was corporeal, and the tumulus was empty when he was wandering.
- The revenant bore traces on its body of any wounds it suffered. (In addition to this, Hrapp is holding Olaf's spearhead in his hand.)
- The revenant disappeared into the ground.
- The haunting ended once the cadaver was completely destroyed— at the moment when the hamr no longer had a material support.

Finally, we are given one more clue, almost in passing: we can read that this or that man had the ability to change shape, and he returned after his death. Such is the case with Thormod in the *Saga of Havard* (chapters 1 and 3), and with Thorkel in the *Book of Settlements* (chapter 93): "Thorkel Farserk had the ability to change shape. . . . He was buried in the enclosure of Whale Island Fjord and returned ceaselessly to haunt his home."

The fact that the dead person could be slain is therefore easily explained: clinical death ends human life, but not the life of the vital principle inhabiting the body, nor that of the inner shape, which goes on living. Because this vital principal is also essentially physical, it can be eliminated in its turn. In fact, the vital principle seems to need material support: it incarnates in the hamr that is one with the corpse.

The human being is therefore not restricted to his body. There is something that "would come back to a notion of the soul as emanation, in favor of each individual, from the spirit world," says Régis Boyer, and this notion is key to the manifestations that people too easily classify as marvels. It explains partially how a dead person can appear in dream and allows clairvoyance and the gift of second sight to be understood, as well as perception of the invisible world and necromancy. Finally, it explains the phenomenon of people marked by death.

All our questions have not been answered. All deaths did not result in revenants and ghosts, and the texts rarely specify if the specter has an inner shape that is particularly strong. For lack of certainty, which is hard to acquire when we are dealing with very ancient beliefs, we can conjecture this: it is possible that this faculty of shapeshifting does not always reveal itself to its owner. On the one hand, there are wizards, magicians, seers, clairvoyants, and so forth who are capable of using it, and on the other, there are common mortals who are ignorant that they have this power at their disposal. In fact, the ability to shapeshift is often connected to witchcraft or to magic, as we can see in the *Book of Sturla* (chapter 289), in which Lod possesses both faculties: *rammaukinn ok fjolkynnigr,* he has "the ability to change shape and is a wizard." The journey of the inner shape (hamfor) could moreover be performed by virtue of magic, as in the story of Ingimund's amulet.

All revenants were not wizards, and therefore not all knew how to make use of their hamr. Some experienced the revelation of their power when they died in particular circumstances. One thing is certain: the *hamr* determining the persona and personality of the man explained the implicit connection between an antisocial and difficult temperment exhibited by those that haunted.

One final observation: the soul remained connected to the body as long as the body had not been destroyed. As vital principle, it prevented the body's decomposition. It remained attached to even the body's smallest piece. Indeed, it was sufficent for a little of the body's ash to be ingested by an animal for the soul to move into another body. The study of revenants therefore opens onto a fundamental aspect of the Germanic mind-set: the union of the dead and fate. This notion of the world demands further explanation.

TEN

The Dead, Revenants, and the Third Function

Among the Germanic peoples characterized by a prelogical mentality, the dead were more or less connected to the fertility of the soil, to its fecundity—in short, to the third function in accordance with Georges Dumézil's classification. If they were good dead who died under normal circumstances and not before their time, they take a place among the ancestors and were reputed to watch over the clan and the family, in accordance with certain rites that testified to the fundamental concept of *Do ut des,* "I give so that you give." In exchange for oblations and sacrifices, the dead granted favor and protection.

The same notion was found throughout northern Europe and, among the problems it raises, that of tutelary spirits and the genies of the soil closely concern our research because they pose the question of the relationship between human beings and the beyond.

The Good Dead and Their Transformation into Good Spirits

In *The Orb of the World,* Snorri Sturluson twice deals with the bond established by humans between a life that has left behind an excellent souvenir for everyone and its consequences on agricultural production. Snorri first reports the example of Freyr, regarded here as just a man among other men and not as a god.

> Freyr took power after Njörd. He was declared Lord of the Sviar and imposed a tribute from them. He was popular and inspired good seasons, like his father. . . . Under his rule began the peace of Frodi [Freyr]. There were then happy seasons for the entire land, and the Sviar attributed this to Freyr. He was therefore worshipped more highly than the other gods as, under his rule, the people were more fortunate than before in peace and good seasons. . . . Freyr fell ill. When the evil struck him, the people sought counsel, letting few people come to him, building a great mound in which they set doors and three windows.
>
> When Freyr was dead, they carried him secretly into the mound, telling the Sviar he was alive, and kept him there for three winters. They spilled all of his tributes into the mound, the gold through one window, the silver through another, and the copper coins through the third. Thus the good seasons and peace continued. . . .
>
> When the Sviar learned that Freyr was dead and that the good seasons and peace remained, they believed that it would continue in this vein as long as Freyr was in Sweden. They did not wish to burn him and called him the god who determines the prosperity of the world. They made sacrifices to him, especially for good seasons and peace.[1]

This extremely rich story presents all details we need to consider—the fertility of the land connected to the persona of the sovereign, the offerings to the deceased, the result of these offerings—and clearly shows how there was born the worship of a dead man whose life vouched for the living condition of people. Snorri's story is indirectly confirmed by a passage in the *Gesta Danorum* (V, xvi, 3) in which Saxo Grammaticus says this about Freyr, called Frotho and the rationalized form of the Danish god Frodi:

Frotho was slain by a sea cow—in fact it was a witch who had adopted this animal form. The greats of the kingdom (*proceres*) removed the entrails from his body and salted them to prevent them from putrefying. In order to continue receiving taxes, they paraded his body in a royal carriage and not on a funeral bed, as if the king was still alive. Frotho's body was carried through countrysides of the land for three years this way, but it decomposed and they were obliged to bury him beneath a mound.[2]

The political intention is obvious: the death of a king was hushed in order to prevent any potential trouble and to ensure the payment of taxes, but this logical explanation actually covers a more ancient and clearly pagan thinking: Frotho, dead, visited his lands. This event must be compared to a passage from Tacitus in which he says that the goddess Nerthus circulates through the countryside in a cart: "These are then days of joy and feasting in the places she honors by her visit or sojourn. The Suevones do not engage in war or pick up arms. . . . It is the sole time when they know and love peace."[3]

Once we know that Njörd, the father of Freyr (also known as Frotho and Frodi), was the Scandinavian god corresponding exactly to the ancient Germanic goddess Nerthus,* the promenade through the country takes on a precise meaning: the land is fertilized by it and peace is assured—the two desiderata of the third function are fulfilled. According to the *Book of Flat Island*,[4] the visit to all of the countryside is also the prerogative of the god Freyr. Snorri and Saxo are therefore following the mythological tradition here, but, turning the god into a man, they are obliged to make him die. Yet the function of this figure does not change whether he is living or dead—his passage through the land is beneficial. We should note that the processions through the fields with relics and the statues of saints are merely the Christianized form of this ancient pagan custom.

---

*Njordr is the Scandinavian form of the Latinized Germanic Nerthus.

In *The Orb of the World,* Snorri provides another glimpse of the worship that a good sovereign can attract following his death, and it indicates the reasons for it.

Of all the kings, Olaf the Black was the most favored by fertile years. When his people learned of his death, and that his body had been transported to Ringerike to be buried there, important men from the districts of Raumarike, Heidmark, and Vestfold went there to claim the body, for they believed that obtaining it would assure them good years of fertility. The cadaver was therefore cut into four pieces: the head was buried beneath a mound in Stein in the Ringarike, and the other parts were buried in each of the districts. These tumuli were called "cairns of Halfdan. . . ."[5]

The Book of Flat Island adds: "Many people made sacrficies to them."[6]

The *Book of Settlements* shows that rulers are not the only individuals to have been in some way deified. It reports: "Because of his popularity, sacrifices were offered to Grim following his death, and he was nicknamed Kambann."[7]

The text does not identify the purpose of these sacrifices made to Grim, but we can say, with no great risk of error, that they were made in seeking to attract his blessings. The sagas offer partial confirmation of this point. That of Hervör (chapter 1) indicates that King Gudmund was buried beneath a mound and considered to be a god. The sagas of Bard tell us this: when Bard died it was believed that he had entered Snow Mountain (Snaefell), and men swore oaths to him as if he were a god (*heitgud*), calling him the spirit of the mountain (*bjargvaettr*) and nicknaming him the Aesir of Snaefell (Snaefellsáss).

The fact the dead were closely connected to the third function clearly springs from a motif that we come across in various locations: the mounds of some individuals remained green through all seasons. The *Book of Sturla* (chapter 75) says this concerning Einar of Laugarbrekka:

"Einar then lived in Laugarbrekka and was buried in a tumulus a short distance from that of Sigmund, and his mound was always green, in winter as in summer."[8] Saxo tells the same thing about Frotho's (Frodi's) tumulus, and the *Saga of Gisli* (chapter 18) says this about the tumulus of Thorgrim, adding: "The folk believed that his offerings to Freyr had earned him the good graces of the god, who did not want him to be cold." The motif is even present in hagiographical legends (*vitae*) to such an extent that we can imagine a borrowing, which is revealing. It testifies to the intervention of higher powers, which is God for the Christians and a deity—Thor, Freyr?—for the pagans.

A final point underscores, indirectly, that the dead had power over the elements. More than once the sagas report that a tempest arises because either an attempt is being made to transport the cadaver to a new location or a revenant makes an appearance. In the *Saga of the Sworn Brothers* (chapter 19), at the moment when men are about to transport the body of the prophetess (*völva*) to Reykjanes by boat, it begins snowing so hard that the water of the fjord turns to ice, preventing removal of the corpse to Olafsdal. The *Laxdaela Saga* (chapter 66) offers us the opposite scenario. Gest Oddleifsson wants to be buried at Helgafell.

> The winter had been very cold, and there was much ice about, and Large Fjord was laid under ice so far out that no ship could get over it from Bardastrand. Gest's body lay in state two nights at Hagi, and that very night there sprang up such a gale that all the ice was drawn away from the land, and the next day the weather was fair and still. Then Thord took a ship and put Gest's body on board, and went south across Large Fjord that day, and came in the evening to Holyfell. . . . In the morning Gest's body was buried. . . . That next night a wild storm arose, and drove the ice on to the land again, where it held on long through the winter, so that there was no going about in boats. Men thought this most marvelous, that the weather had allowed Gest's body to be taken across when there was no crossing before nor afterward during the winter.[9]

Here we can compare the state of the weather and the appearances of Thormod and Glam: snow and storm precedes or accompanies them. For us, people of the twenty-first century, it is obvious that storms have the power to inspire phantastical visions, but during the tenth and eleventh centuries, this was not how it was, and storms were viewed as the intervention of immanent powers, spirits, or the dead. If the dead person could intervene this way with the elements, he was necessarily connected to the fertility of the soil and to the fecundity and the well-being of grazing animals. Everything fit together in that time's mind-set.

The good dead therefore rejoined the ancestors in the mountain or some other place. The good dead became tutelary spirits such as Bard, "spirit of the mountain" and "god" (Aesir). I believe it is possible to interpret in the same way two mysterious figures who appear in the *Saga of Christianity* and in the *The Words of Thorvald*. The first text relates:

> Gilja was where lay the stone to which the relatives of Kodran had sacrificed and in which they said dwelt their protector (*ármadr*). Kodran declared that he would not be baptized before learning who had the greater power, the bishop or the protector in the stone. After this, the priest went to the stone and sang above it (the holy offices), until it exploded into pieces. Kodran deemed then that the protector had been vanquished. He had himself and his entire household baptized.[10]

Let's keep in mind the designation of the tutelary figure, ármadr, formed from *madr,* "man," and *ár,* "year, good year, fertility, spring," which is found in the phrase of invocation—"for a fertile year and for peace" (*til árs ok fridar*)—that is addressed to the god Freyr at the moment a sacrifice is made, as confirmed by Snorri in the *Saga of Hakon the Good.*[11] *The Words of Thorvald* makes explicit the connection between a tutelary spirit such as this one and the third function: "When he was asked to convert, Kodran declared he had a seer (spámadr) who revealed the future to him, told him what he should do, and watched his flock. This figure also lived beneath a stone, and holy water sent him fleeing."[12]

It is curious that it would be the *Saga of Christianity* that preserved the term *ármadr* and that it was *The Words of Thorvald* that demonized the supernatural being more by designating it with *spámadr*—by therefore making it leave the otherworld to introduce itself into the human world.

All tutelary spirits were not the dead. Regrettable confusion and combinations had been produced by virtue of the fact that some dead individuals were transformed into land spirits (landvaettir) whereas others existed as the spirit of place (genius loci)—those who inhabited the stones and groves and springs and mountains and who were somewhat similar to the small Greek demons from the Hellenic period (when fauns, satyrs, sylvan spirits, or dryads populated nature). In the north, for example, there were alfes and dwarves. In the *Saga of Kormak*, Thordis, a wizard, recommends that the gravely wounded Thorvald, who is slow to heal, go pour the blood of a bull over a mound in which alfes are said to live.[13] The *Book of Sturla* indicates that Thorir Snepill "worshipped a grove of trees" (*hann blótadi lundinn*), and we can also recall this passage from the laws of Ulfljot:

> The first of pagan laws said that one should not be at sea in a ship with a figurehead, and if there was one, it should be removed before arriving in sight of land, and to not moor a ship facing toward this country with figureheads with gaping jaws or hideous grimacing faces, at the risk of terrifying the tutelary spirits of the land.[14]

Doubt was permissible in certain cases where it was impossible to know with exactitude which tutelary spirits were involved. In the *Book of Sturla,* however, the text appears to establish clearly an implicit relationship between them and the dead: "Ölvir, son of Eystein, took land to the east of Grimsa. No one had dared colonize this region because of the land sprites there ever since Hjörleif had been killed."[15]

Widespread anarchy therefore reigned over the world of land spirits because tossed together pell-mell were the dead, alfes, dwarves, giants, and tutelary spirits—hence the difficulty of identifying an individual spirit met here or there. O. Briem thinks that it was Christianity that gave to the creatures of low mythology and figures of folk belief the figure of the living dead, the revenant (draugr), which in his eyes explains the confusion that rules in the world of spirits. The point is still a subject of controversy, and for other researchers what we have here are authentic vestiges of paganism.[16]

Yet lasting—and we might add, diplomatic—relations were established between men and the spirits. In fact, a passage from the *Book of Settlements* says:

> One night, Björn dreamed that a dweller of the mountains (*bergbúi*) came to him to offer to form an alliance with him, and he heard himself accept this offer.
>
> After this, a billy goat came to his nanny goats, and his herd multiplied so rapidly that he became quite rich. He was nicknamed Björn of the Billy-Goat (Hafr-Björn). The folk gifted with second sight (*ófreskur menn*) could see that tutelary land spirits accompanied Björn to the assembly and Thorstein and Thord when they went hunting and fishing.[17]

The "dwellers of the mountains" is the name that generally designated giants, as shown in D. Strömbäck's study.[18] Yet I, along with Régis Boyer, believe that what we have here are telluric spirits, in conformance with the second part of the text. But the dead also live in the mountains, and it is possible to be confused. One detail, however, speaks in favor of the interpretation of the bergbúi (the dweller of the mountain) as the dead: he visits Björn in a dream. To my knowledge, this motif does not apply to tutelary land spirits (landvaettir, as opposed to fylgjur).* This point deserves much more extensive study.

---

*Which also appear in dream.

A Revenant of the Third Function

In the legendary *Saga of Saint Olaf,* written in the Trøndelag in Norway around 1250 and based on older sources, we find an excellent illustration of a dead individual acting in the context of the third function. In a gripping combination of pagan and Christian traditions, the saga offers us this story.

A man named Rani . . . dreamed that a man came to him wearing a cape of rich cloth and a red habit bordered with ermine, a gold ring on his hand, and a sword at his side. "Are you sleeping, Rani?" he asked. Rani answered that he was awake. "No," said his visitor, "that is not true, even if you undoubtedly think so. King Olaf the Fat has come (meaning Olaf Alfe of Geirstad). I want you to take a trip at my request. I have chosen you to open my tumulus at Geirstad. This will not be hard if you heed my advice. You must bring fire, a stake, and a rope with you there. Attach the rope to the stake and lower yourself into the mound. You shall see a man there dressed like me. Approach him and take his ring, his cape, and his sword. You shall see several men at his side. Act fearlessly and no harm shall befall you. Then, cut off his head. It will be easy. If you recoil from that, you will draw punishment upon yourself, but if you listen to me, good fortune will accompany you. Before decapitating him, [also] take his belt and cutlass. Once that is done, it is time to leave the mound."[19]

All the details are important, and those concerning the clothing of the deceased allow the realization that the visitor is none other than the dweller in the mound. It seems that a determined attitude should intimidate the other inhabitants of the cairn, and the wish of King Olaf the Fat is accompanied by a threat and a promise, a new proof of the powers of the deceased. Let's now look at the explanation for this odd request.

"You shall then go to Upplönd [in central Norway], to the home of Gudbrand Kula, as a great event is taking place there. Asta, his daughter, is feeling her first labor pains and it is her first child. Gudbrand is worried for her. . . . Put the belt on Asta,* that shall aid her to give birth. . . . As reward for your service, ask that you be allowed to name the child."[20]

Of course, Rani obeys, and Asta gives birth without difficulties. Gudbrand presents the child whom Rani picks up and baptizes in accordance with pagan custom, giving him the name of Olaf.

The revenant who appeared in dream to Rani is therefore Olaf, the brother of Halfdan the Black whom we encountered earlier. He uses Rani as an instrument of his will, desiring to facilitate the birth of Asta's child, for he knows that the child will be the next sovereign of Norway and will bear his name. The pagan notion of the transmigration of the soul and the transmission of the deceased's capacity for luck through the intermediary of the name is particularly well illustrated here. But the ancient beliefs have been twisted. The intention is to show that a child born under such auspices can be only an uncommon individual, a saint. Nonetheless, the notion of revenant remains, clearly established by the rape of the mound as well as by what Rani observes when he decapitates Olad Alfe-of Geirstad: "He had the impression of striking in the water" (*oc var, sem I vatn brygdi*). We have encountered this phenomenon in other texts and even in England, where the tailor has the impression he is striking a sack of peat. This characterizes the "consistency" of the dead. Furthermore, it is significant that the dead man asks to be decapitated because, compared to what we know of the hamr, we find confirmation here of an essential detail: decapitation is necessary to allow the vital principle still attached to the nondecomposed body to escape so that it may enter another body—in this instance, the body of the newborn. The granting of the name is the concrete manifestation of this underlying thought.

---

*This custom is vouched for in Scandinavia before Christianity. It was resumed by the church, and during the Middle Ages, pregnant women were girded with the belt of St. Foy or St. Marguerite.

The Wicked Revenants

The dead who caused harm, whose exacting did not stop with their death, confirm—though in a negative fashion—the bonds uniting the dead and the third function. In accordance with a veritable constant, they attacked people and threatened the existence of the clan. Thorolf Twist-Foot bespells the oxen that have pulled him to the tomb; the livestock that approach his tumulus bellow and die, and the birds that alight upon it perish. Thorolf kills shepherds and sheep, scatters the animals, and attacks the mistress of the house, who eventually succumbs. The farms of the valley are abandoned (*Eyrbyggja Saga,* chapter 34). Glam slays the shepherd Thorgaut, then Thorhall's cowherd, and ravages the farms (*Grettir Saga,* chapter 33). Hrapp brings about the death of most of his household, causes the neighbors harm, and customarily attacks the herdsman (*Laxdaela Saga,* chapter 17 and 24). Thormod prevents Brand from gathering up his flock that comes down to the beach during bad weather (*Havardar Saga,* chapter 3).

In other words, wherever a revenant raged, the earth became a desert—that is, the earth no longer bore fruit. The countryside was literally cursed, hence the temptation to which men easily succumbed: They transformed the evildoing dead into demons—and in this they were helped by the church for whom tutelary spirits and revenants were pagan devils. The harmful dead became trolls,[21] a term used originally to designate giants and today elves or sprites, and, under the church's influence, all beings that the clerics could consider demons. In the *Saga of Hörd,* Soti is called "large troll," and the ancient laws of the Gulathing used the phrase "to be seated outside to awaken the troll" (*utiseta at vekja troll upp*) to designate necromancy. This incorporation was so common that it compels Georgia D. Kelchner to establish that trolls and the spirits of the wicked dead were identical.[22] In order to eliminate revenants from the texts, the clerics had an excellent linguistic tool at their disposal. They had only to erase certain portions, certain details of the story—to make the word *draugr* (living dead, revenant) disappear, and then to replace it with *troll.* The history would then concern only the battle between a man and a demon.

This third function, which is the sphere of action of the dead, casts a sharp light on several details from our textual evidence. We can easily understand why men established their homes near the places where the bodies of their ancestors expired: the deceased had selected a place that was most apt to guarantee the wealth and prosperity of the family. We grasp why Tungu-Odd asks to be buried on the Skaneyjarberg in order to be able to watch over the region: he is keeping watch to ensure that human affairs run smoothly.* What's more, Odin, the god of the dead, presided over commerce. He was the god of cargo (*farmatyr*), thus connected to the third function.† The Roman writers merged him with Mercury. Isn't this god, like Odin, a psychopomp? The further the investigation is pushed, the more obvious becomes the link between the dead and fertility, even when elements foreign to the third function intervene, like that of the dead man who asked to be interred at the edge of the sea in order to repel, with weapons in hand, any potential invaders. Won't the warrior who has found a glorious death assure the peace without which there could be no harvests or well-being?

---

*In the *Saga of Ragnar Hairy-Breeks* [*Ragnars Saga Lóðbrokar*] (Copenhagen: Olsen, 1906–1908), chapter 18, Ivar the Boneless (*beinlauss*) says shortly before dying: "Bury me where the kingdom is most exposed to enemy raids. I hope that those who then disembark shall not carry off the victory." The text adds: "When William the Conqueror landed in England, he had Ivar's mound opened and burned his nondecomposed body in a large bonfire. Only after that did he penetrate into the land." The Celtic literature of the Middle Ages offers us the examples of King Guortigern and Loegaire MacNeill, who had themselves buried standing upright and bearing arms in order to terrify any potential enemy. In the *Mabinogion* of Branwyn, the head of Bran the Blessed is buried beneath White Mountain near London with its face turned toward France.

†This is confirmed by the toponyms ending in –*vé/vi*, "sanctuary" (Odinsvin, Norway), –*akr*, "field" (Odensakr, Norway), –*salr*, "enclosure, hall" (Odensala, Sweden), and –*lundr*, "sacred grove" (Odenslunda, Sweden). In Iceland we find the place-name Odáinsakr.

PART FOUR

ELEVEN

Disguised Revenants

For Christian writers, the easiest means of evicting revenants was ruse. They dressed them up as demons or as apparitions that took place in both good visions and diabolical dreams—at least when recuperation was possible. When revenants appeared in a well-known popular narrative, when they were a constituent element of the story, their real nature could be brought to light only if we have points of comparison and reference. If English literature is so poor in revenants, it is because the clerics more or less transformed them happily into demons or monsters.

Grendel and the Trolls of Bard's Vale

Beowulf, an epic preserved in a single manuscript written around the year 1000 but referring to facts that date generally from the sixth or seventh century, includes two episodes that researchers have long identified as ghost stories: the battles of Beowulf against Grendel, and the battle against Grendel's mother.

> Hrothgar, King of the Danes, commanded the construction of a large feast hall, Heorot. Grendel, a monster with a human face but gigantic in stature, lived in the surrounding marshlands, a place traditionally

regarded as the home of spirits. As night fell, he lurked near Heorot, and when the Danes fell asleep after the feast, he entered, hurled himself upon them, and carried off thirty warriors. The same thing happened the next night, and twelve years fly past in the same way. Heorot is abandoned because no one can put an end to Grendel's foul deeds. "They promised to make sacrifices in their heathen temples and prayed to the murderer of souls (in other words the devil for the Christian author) for help against this calamity."[1]

Beowolf, a warrior in the service of Hygelac, King of the Geats, hears stories about Grendel. He leaves Sweden with fourteen companions to offer his service to Hrothgar, and proposes to him that he confront the monster. Hrothgar accepts, elated to find a champion, and he leaves Beowulf and his companions alone in Heorot. That evening, Beowolf strips off his armor and abandons his weapons because he wishes to fight Grendel barehanded. He then goes to bed.

Grendel enters, seizes a sleeping Geat and devours him, then attacks Beowulf, whom he grapples with physically. The battle is terrible: The hall shakes and the benches are torn from the walls. In the clutches of the strongest warrior of the age, Grendel lets go a dreadful wail of distress. Beowulf's companions hurl themselves on the monster, but their weapons do even not pierce Grendel's skin. They do not know "that no sword, even the best in the world, could touch the miscreant, for he had laid a spell on all weapons."[2]

With one final effort, Beowulf manages to tear off one of Grendel's arms, and the monster flees, mortally wounded. There is then great rejoicing in Heorot.

Let's look at this story to see what allows us to identify Grendel as a revenant: He comes out only at night; he does not use weapons but uses his hands and fingers, which are like talons; he devours the living—as Aran would do if Asmund would not defend himself; he is much larger than any man, and the same is true for his weight—when he enters, the room shakes. He lives in the fens and marshes, where, Tacitus reports, at an earlier time criminals were thrown. Discoveries of cadavers in the peat bogs of Jutland and northern Germany confirm this fact and show that the return of these dead men was particularly dreaded. Out of the twenty-one bodies collected at these sites, four had been impaled inside the pit, four others may well have been, and one had its head shattered and wrapped in linen.[3] Iron cannot bite Grendel, and the explanation offered—sorcery—conforms with the clerical interpretation of inexplicable phenomena.

The next night brought horror with it: Grendel's mother entered Heorot to avenge her son, and she carried off one of Horthgar's best-loved counselors. Beowulf promised to go slay her. She lived in vague and poetic surroundings, "a land of mystery with wolf-haunted hills, windswept crags, and a dangerous path through the marshes where waterfalls disappear beneath mist-shrouded rocks and the river flows underground. . . . Above it are frost-covered groves, trees hanging by their roots overlooking the dark waters. There, every night, you can see a terrible and mysterious thing, fire upon the waves."[4] Accompanied by Hrothgar and several men, Beowulf made his way to the swamp, and, taking the sword Hrunting, which had been lent to him, he dived into the lake. It took him a good part of the day to reach its bottom.

Grendel's mother seized him and dragged him into her underground cavern, where no water penetrated and a fire was burning. Beowulf struck her with his sword in vain. She wielded a cutlass but the hero was protected by a coat of mail. Catching sight of a large sword, "the work of giants," in the cave, Beowulf seized it and dealt a mighty blow to the monster, who then collapsed. He then explored the premises and found the corpse of Grendel, which he decapitated. During this time, the warriors waiting with Hrothgar saw the water suddenly turn dark with blood, and concluded that the valiant warrior had found his death. They all left except for the Geats. Beowulf made his way back to the surface of the lake with

Grendel's head and the hilt of the sword Hrunting, whose blade melted away at contact with the monster's poisoned blood.[5]

Examination of this extraordinary tale through which passes an admirable epic breath shows that words designating Grendel are those the clerics used to describe a monster or a devil. The vocabulary essentially reflects the predatory nature of the characters.* They are hostile beings, enemies of the human race, devils. More interesting are the designations *foreign spirit* or *strong, furious,* or *ferocious* that suggest a nuance of otherness, of monstrousness, well commentated by the narrator, who makes successful use of a fable: "[T]hey are all children from the lineage of Cain, from whom emerged all the monsters, elves, goblins, giants, and evil spirits."[6] The combination illustrates that some terms are veritable catchall phrases. But the scribe has let a few traces of the ancient beliefs survive. First, there are two mythological notations—*eoten,* "giant," which is repeated twice, and *thyrse,* "giant," "monster," "magician," or "wizard," which in English dialect shares meaning with "ghost," or "sprite," and "elf" (*thurs*). The two terms, *eoten* and *thurs,* refer to the trolls of Norse literature, even to tutelary spirits. Next come the lexemes *angenga,* "solitary," and *sceaduganga,* "walker in darkness." These two compound words are formed with the help of the verb "to go" (*gangan*), and we can recall that in Norse "to haunt" is *ganga um* or just simply *ganga,* and that in northern Germany the folk name for "specters" is Gonger (*Gänger*), "one who goes." Furthermore, if Beowulf does not regard Grendel's cadaver as still posing a danger, then why does he cut off its head? This measure is applied to an evil dead person. The comparison of the Anglo-Saxon text to an episode from the *Saga of Grettir* confirms the indirect evidence of the nature of Grendel and his mother.

Among Grettir's exploits that remain famous is his fight against Glam[7] and against the revenants of Bardardal, which presents disturbing analogies with Beowulf and, like the Anglo-Saxon epic, includes two parts.

---

*Sceada, scatha, German *Schaden,* "damage, harm."

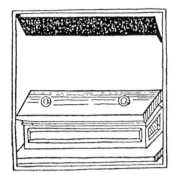 

Medieval depictions of revenants. They are devils.

Thorstein the White lived in the Bardardal, south of the Eyhardal River in Sandhaugar, with his wife and their children. It was said that the place was haunted. During Christmas, his wife went to Midnight Mass and her husband remained at the farm. When everyone was in bed that night, a loud crashing noise was heard in the middle of the night in the hall, heading in the direction of the farmer's bed. No one dared get up to see what was happening. When Steinvor returned to the farm the next morning, she found that Thorstein had vanished without a trace.

A year went by, and that winter, Steinvor wished to go to Christmas Mass again. She commanded the farmhand to remain in the house. He obeyed but with great reluctance. When she returned from the church, there was no sign of the farmhand, but there were traces of blood on the front door. It was thought that an evil spirit (*óvaettr*) had carried him off like Thorstein the previous year. The news spread and reached the ears of Grettir, who set off on the road to Sandhaugar. He arrived at the home of Steinvor on Christmas Eve. She offered him hospitality, and he suggested that he guard the house while she went to Mass. She accepted.

When evening came, Grettir ate his fill then called the farmhands back into the common room; built a barrier wall in the middle of it that was too high for anyone to get over; then stretched out, still dressed, on a platform near the entry. A light that faced the door was burning. Toward midnight, Grettir heard a loud noise, and immediately after, a female troll (*trollkona*) entered the room with a trough in one hand and a large knife in the other. She saw Grettir and hurled herself upon him, but he leapt up and confronted her. The battle was dreadful; everything was smashed to pieces and the barrier wall was destroyed. The woman troll tried to drag Grettir outside, but he resisted with all his might, hanging on to the door-frame. When that finally gave way, they both found themselves outside, and the female troll succeeded in pushing Grettir to the river above the chasm. Gathering his last strength, Grettir was able to free his right hand. He drew his short sword, struck the female troll in the shoulder and cut off her right arm. She fell into the chasm and disappeared beneath the waterfall.[8]

Two different stories paint a picture of his disappearance: "According to Grettir's tale, when the female troll felt her wound, she leapt into the chasm; but the people of Bardardal said that, surprised by daylight, she jumped after he had cut her arm off and changed into stone. One can still see the shape of a woman in a rock on the cliff."[9]

The petrification of the female troll is a clear sign that she belongs to another world, but ordinarily only alfes and dwarves turned into stone when struck by the light of day—which underscores yet again what a confused representation medieval men had of supernatural beings. The other details of the narrative clearly show that the female troll is a revenant: She appears only at Christmas and, like Glam for example, she is of greater than normal size. Finally, she attempts to pull Grettir outside of the dwelling. With the second part of the text, we come back to the story of Beowulf, but everything is much more specific.

To prove to Stein, the priest of Eyjardalsá, the veracity of what occurred Christmas night, Grettir left with him and descended into the chasm with the aid of a rope that the churchman had to watch.

Beneath a jutting rock concealed by the waterfall, the hero found a cave. He entered it. A large fire was burning inside next to which a giant of colossal size was lying. The monster saw Grettir, leaped up, and grabbed a weapon. The valiant warrior cut through its shaft with his sword. The giant then tried to reach for a sword hanging on one of the cavern walls. Grettir stabbed him, slicing open his body. His entrails fell out into the water and the current carried them away. When Stein saw the bloody water, he believed that Grettir was dead and he ran away. Grettir stopped stabbing the giant once he was certain he had truly slain him. He explored the cave, and found much treasure there and the bones of two men—those of Thorstein and the farmhand. He put them in a sack and carried them off.[10]

What are the coinciding points of the saga and *Beowulf*? The two heroes confront two revenants, a man and a woman, who devour men. There is a reversal of the monsters' entrances onto the stage in *Beowulf*: It is the male figure that first appears.* Beowulf and Grettir fight the first time in a dwelling and the second time in an underwater cave. In each story the first revenant loses an arm and disappears, and the second is killed in the fire-lit cavern in which are found riches and a sword hanging on the wall. In the saga it is the giant that tries to possess the sword, in the epic it is Beowulf. Those awaiting the courageous warrior's return believe him dead on seeing the water colored with blood. In addition, we can note several lexical observations: In each text a *hapax legomenon* appears. This is a name for which we know of only one example—it designates the sword that is taken from the dead character. It is *hæftméce* in Beowulf (verse 1457) and *heptisax* in the saga, and it concerns the same weapon, a kind of sword (*sax, méce*) with a long shaft (*hæft, hepti*). There is yet one more lexical similarity: Grendel is called *eoten* (*Beowulf*, verse 421), which corresponds exactly to the designation of the second giant in the saga, *jotunn*.

---

*Note the discomfort of the English narrator (verse 1282–87), who seems to find this order abnormal.

The two narratives therefore go back to a common tradition, Scandinavian undoubtedly, inasmuch as we find their traces in other sagas, notably that of the handsome Samsun, in which a female troll pulls the hero beneath the waves,[11] as well as in folktales. The narrative framework is well preserved, but the nature of the protagonists has changed: in folktales, the revenants have turned into giants, and in *Beowulf*, with the long descent of the Swedish warrior to the bottom of the lake we tumble into the domain of the marvelous. The saga provides a much more plausible topography of the sites. Even today, in Iceland, there is the waterfall Gódafoss, Cascade of the Gods, behind which opens the cavern where Grettir's combat took place, and not far from there, a locality bears the name of Grettir, Grettistödvar.

In all of this emerges one intriguing question: Why were the revenants replaced with giants?

From Revenant to Giant

Medieval literary works inform us that little is left to chance and every detail carries a meaning. The replacement of revenants with giants could not be the fruit of chance. It must have covered a very ancient reality, inasmuch as Grendel is already a giant—even if this reality was no longer perceived during the twelfth and thirteenth centuries and was nothing more than the flotsam of a vanished age. In the current state of our research, we can formulate only hypotheses, but scattered motifs inspire reflection.

During an ancient period, before literature had commingled them, the giants formed several races whose names have been preserved in the vocabulary. First, there were the trolls (*trollar*), incorporated with demons and about whom we know little; and the *jotnar* (sing. *jotunn*), the giants who were the original constituent elements of the physical world. The jotnar derive their name from the verb "to eat" (*eta*), and their exact counterparts are the Anglo-Saxon *eotenas* (sing. *eoten*) about whom, again, we know nothing—which would tend to prove their great antiquity. Next come the thurses (*thursar*), also called "frost giants" (*hrimthursar*), referencing the primordial giant Ymir. Their name appeared in England before the tenth century under the form *thurse,* and in Germany under the name *Durs* or *Duris,* which speaks in favor of a belief common to all Germanic peoples. In Scandinavia and beyond the Rhine, there were the *risar* (sing. *risi;* German, *Rise*), often called "mountain giants" (*bergrisar*) after their habitat. Norse used yet other names of murky etymology: *flagd,* "giant, wizard," and *gygr,* "giantess." *Gygr* should be compared to the English dialect name *gyre-carling,* "witch," and also prompts mention of the Orkney Islands, where *geyar* means "diabolical."

With the differences blurred or no longer perceived, narrators had a tendency to substitute these names for one another, and only the texts going back to what may be oral traditions from the Early Middle Ages still ever so slightly distinguish between them. It so happens that the glossaries of Beowulf and the saga offer us the names *jotunn/eoten, thurse,* and *troll.* Therefore, we must discern if there was a connection in these long ago times between the dead and the giants.

Closely connected to the earth, they lived in the mountains, like certain dead; or toward the north, where the empire of the dead is located; or even toward the east, in a cold, desert land among the mountains and glaciers, somewhere between northern Russia and Greenland, in that territory that folk songs later called the Land of the Trolls (Trollebotn), where "day never comes" and where "the sun never shines."[12] Régis Boyer concludes from this: "Thus to the extent where they are literally confused with the land, they would fall directly under the heading of manism or worship of the dead."[13]

From the light cast by numerous clues, we can postulate a relation between giants and the dead. Giants strove to fulfill their wish of taking possession of the sun—perhaps to extend shadow over the earth and bring about the disappearance of that light that prevents them from acting and that sometimes petrifies them. When Brynhild goes to the kingdom of the dead, whom does she meet? A giantess, and the last words Brynhild addresses to her are: "Sink, giantess!" (*søkkstu, gygiakyn*)—in other words, go back beneath the ground, beneath the stones.[14] The giant who in the form of an eagle raises the winds is named Hraesvelgr, which means "Swallow Corpses," and one metaphor for "Hel, goddess of Hel," is Hvedungs Maer, which means "daughter of Hvedung." Hvedung, as it happens, was a giant. The belief was that at the end of the world, during the Twilight of the Powers (Ragnarök), the giants would leave their isolated lairs by using Nagalfar, the boat made from the fingernails and toenails of dead men.[15] Surt the fire giant is called "god of the dead."

> *Surt arrives from the South*
> *With the death of branches (fire)*
> *The sun emanates*
> *From the sword of the god of the dead.*[16]

This giant slays not just any god: he kills Freyr, who represents the third function, which amounts to saying that he puts an end to all fertility and fecundity.

Beyond these disturbing points, language plays a role here again. The glosses in Old High German give *Durs* (*Thurse*) for the Latin lemma *Dis* and *Orcus*[17]—so *Dis Pater* is a god of the dead and *Orcus,* who is represented as a bearded, hairy giant on the funerary paintings of Etruscan tombs, and who became the *ogre* of folk traditions, is another. In Old English, *dyrs* is rendered by Orcus and "devil of hell" (*heldiobul*), or by *thurs* (*kyrs, Orcus odd heldeofol*).[18] It is undoubtedly the Christian meaning of *demon* that permitted these names to remain—all too rarely, alas—but it is revealing to see Caesarius of Heisterbach present a revenant accompanied by a giant: "Not so many years ago, a rich vassal of the Duke of Bavaria died. One night, the castle in which his wife was sleeping was shaken so strongly that it felt like an earthquake, and then the door to her chamber opened and her husband entered, led by a coalblack giant, who was holding him by the shoulders."[19]

What's more, the leader of the Infernal Hunt is, in the Germanic countries, a giant called Dürst in Alemanic Swiss. There may yet be even more interesting crosscurrents.

In the *Sayings of Alvis,* the alfe or dwarf who bears this name attracts these words from Thor because the narrator does not seem to have a very clear idea of what the two concepts—that of the alfe and that of the dwarf—define.

> *"What kind of man is this?*
> *Why are you so pale around the nose?*
> *Have you spent this night among the corpses?*
> *It seems to me that you have the*
> *Look of a thurse."*[20]

Alvis can be translated as All Wise—and a kind of wisdom belonged especially to giants, such as Mimir, or Memory, whose head Odin consults,[21] and Vafthrudnir, with whom he has a long oratory contest to see who knows more.[22] According to an idea that was widespread among the Germans and Celts, all wisdom dwelled in the lower world, which is often cited as the source of knowledge and art.[23] This notion goes hand in hand with another idea that maintains that death precedes life. Because death is identical to night and life is identical to day, these peoples counted time in nights rather than days.[24] We can compare this to Scandinavian cosmology: The giant Ymir is the originator of creation. In Nordic mythology, the giants are the keepers of the science of runes, and one of them, Sutting, is the keeper of poetic knowledge. As the world's first inhabitants, they [the giants] knew all its secrets. They thus maintained many close ties with death and the otherworld—with, for instance, dwarves and elves.

We should note another revealing detail: it was believed that dwarves led humans into the kingdom of the dead, but giants accompanied them when they returned from it. King Hurla disappears following a dwarf, and in *The Counting of Ynglingar* by Thjodolf Hvinverski (ninth century), King Sveigdir disappears into a boulder when pursuing a dwarf.[25] There is also the example of Theodoric of Ravenna, who, an old legend tells us, vanishes when following a dwarf and "no one knows what became of him, if he yet lives and where he may have gone."[26]

But in Caesarius of Heisterbach, a giant stands at the side of a revenant, and we find an odd tale in ancient Irish literature, *Finn and the Phantoms,* that shows us how giants were connected to the otherworld.

> Accompanied by his sons Oison and Cailte, Finn arrived in a sparsely populated region, Valley of Yew, where they sought shelter for the night. The three spotted a house from which moans and cries were emitted. A giant was standing in front of the door and bade them welcome. A fire in this dilapidated dwelling was giving off a thick smoke, and they saw an old woman, completely black, with three heads. One head was laughing, one was weeping, and the third was sleeping. There was also a headless man with a single eye on his chest.[27] The giant asked the old woman to amuse their guests. Nine bodies rose from one side and nine heads from the other, uttering terrible cries. The giant then killed Finn's horse, cut it into pieces, and roasted it in the fire. Finn refused this food, which made the giant angry and made the fire go out. Finn and his companions were soundly beaten, and they sank into a kind of lethargy. When they woke up, there was no sign of the house or the monsters, but the horse was alive. Finn put his thumb to his mouth and learned, thanks to this magic action, what just happened to them: the three phantoms of the Valley of Yews had assaulted them.[28]

These are clearly beings from the beyond. Their monstrous nature makes them akin to the Fomorians, a name translated by giants in the *Topographica Hibernica* by Girauldus Cambrensis.[29] Their disappearance and, most important, their connection to the horse—the offered meat clearly seems to be a religious meal—provide the final proof.

Fictional Examples

Few revenants appear in the medieval literature meant to entertain, which is all the more surprising because we know, through the exempla, that they did exist, however marginalized. Like other literary genres, the romance disguises revenants and uses them simply as wondrous motifs that sometimes confer a mythical character onto the narratives. In *Wigalois, Knight of Fortune's Wheel,* written by Wirnt von Gravenberg around 1210 after a now-lost French source text, we read this interesting story:

> Wigalois was on his way to confront the usurper Roaz and return the country of Korentin to Larïe, its legitimate sovereign. He met a crowned animal who, through its behavior, invited him to follow it—a well-known motif in folktales. Winglois reached a castle surrounded by an atmosphere of intense heat, crossed through it, and found armed knights. Because they appeared hostile to him, he attacked them, but his spear started burning when he wounded them. Still following the crowned animal, he made his way to the land of Korentin. In a meadow stretching out in front of a fortress, the animal took on human shape—that of King Lar—the former ruler of the country and Larïe's father. He informed Wigalois that the region was once a true paradise, but a dragon named Phetan had chased away its inhabitants and turned it into a marshy moor (*wildez moz*). The deceased king asked the hero to slay the monster that Roaz could not succeed in killing because, as a usurper, he was not permitted to regenerate the land. "You shall win the hand of my daughter Larïe," said Lar while giving Wigalois a spear (*glavie*) that an angel was said to have brought him and which was the only weapon capable of killing the monster. Wigalois slew Phetan, bringing an end to his depredations, and the land could once again be cultivated.[30]

The Christian influence is quite pronounced in this text. The fire knights are sinners condemned to burn eternally, and King Lar is a victim of divine wrath: "I deserved His wrath and the blow that struck me down, and my soul is lost unless He take pity on me," he tells Wigalois. From the narrator's point of view, the transformation into an animal and the sovereign's wandering are therefore a punishment, a purgatory. But the Christian dressing hardly masks the pagan foundation. In fact, while narrative motifs change, the structure and function remain. The dead man is totally committed to the third function and fights to reestablish peace, to restore the rightful ruler, to restore fertility. It is certainly not coincidental that Roaz is incapable of killing the dragon. As an illegitimate king, he lacks the ability to restore the land to agriculture. In the background stands out the ancient notion that the land is connected to the person of the king and even to his health. In French Arthurian literature, the infertile soil, the *terre gaste* ["waste land"], is the direct consequence of the wound suffered by the Fisher King.*

Other revenants, "spirits of the dead" (*der toten geist*) appear in *Wolfdietrich,* an epic recorded around 1300. Traces of a curious scene that is at least a half century older than the work itself can be found in the *Song of Ecke.*[31]

After the death of his wife, Wolfdietrich decided to become a monk—for the theme of monkhood was to atone for sins and guarantee the salvation of the soul. Imagining that the customary penitence would not bring him redemption, he asked the abbot for "a harsh penitence that would deliver him from his sins in one night." His wish was granted: he had to spend the night in church alone and once more confront all his enemies—all those he had slain when he lived in that century. With the fall of darkness, Wolfdietrich was

---

*This sovereign is also called the Maimed King and Pelles; he is the guardian of the Grail. See Chrétien de Troyes, *The Story of the Grail,* and its continuations by Manessier and Gerbert de Montreuil, as well as Michka, ed., *Prose Lancelot,* 9 vols. (Paris/Geneva: Droz, 1978–1983).

attacked by the dead and was saved only by the arrival of the monks coming to sing Matins.[32]

Nothing justifies this passage unless it is the narrator's desire to give his hero expiation worthy of his courage. He thus turns to revenants, and the passage is reminiscent of the story that Wace tells in the *Roman de Brut*.

The kinship of Celtic and Norse traditions is striking, so is it not at all surprising to discover in the literature of green Ireland a trace of revenants and ghosts. But myth overlays this trace almost completely, and understanding the narratives, discovering the true nature of the characters acting on their stage, often necessitates knowledge that is exterior to the text.

A quarrel broke out between King Mongon and the poet Forgoll over where Fothad Airgtech, the ruler of Ireland slain by Find, had met his end. Forgoll threatened dire curses upon his adversary if he could not prove in three days that Fothad perished in a battle on the banks of the Larne in Ulster and not at Dubtar in Leinster. The sun was

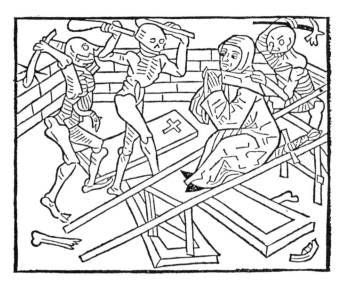

Wolfdietrich's battle against the revenants

setting upon the third day, and Mongan's wife was despondent at seeing no savior arrive. "Do not torture yourself," said the king, "he is
not far; I hear the sound of his feet in the Liffey River. Do not weep,
wife. I hear his feet moving through the water of the Boyne River. . . .
Cailte arrived from the north, holding the shaft of a headless spear in
his hand. Using it as a pole, he vaulted over the three moats and three
earthen ramparts that formed the wall of the fortress, and entered the
palace. He then revealed how Fothad died.[33]

We should now pay close attention to the description of the scene,
for each detail is fraught with meaning.

"We were with thee," said Cailte, addressing the king. "We were
with Find" "Know, however," replied Mongan, "that you do wrong
in revealing a secret." But the warrior Cailte continued: "We were
therefore with Find. We came from Scotland. We encountered
Fothad Airgdech near here, on the shores of the Ollarba. We gave
him furious battle. I cast my spear at him in such a manner that it

The danse macabre reflects one of the avatars of the belief in revenants.
(La Danse Macabre, *Paris, Guyot Marchand, 1485*)

passed through his body, and the iron point, detaching itself from the staff, became fixed in the earth on the other side of Fothad. Behold here [in my hand] the shaft of that spear. There will be found the bare rock from the top of which I let fly my weapon. There will be found a little farther to the east the iron point sunken in the earth. There will be found again a little farther, always to the east, the tomb of Fothad Airgdech. A coffin of stone covers his body; his two bracelets of silver, his two arm-rings, and his neck-torque of silver are in the coffin. Above the tomb rises a pillar-stone, and on the upper extremity of that stone, which is planted in the earth, one may read an inscription in ogam: *Here reposes Fothad Airgdech; he was fighting against Find when Cailte slew him.*[34]

The battle on the banks of the Ollabal took place around 285, and Mongan, a historical figure, died in 625. The secret he alludes to is this: Mongan has already lived an earlier life under the name of Find mac Cumaill, and Cailte was one of his companions in that life. Both took part in the battle where Fothard was killed. Cailte is clearly a revenant, and he comes so that truth may triumph.* If we do not know that Fothad died several centuries earlier, Cailte cannot be seen as a visitor from beyond the grave.

If we wish to find the revenants beneath their various disguises, we must start from the function of the figures who at first sight belong to the realm of legend or are from the world of fantasy. Of course, we shall not obtain a historical image of the belief in revenants, but a fictional reflection testifies occasionally to the knowledge—the infatuation—of an era regarding specters. We should pay particular attention to the battles that pit a knight against a devil in a cemetery. We know of two, in the romance *Amadas and Ydoine* (composed between 1190 and 1220) and in *The Perilous Hearth* (from the end of the thirteenth century). In

---

*A motif we see again in the lais of the twelfth and thirteenth centuries, like that of Lanval, for example, where the fairy emerges at the spot named to prove that her lover has not lied.

The Perilous Hearth, Gawain confronts a devil, presented as the demons of courtly literature, to free a lady imprisoned inside a tomb by enchantment and sorcery (*caraude et sorcerie,* verse 1194).[35] It so happens that this tomb is the dwelling of the evil being (verse 1223). The text displays a surprising incoherence: Gawain kills the devil, which is already noteworthy, but his body does not vanish, leaving nothing behind but a foul odor—which is even more remarkable. Moreover, two details clearly recall what we saw earlier concerning Glam: Gawain forces his adversary to retreat—his heels bump into a gravestone and he falls over backward, and Gawain wounds then decapitates him (verse 1403). One final vesitage of an undoubtedly ancient tradition calls our attention: this devil had devastated the land (*gastoit le païs,* verse 1438).

These elements are insufficient for asserting peremptorily that in this story we are in the presence of a revenant, but they display too much consistency with the facts of revenants not to belong to an older story, perhaps from oral tradition, that provided the subject matter for a chilvarous adventure. We can see that, depending on the art of the storytellers, the revenant could be so firmly transposed into the fictional realm that it was hardly recognizable.

All our witnesses agree on one specific point: revenants fit within a specific culture from which it is impossible to separate them—that is, they form a perfectly consistent set of details closely linked to the beliefs of the time, religion, and a people's notion of the world. Their incorporation into devils, monsters, giants, or more or less mythical knights and their transformation into literary motifs is the logical consequence of the battle led by the church against these dangerous elements beyond its control. The church deemed these elements dangerous for souls, and it twisted them to its own advantage by putting them on the right path and fitting the belief in ghosts between the worship of saints and the liturgy of the dead. It is expected that the writings would be altered by clerics, but the oral traditions were not codified in this way. What became of them?

TWELVE

Perspectives

What remains in our memory of the revenants of long ago times? Has their nature changed? Using a corpus of about one hundred texts, I have attempted to see this clearly and classify the data.

Starting in the sixteenth century, a tradition frequently cropped up that offered a fact that was vouched for until the nineteenth century.

Between Lindholm and Massbüll in the Tondern District (Schleswig-Holstein) a ghost carrying a spear wandered every night. To late passersby he shouted: "Where should I put it?" One day, a farmer had the courage to answer him: "Put it where you found it." The specter thanked him and told him he had been waiting for this answer for a hundred years and disappeared.[1]

In a field near Eger, a ghost in human form could be seen; the people of the area called him the Junker Ludwig. It was said that an individual by this name had moved the boundary markers of a field and returned shortly after his death to haunt the area, especially around where the boundary marker had been moved.[2]

The will o' the wisps you see on shores and embankments were believed to be surveyors who marked out lands dishonestly. The surveyors were condemned to return to guard the borders.[3]

Connected to this group of stories are those concerning phantom laborers. Because they plowed and seeded several furrows on their neighbor's property, they had to return to work the fields during the night or else harrow them. Also part of this group are all stories of land theft, whether or not the land could be farmed, as shown by this tradition:

The owner of Südergard dishonestly took possession of a peat bog belonging to the domain of Kürbüll (Schleswig-Holstein) and, after his death, he found no rest and appeared ceaselessly to his heirs. Weary of being pestered in this way, they interrogated the revenant, who answered: "I will never find peace in the grave as long as the peat bog has not been restored to its legitimate owner." The heirs refused to grant his wish. "It is better to have a damned soul in the family than disgrace," they told themselves. They then buried the deceased beneath a stake at the door to the sheepfold. Because the stake hampered the passage of people through the door, it was often jarred. One day, when a serving maid stumbled against it violently, a voice rang out: "Yet another blow!" The stake was then hammered all the way into the ground.[4]

The stories of this type require several layers of interpretation. At first glance they fall into the realm of those messages generated by human society inviting each of its members to respect the honor code and the good mores and laws of a given era. We could describe this as education through storytelling, or fear-based pedagogy: give thought to your eternal rest before behaving dishonestly. There is therefore a language that fairly well covers that of the medieval church, which sought to make use of the dead to instruct the living. The story also carries interesting testimony concerning the breakup of the family unit during the nineteenth century and the disappearance of respect for ancestors. The dead man is just that—a dead man—and his wishes are no longer of any importance. His descendants do not hesitate to get rid of him by nailing him into his grave. But the fact is that all these examples lie over a much older reality, and we should not stop at the first interpretation, which is merely the ultimate form taken by a belief that has come from antiquity.

In an earlier age, the earth or the domain was sanctified. If we use Rome as a reference, we can read the following passage from a surveyor's manual: "Every domain owns three sylvan spirits. One, the domestic, presides over the procession; the second, called agreste, is dedicated to the pastures—thus to the livestock; the third, called oriental, is placed at the borders of the fields, inside the sacred grove (*lucus*)."[5]

The Roman surveyor to whom we owe these clarifications, adds: "Why is it customary in all rural properties to honor Sylvanus? It is because he was the first to lay down a stone to mark off the boundaries."

The person who moves a boundary marker is therefore committing a sacrilege because he is stealing from the protective deity the land it has under its protection. A sacred character is conferred upon land holdings, and this can irritate the small god of the lucus. We should note a curious survival in the French countryside: Quite often, in the midst of a completely cultivated field, a bothersome grove is left, and the laborers have to work around this grove. When asked why this grove was left, the peasants could not provide us with any satisfactory answers. Some were even contradictory. "It is for the game," one said. "It is for the birds," said another, but birds would eat the seedlings. The land is therefore sacred in Romanized countries. Does this hold true for the Germanic peoples?

The boundary of a domain is marked by an earthen embankment or by a hedge. Old High German offers us two terms for these: *hegge/hegga* and *zûn.** Hegge comes from the Indo-European root word *kagh* or *kagio* from which also comes *Hain,* "the sacred grove," and which means "enclosure." The word that engendered several Latin lemma[†] also attested for "town" (*urbs*) and once for "region bordered by a for-

---

*Norse *agi,* Old English *hecge.*

†For example: *indaggo, agger, valum, caulae.*

est" (*circuito regio in silva*).[6] *Hegge* soon came to designate the thing that marked off a space, meaning the hedge, out of confusion with *zûn* (Norse *tún;* Old English *tyn*), today's *fence.* The domain that is marked off this way is sacred in accordance with the testimony of numerous texts. When the town of Bobbanburg, the current Bamborough, was founded in 547, the English chroniclers wrote: "It was first surrounded by a hedge": *seo waes aerost mid hecge betyned.*[7]

We must take note of the choice of terms: *hecge* and (*be*)*tyn.* From *tyn* comes the word *town.* Now we know that the foundation of a city is a magical and religious act accompanied by the consultation of omens, and the nature of this act took place in the two names that were retained. Moreover, it seems the chroniclers would not have taken note of an event of no importance. They would have been satisfied with saying "In this year this city was founded . . ." a common phrase in Anglo-Saxon chronicles. A study of place names conducted in different Germanic countries confirmed more than one case in which the settlements were placed under the protection of a god: Torstuna was the town of Thor, Fröstuna that of Freyr, and, in France, Lugdunum (Lyon) was the city of the Celtic god Lugh. It so happens that dunum etymologically corresponds exactly to the Germanic *tûna* from which *zûn* was derived.

In Scandinavian countries the sacred nature of the domain has been clearly confirmed, notably that of the enclosure (*tún*) that Régis Boyer defines.

> It is the small enclosed field, object of all the concerns of the household located there, today as in the past, in front of the house or farm in all Germanic countries. Once upon a time a sacred value was attached to this *tún.* Also raised there were one or two preferred animals who also benefitted from a more or less sacred character.[8]

The equivalent of the three *sylvanus* of the Roman *possessio* is the tutelary spirit (landvaettr, genius loci). We can add that the sacred character of the domain extends an arrow's flight beyond its strict boundary.

According to Nordic laws, the outlaw loses his immunity (*manneshelgi:* the part of the sacred in an individual), and thus becomes *óheilagr** when off his land and the space marked by the flight of an arrow.[9]

In England, a portion of land called "the good man's field" (*gudeman's croft*) was allowed to survive into the seventeenth century. This was a piece of land that was never plowed or planted and was instead allowed to lie fallow. No one harbored any doubt that it was reserved for some spirit or demon. What we have in *gudeman* is not the adjective *good* but the Anglo-Saxon noun *god* (the Germanic *Guda*).

All these testimonies point in the same direction. We might therefore conclude that the theft of land was a sacrilege and that the guilty parties were, in ancient times, persecuted by the spirit of the land, then, after conversion to Christianity, were punished for having sinned against the ninth commandment. If we accept the presence of genius loci inside the enclosure, large areas open to future research. Wizards were known as "hedge riders" (Norse *tunridur*; Middle High German *Zûnrîte*), and in nineteenth-century Vastergötland (Sweden), the witch or wizard was believed to ride a wooden stake from the hedge.[10]

Another kind of narrative—this one falling into the category of the educational and edifying tale—presents revenants as men who, during their lifetimes, caused harm to others.

In Dielingforf, near Melle, the farmer Potthaf haunted his attic. Formerly, he had cheated his customers on the quantity of wheat he sold them, and now he spent all his nights measuring his grain.[11]

Between Dassel and the Möosberg, in Sievershausen (Lower Saxony), walked a headless ghost who stopped the passersby and asked them for a toll. It was said he had been a miser who had wrested hard-earned money from more than one person.[12]

Heilagr, "sacred," *ó*, privative prefix, thus: "stripped of its sacred nature."

The warnings given by sometimes ill-defined specters are in the same spirit. In the Hildesheim region, someone named Huckup hurled himself on the backs of woodland thieves and let them go only when they left the forest. He slipped into the basket of the farmwife who sold her milk and butter for more than their worth. Perhaps he symbolized the weight of remorse. The message is clear: any misdeed will be paid for in the coinage of postmortem peace.

A group of stories reflects the theological discourse fairly well, but ethnographical touches are as numerous as they are old.

Gerhard Heisius, pastor of Arbergen at the beginning of the eighteenth century, was a man of pitiless severity. He did not rest in peace. His ghost was exorcised and his body was buried in a woods near Thedingshausen.[13]

The prior of Loccum Monastery wallowed in luxury. Once he died, he returned to haunt the monastery where he had met his end. His body was carried into a wood, and the haunting ceased.[14]

A farmer committed suicide in Bassum. When he came back, he was buried beneath a large rock in the forest. He emerged every three years and returned to travel toward his former home at a flea's pace. It is said that once he reaches it, he will find peace. It is also said that he has carried off people behind the hedge on more than one occasion.[15]

An atheist who was living in Vollerwick on the Eider sold his soul to the devil. After his death, he returned and carried his body off beyond the dike. Every night, he gets a little closer to his farm and has already made his way to the first furrow carved by the plow. When he reaches the second, the dike shall burst.[16]

In addition to this family of texts, we have all those that report a dual punishment: that of the deceased and that of a living individual who behaves badly.

> In Kampehl near Wusterhausen on the Danube, the body of the lord of Kahlebuss, a murderer and traitor, did not rot in the grave. He haunted a bridge between eleven and midnight, when he jumped on the backs of passersby. In 1806, two soldiers opened his coffin, pulling out the corpse and injuring it before placing it back upside down, daring it to come visit them at their campsite. The next morning one of the two men was found dead—with a broken neck.[17]

Yet even more revealing is the following story collected in Uri Canton, in Alemanic Switzerland. In it we find the principal elements that exist in the Norse sagas.

> A revenant was slaying cowherds and beasts in an alpine pasture, and the domain's owner could no longer find anyone who would climb up there during the summer. One day a stranger arrived. Once informed of the situation, he declared his readiness to climb up to that meadow and bring with him some dozen cows.
>
> The first night he noticed nothing out of the ordinary. On the second day a stranger appeared and hampered him in his work. The cowherd quietly told him: "Get out of my way. I have enough to do," and the stranger vanished. He reappeared the next night, up to his old tricks. "Help me instead of constantly stepping on my feet," the cowherd told him. The revenant got to work and helped the cowherd all summer, but when the time came to separate, he began weeping and said: "I must now stay here all alone and the winter is so long." "You can come back down with me," the cowherd told him. The revenant accepted. No one saw him at the farm, but because he was sharing the cowherd's sleeping quarters, the farmer overheard his employee's conversation and questioned him.

"I am with the ghost," was the answer, "and it is thanks to him that there is so much milk and cheese." The ghost was asked what could be done to help him. "Once I was a cowherd here," the revenant responded, "and it was my fault that the farmer lost so much milk. He was the grandfather of your master. If he forgives me, I shall be delivered." "Why did you slay men and beasts?" "They cursed me, and that put them in my power." The farmer gave his forgiveness and the revenant appeared one last time. The cowherd extended his hand, but the ghost would not touch it. He then held out a shingle to the revenant; the latter touched it and vanished. The shingle was completely burned.[18]

In addition to the dead man's obvious connection to the third function, the story includes a lesson: The living should behave properly to the dead. Any wicked word or action calls down a vengeance that here takes the form of death. The final observation underscores the danger that accompanies apparitions and is reminiscent of the medieval exempla in which the damned seek to display the torture they are undergoing beyond the grave: they are burning. Revenants are therefore seeking to make up for the sins they have committed, as is illustrated by a Danish folk song.

His Lordship Morten von Fugelsang had just been buried, but before it had even reached midnight, he mounted a horse and pursued the younger Folmer Skiødt: "Listen, stop and speak with me! I promise, on my faith as a Christian, that I am not trying to trick you."

"Listen, Lord Morten, how can you be riding like this? No later than yesterday we buried your body."

"I am not riding like this because of trial, I am not riding like this because of a judgment. I am riding like this for a small enclosure that was obtained with a (false) oath, to increase the size of the Fugelsang.

"I am not riding like this because of quarrels; I am not riding like this for gold so red. I am riding like this for a small enclosure that belongs to two orphans. Tell my good lady Mettlille, when you get back to my house, that she should truly return the enclosure! Then my soul will be able to find peace.

"Tell my good lady Mettlille, so that she will believe you, that my pants are outside the door to her room.

"My pants are outside the door to her room. Before the arrival of midnight, they shall fill with blood." Lady Mettelille returned the enclosure and Lord Morten was able to rest in peace.[19]

Homicides give rise to a large number of traditions, not all of which are equal in value. I include only those that bear credible information.

A woman drowned in a lake in the domain of Wittwein, in the Ruppin District in the Mark. She returned ever since, a white shape floating over the ground that would suddenly vanish.[20]

On the road from Kolow to Hökendorf, near Rügen, a man was murdered at a place called Sprockenkreuz. Everyone passing by this place would toss some twigs or branches on the spot because the ghost of the dead man would attack travelers.[21]

Could this tossing of branches be a form of sacrifice or exorcism?

Between the village of Altenhagen and the town of Spring (Lower Saxony) was the site to which the Lord von Sehminne returned. He appeared in the ruins of his castle with a terrible noise accompanied by the clinking of weapons and armor. It was said that he had been slain by one of his neighbor's knights.[22]

The majority of the traditions cited, some obviously of medieval provenance and others more modern, provide fairly good matches with the much older information, as well as the role played by forest, stones, stakes, and bridges. The revenant was rarely immaterial, and when he jumped astride the back of a passerby, that individual felt his weight. The motif appears too frequently not to cover a belief well vouched for throughout northern Germany. Schleswig-Holstein, the former earldom of the Mark (Westphalia), and Lower Saxony offer a group of ghost stories that are almost as rich as those collected in Armorican Brittany by Anatole le Braz. It is enough simply to read the works of writers native to these lands to be persuaded of the perennial nature of these traditions.[23]

The dead are definitely alive, and in the former Mark it was said they went to Naberskrooch, near Neu-Ferchau village, to spend the money that was placed in their coffins. This site is also claimed to be a meeting spot for the dead.[24]

Many hauntings were explained by a lack: The dead were dispossessed or a final wish of the dead was not respected. These are particularly good candidates for afterlife wandering.

In 1587, the judge of Gardelegen granted a farmhand the doublet of a roué. That very night the damned soul appeared to the farmhand and demanded his garment.[25]

A man from Joachinstal in the Angermünde District removed his wife's wedding ring from her dead body. The woman returned ceaselessly, demanding it, and the widower eventually dug a hole in her grave and placed the ring inside it. The haunting ceased.[26]

An elderly woman in the ancient town of Stettin made a shroud from expensive cloth and gave it to her neighbor, asking the friend to place it on her after her death. The neighbor thought the cloth was extremely beautiful and kept if for herself. After her death, the dead woman came to her ceaselessly, asking for her shroud, and this continued until she regained possession of her property.[27]

We could certainly explain this kind of story using psychoanalysis: its origin is a feeling of guilt reinforced by the fact that an individual has wronged the dead.

The dead can also turn into revenants under the pressure of events, especially when people dear to them are unhappy. The living's lack of affection compels the departed to intervene. A Danish folk song explains this wonderfully.

> *Dyring's wife died, leaving behind seven children. He*
>   *remarried,*
> *But his new wife was a cruel stepmother:*
> *It is late in the evening and the children are crying;*
> *In the ground below, their mother hears them;*
> *The woman lying in the earth hears them:*
> *"Of course, I must go see my little ones."*
> *God granted her permission to go to their bedside, but*
>   *she had*
> *To be back before the cock crowed;*
> *On weary limbs she raised herself,*
> *The wall and gray marble opened before her.*
> *She consoled her children:*
> *One, she brushed her hair,*
> *Another her hair she braided,*
> *She lifted up the third, and the fourth as well*
> *And on her knees she set the fifth . . .*
> *She asked her eldest daughter to go get her father, and*
>   *when he entered*
> *The room, she said:*
> *"If I have to come back here again,*
> *Much woe shall befall you,"*
> *And the threat hit home.*[28]

Maternal love can give way simply to love, and the *Song of Master*

Aage shows us how Aage returned to ask his fiancée Elselille to stop mourning him.

> *Every time you rejoice and your heart is gay,*
> *The inside of my coffin is filled with the petals of red*
> *roses;*
> *Every time you lament and your heart is sad*
> *The inside of my coffin is filled with coagulated*
> *blood.*[29]

We should realize that the human mind believes somehow that mourning is more tolerable. Yet stories tell that the tears of the living are intolerable to the dead, and this belief has even been pushed so far as to claim that if these tears fall upon the eyes of a dead person, that individual will come back to life.[30] In one tale, a small child comes to ask his mother to stop crying because his shroud is soaked and only a surface the size of a fingernail remains dry. When it too is wet, he will no longer have any rest. In another, two young children appear and compare their mother's tears to blood.[31]

The living who find themselves in a difficult situation still make an appeal to their dead ancestors, but the motif belongs to folk traditions only as an echo of the past.

On the death of her godfather Gertrude received all his property, but an earl wished to carry her off and to ravish the land. Gertrude used necromancy to contact the dead man and ask him for help. The dead man rose and accompanied her. Everyone hid when they saw him except the earl, and battle was joined. Close to succumbing, the wicked man asked: "Gertrude, Gertrude, enjoy your property in peace and deliver me from this dead man!" Thanks to her book (of magic), she was successful, but her godfather requested a gift and she had a chapel built over his grave.[32]

All the stories we have examined up to this point contain an explicit or implicit interpretation, but next we find tales that record well-known incidents in a region—but they offer no explanation or solution.

The night following his burial, several people spied Count Lynar making his way through a crossroads, riding a black horse.[33]

In the Pfelder Valley (Tyrol), the ghost of a female cowherd was haunting a chalet, lighting the fire and washing the milk churns and vats. Hunters took shelter there one night. They were awakened by the revenant, who was cooking a hearty soup and, with a gesture, invited them to join in. They did not dare go near it, and the ghost disappeared with a sigh.[34]

If we compare the ethnographical data of these narratives and that of the ancient Germanic literature, it is obvious that we can find important surviving beliefs, the most disturbing being the absence of any pronounced border between life and death. The dead remain attached to the earth, to their home, and—something new—to the very site of their death. Nowhere can we read of the obsession of the decomposing corpse, the skeleton rattling his bones in a *danse macabre*. The revenants have a body, at times they speak, and sometimes they kill or ask for help. What has been best maintained is their bond with the third function.

The cross planted where a dead person spoke while being carried to the grave was the object of the villagers' care. If it fell down, the sheep would die from illness or accident, and this would continue until another cross was set up.[35]

What is most surprising is the weak role played by Christianized ghosts. This leaves the impression that with the church losing influence over the course of the centuries, the ancient beliefs—never totally forgotten—have experienced a rejuvenation. In the final analysis, when we review the corpus of collected stories, the devil practically never puts in an appearance—which is stupefying—purgatory is cited only once, and when churchmen step in, it is to come to the aid of people seeking to rid themselves of the recalcitrant dead.

The elimination of revenants is no longer as barbaric as in the eleventh and twelfth centuries: they are no longer decapitated, but their bodies are still buried beneath a stake or their bodies are carried a long way off and mislaid.

> It was thought that the old barber had been buried once and for all, but when the villagers returned from the cemetery, they saw the dead man laughing in the window of his house. His heirs did not find this amusing and ran to summon the pastor. He addressed the revenant, but to no avail. They next went to the Minden city fathers who had a better idea of how to handle the situation. They laid the old barber in a copper coffin, then carried it along a zigzag path through the hedges and fields, and buried the body on the other side of the Ils River. Nothing would ever grow again in the places where they had passed through the hedge.[36]

Each region has its own methods: In eastern Prussia, revenants are tossed into the Haff, and in Frisia they are left on the Wattenmeer, a strip of land left uncovered when the tide goes out, the same spot where criminals were buried one thousand years ago. It is believed that "he who is banned there can never return."[37] In Schleswig-Holstein, burial beneath a stake was the prevailing custom until fairly recently.

The irksome nature of ghosts and revenants emerged more in nineteenth-century folklore traditions than in the Middle Ages. The dead were expelled into the otherworld, and their descendants no longer felt responsible for meeting the requests of their deceased ancestors, even claiming that the apparition was a diabolical illusion. The family unit no longer included the dead and the living in a single community. We can sense, at this time, a desire to put everything in its place, to shut the door between here and the beyond, to make definitive the character of the dead, finally to be emancipated from the dead who, if they returned, would occupy a position they did not merit. Eventually, the young villagers did not hesitate to steal the shroud that the ghost left hanging from the door of the cemetery,[38] the fiancée refused to enter the tomb when her lover came looking for her,[39] bold souls invited the dead to dine.[40] The mind-set had changed—the dead had become undesirable and people seemed to dread them less.

The results of the investigation by Aniela Jaffé and the Schweizerischer Beibachter, published in 1958, show additionally the predominance of dream:[41]

- The dead appear to their close relatives and friends.
- Most often, an apparition signifies the imminent death of the witness of the manifestation.
- Ghosts are nothing more than ectoplasm.
- The ghost manifests at the moment of death; often, moreover, it comes to take leave of a person dear to it.

These characteristics are evidence of the final transformation of revenants: they have turned into nothing more than precursory signs and are no longer worthy of their name.

We should however refrain from generalizing too broadly because not all rural locales have experienced the same changes and evolution, and it is obvious that the denser the communication network and the stronger the industrialization process, the more widely ancient beliefs have been erased. We cannot compare an isolated valley to a plain full of people. In addition, it is likely that the countryside has played a large role in the survival or disappearance of revenants. If they have found refuge today in Scottish manors lost on the moors, in the mists of the Baltic Sea, in the dusty haze of Icelandic geysers, or in the mountains of Norway or the Alps, it is not by chance. They exist wherever a human community lives closely connected to nature or withdrawn into itself.

The farmer, the mountain-dweller, and the sailor have experienced ghosts and tend to believe in them.

More than any other people, Icelanders have preserved a kind of gift that gives them foresight of things to come and the ability to see revenants. Kristjan Thorolfsson woke up suddenly during the night of September 15, 1936, without knowing why, awakened his brother-in-law, and went out with him. Breaking up on the reefs before their eyes was Jean Charcot's crippled ship, the *Pourquoi Pas*. In the story of the events Thorolfsson gave to a Heykjavik newspaper, the *Morgunbladid*, there is one passage that deserves to be highlighted.

We had brought twenty-two bodies back to land and laid them out on a hill called Borgarlaekur, located just south of the farm, and they stayed there until they could be transported to Reykjavik two days later. I had no problem walking among the dead; even all alone at night I had no fear. This was how it was during the two days they remained there because there were sheep to look after in the pastures of the Hölubjarg, and to get to these pastures every evening, I had to pass by the bodies of my French friends. This did not scare me in the least. It was only after they had been taken away that I felt a kind of fright when passing that way, and I did not like being alone. I felt a kind of emptiness inside. . . . But you can call that fear, I don't know.

The reason could be that my dog, a good and loyal friend, scared me a little at night after the bodies had been carried to Reykjavik. Our route passed by the Borgarlaekur, and all at once the dog began barking. Although I did not see anything, he is not stupid. I do not think though that you could say the spot was haunted, although I did catch sight of something that looked like revenants near the farm. It was not at all surprising because there were so many bones and body parts found on the shore. And they were all buried in a mass grave; but I saw very little, a couple revenants, that's all. I do not like to talk about it.[42]

We can note the sobriety of the story and Kristjan's reluctance to admit he saw revenants. This reticence could give the impression that ghosts and specters have disappeared. In fact, they are only waiting for a propitious moment to quit their forced retirement and let their presence across the centuries be known. Anyone who travels through the countrysides and knows to listen to the older folk will discover that revenants have not completely vanished.

Revenants have therefore left the shadows in which they have been hidden and have yielded a large part of their secret, pulling us along the traces of ancient beliefs that are little known today, back to a civilization where they had a place. Well anchored in a specific mind-set, connected with beings from high and low mythology, integrated into rural space, having power over the fertility of the soil and the health of livestock, they are neither patched-on limbs or literary stereotypes. They form part of the family, the clan, and the countryside. Endowed with extensive powers, they are both feared and honored; their visible or invisible presence inspires their relatives to maintain family virtues and traditions.

In terms of an evolution, having suffered the outrages of time and history, revenants have lost almost everything that distinguished them: their physicality and their powers. They no longer kill or threaten, nor do they perform domestic tasks. They are no longer the tutelary or wicked spirits of an earlier age. Ordinarily, they appear mute, using their eyes or gestures to express what they wish to say, but they no longer have the power to express themselves with words because they are no longer of this world. They inspire pity or affection when coming to take leave of their children. The deceased returns in search of his or her spouse, the friend shows himself one last time. The last bonds that join the dead to the living are most often those of love.

Currently, revenants are in the final stages of dying, slowly fading away as the family unit dissolves, ancestral traditions vanish, and death becomes the business of specialists. Death has become anonymous, as feared by the poet Rainer Maria Rilke—people no longer die at home, surrounded by family, but in hospitals or hospices, from where they are taken to stone gardens on the periphery of the community of the living and are no longer huddled around the church in the very center of town. How are they to return, and, more important, why should they come back if the living let the dead know in this way that their disappearance is a definitive one? The treatment the dead receive is related to the reduction in hauntings.

Except in Sicily, Romania, and Hungary, and in the Tyrol, where candles still burn day and night in the lanterns left on the graves, the dead are the outlaws of society. They are no longer cherished as before. Cemeteries are no longer meeting places where people go to share the latest news with the dead. Once upon a time, people would sit upon the cairn of the dead at times when important decisions were made; the memory of the dead was passed down from one generation to the next, and their names were borne by their descendants. Today, there are no longer any feasts or toasts in their honor, no more oblations, no more requests for help, no more confidences, no more visits—no more community. The attitude of men is responsible for the extinction of revenants. Because it is no longer a reality, the figure of the dead person no longer obsesses anyone to the point that it takes on material shape. This figure is no longer a guarantor of the social order, whereas it once compelled the living to respect laws and commandments, religion and tradition. By losing this role, ghosts and revenants have lost their place in society. The door to the otherworld has closed, and the beyond keeps our elders for eternity.

Afterword

For a Westerner living today, it is hard to imagine that ancient cultures were incapable of even conceiving the notion of nothingness and that this mental category was simply absent from their world. This was the case, however, in the Middle Ages, and most particularly in the Germanic world. There is also something else: the idea of temporality that we have manufactured, of how it is established, of its total cessation, as we all know, is something that exclusively haunts the modern mentality. History, as a science, would not have assumed the astonishing importance it has today without this temporality. The *Völuspa,* the gem of the *Poetic Edda,* introduces history into its story of the mythic events of the world with the battle of the Aesir against the Vanir, but Ragnarök, which it describes in apocalyptic terms, is not viewed even for an instant as an ending. To the contrary, it is immediately followed by a universal regeneration that relaunches the destinies of a primordial couple eloquently named *Lif*—Life—and *Liffthrasir*—Undying or Greedy to Live.

This is the first point: Death—that absolute and definitive rupture, that glacial silence beyond call or echo, that irreparable void that our nihilism tends to make of it—does not exist. It is only a passage, a transmutation insofar as the essential remains—Life—are concerned.

230

If there is any theme that Christianity was able to exploit so admirably, it was definitely this one. But the idea, an Indo-European legacy, is not a new one, and the Germans had practiced it for a long time, as did so many other people reputed to be "barbarians." In fact, these people were evolving constantly in a dual world (for the sake of simplicity, let's say *spiritual* and *material,* but this dichotomy is meaningless). And this world was haunted, in the etymological sense of the word (it is not immaterial that this etymology is Germanic) by the dead transformed into spirits passed on to another state, living another life in permanent conjunction with "contemporary" humans and always capable of either giving them information or ceding to their imperious requests. This is something that Claude Lecouteux sees quite well in his cautious, poised, well-thought-out, and admirably documented way. There is neither life nor death. There are two modes of life. What we find convenient to call death, assuredly an inevitable necessity, begs for neither emotionally moving lamentation nor romantic revolt nor ontological despair—and least of all that relish for the absurd that we have finished by turning into a literary myth. The people of the Middle Ages had no fear of death: they dreaded the dead—some of the dead, in any case— and this is the entire aim of the book you have just finished reading.

The second point is perhaps even more original, and if I may say so more exemplary, even though it basically takes us back to the first point. The *Weltanschauung** that Claude Lecouteux defines so exactly, even in its deepest layers, lacks all knowledge of our idea of solitude— so much so that the worst penalty the many legal codes of that time [the Middle Ages] could envision was not death but expulsion from the group, the reduction to the state of "wolf" (*vargr*), the radical eviction. The Icelandic sagas are eloquent on the point that the individual could easily strive to assert the prerogatives of his powerful personality, even, sometimes, to the detriment of others, but he had no notion of himself outside of the community in which he lived. He lived in reference to

---

*[*Weltanschauung* is a comprehensive conception of the world from a specific point of view. —*Ed.*]

this community, and his notion of his identity was filtered through the way he looked at the community. Through a sure and innate science, he knew that no one could be great for himself alone. When he attained literary awareness, everything he wrote, whether skaldic poem or saga, would primarily be a celebration of this belonging to something greater, to his dependency upon it. But what is this thing that he belonged to and is dependent upon? It is the family, the clan. This essentially rural world living, by virtue of obvious geographical necessity, in widely scattered dwellings has always, it seems, consisted of small units joined by ties of blood. The town and even the village are recent apparitions. The center of all activity long remained the "farm" (*baer*), with its numerous buildings. It is inside it that the family (in the broad sense) sheltered; that a man was born, grew up, lived, and died. He was defined only in relationship to it, from the moment his father, by giving him a name that brought to mind that of his parents or some ancestor, ritually integrated him into the family until the day of the "funeral banquet" (*erfi*) that would legally and precisely establish his transition into the state of ancestor, while authorizing his decendants to maintain its continuity. If, in order to create a quasi-absolute criteria, it would be necessary to isolate one component of medieval society, it would undoubtedly be this notion of family (*attr*) that immemorially carries a certain quantity of destiny ratified by memory—that is, a part of the success, prosperity, or even honor, of the ability to survive . . . everything conveyed by the archaic and alliterative phrase *máttr ok megin*. What makes the value of a human being, what gives basis to his sacred inviolability, *mannhelgr*, to which Claude Lecouteux brings all the requisite attention to bear, is just this: a human being's part, duly based on law, inside a familial community.

This family, let me repeat, is not limited to the living (I should write "currently living")—not by a long shot. One feature here should hold our attention: Claude Lecouteux is a great specialist in monsters and other supernatural creatures that inhabit the ancient and medieval world. And if we stick to the Germanic world, it is worth noting that all of these entities can pass for the spirits of the dead: the giants, who are the original dead, those who presided over the formation of the world (which in truth is made from their substance) and have retained the knowledge of the origins, *in illo tempore* as Mircea Eliade liked to say; the dwarves whose very name (*dvärgr, Zwerg,* meaning "twisted ones") is fairly reminiscent of cadaverous postures and that represent, in accordance with the *homo-humus* valence, the fertile dead, both from a flatly realist point of view and by virtue of the intellectual or spiritual inspiration conferred upon them by the texts; the *landvaettr,* Scandinavian version of the genius loci, or the tutelary dead of a particular setting; the alfes who, although somewhat impure, could perhaps be the tolerably easternized faces that assume, to the exclusion of others, the dimension of the mind of the dead; and the trolls who correspond best to our current representations and would be the dead monsters, for various reasons. Claude Lecouteux elucidates them all with splendid mastery. But before getting there, what a universe beyond the grave, what a literally haunted world!

The point is that the notion of *ancestor* exists here in every form. It is for this very reason that the tomb had all the aspects of an actual home—it was provided with all the necessities, all the possible pleasures, that the living enjoy. And by virtue of the fact that this tomb (*haugr, hörgr:* mound) was placed within the borders of the farm, there was no reason to separate the dead from the familial community. They remained an integral part of it and never left. Symbiosis is guaranteed. We shall see that more must be said: the osmosis is permanent. One of the major difficulties Christianity encountered in Germany was its wish to "exile" the dead to a cemetery around the church. One of the most alarming symptoms of the complete loss of the sacred meaning of life displayed by our empty era is that the dead have been relegated, anonymously or almost anonymously, simply anywhere in our sprawling urban areas.

This brings us to the central notion that serves as the subject of the fascinating study you have just read: the idea of the ghost or revenant.

Let's say for the moment that just as the living's sole purpose is to perpetuate the long chain of ancestors, the true destiny of a dead person is to become an ancestor—to reincarnate and resurrect, or, in any case, to continue living among his people or to come back to them. He is most definitely dead, yet the dead person leads another kind of life that is not at all incompatible with our own. And he does so in two ways that are so easy to confuse that only modern thought has been able to isolate them, for the language has only one word for designating this second state (secondary state?): *draugr*, revenant, ghost.

I do not know—and good academic that he is, Claude Lecouteux takes pains to avoid coming to definite conclusions—if it is necessary to introduce at any price the so-called two-cultures theory that is presumed by some to have been a source of conflict during the Middle Ages. One culture would have been material and based on pre-Indo-European notions of corporeal realities. It would have made the revenant a *lebende Leiche,* a living corpse. The other culture, more recent and visibly Indo-European, was more spiritual and oriented toward the notion of "soul." This opposition could even have been one that pitted a sedentary, agrarian mentality against one that was pastoral and nomadic—distinctions whose reflections are found in tests such as the *Saga of Egil; Son of Grímr the Bald,* with its two personality types; or in a mythology that envisions its pantheons in adversarial pairings (Odin-Loki, Thor-Tyr, and so on). This opposition does not prevent the fact that the draugr is represented by two very different appearances, which are reflected by the very title (*Ghosts and Revenants*) chosen by Claude Lecouteux [for the French edition].

I do not know if it is necessary to search so far afield for the reason behind this dualism, which is incontestable. Excellent pages concerning the soul as the ancient Germans understood it provide us with extremely interesting reading. This study calls for one additional clarification. Of the three words that strive to define this notion—*hugr, hamr,* and *fylgja—hugr* seems clearly to connote a more spiritual definition. *Hamr* and *fylgja* designate in flat realism the placental membranes that mold the shape (*hamr*) or accompany (verb *fylgja*) the ejection of the newborn. This would explain the double hold that would next be at work in the idea of soul. But, getting back to the definition of the soul, there is no disparity. *Hugr* reflects in a very orthodox way the spirit of the ancestors that timelessly "animates" a given family. *Hamr* and *fylgja* convey the same representation, but strictly invisceral. In one case like the other there is—forgive me for this neologism—necrophany.

And the draugr, phantom (phantasma), or revenant is always necrophany. Let me repeat: The dead person is not dead. He leads another mode of life that conjoins with our own in two different ways, which impartially go back to the fundamental worship of the ancestors, the veritable *nucleus* of these mentalities.

If he chooses, so to speak, the spiritual path, he will manifest—through dreams, apparitions, and reincarnations—all phenomena that this work analyzes extensively. This would be, let's say, the Odinic aspect of the matter. Odin is not so much the god of the dead—he never officially bears this title—as he is lord of the draugr—*draugadróttin*. These are the ones he leads in the Wild Hunt so dear to Norwegian folklore, he is the great psychopomp of this religion. Nothing even forbids viewing the Valkyries, who are certainly not at all what a Wagnerian pictures, or the *einherjar*, those elite warriors with which Odin-Wotan populates his Valhöll-Walhalla with Ragnarök in mind. These elite are a select class of draugr who are specialized in some way in the duties of service. In truth, the draugr-ghost does not stand out so much to the modern reader as something strikingly original because of its relative conformity to what we are accustomed to, except on the level of the motifs that compel the draugr-ghost to intervene, a subject we will revisit.

On the other hand, the draugr-revenant does threaten to teach us something new, and if anyone needs an inspirational reason to read Claude Lecouteux's rich work, it would be this one. The dead-though-never-dead man is able to intervene physically in the world of the living. He fights like a man—indeed, he sleeps, eats, and leaves behind an easily identifiable trail even when he is carrying his head in his arms, like

Klaufi of *Svarfdaela Saga*. In the saga that bears his name, Grettir, the Hercules of Iceland, spends an entire night besting the draugr Glam and will remain marked by that dreadful battle for the rest of his life. Even though the draugr can be impaled, decapitated, and, if need be, burned, he still may be able to find a way back, as in the case of one revenant whose ashes were reincarnated in a hot-tempered bull. This is the real revenant that inspires fear—not out of fear of contamination or lamentation of this individual's death. What L. V. Thomas says in *Le Cadavre* (Paris: Payot, 1980)—"a cadaver is a presence that manifests an absence"—does not apply here. But the revenant inspires fear because the hauntings, *reimleikar,* always mean there is a breech in the very principle for which the familial community is the seal—which is to say, a breech in the law.

This is the third point that I wish to touch upon here. It is true that the draugr is a dead individual who is discontented with his lot—but why? The quick answer: because he died a bad death, which is to say one not in conformance with ancestral and clan law. There has been a deviation of form either in his death or in the way the survivors behave toward him or toward what has always been the law of the family. In short, his sacred immunity, his mannhelgr, evoked earlier, has been slighted in some manner. This is an intolerable stain; he cannot assume properly the new state of life he has just entered. Let me underscore this point: The mannhelgr is founded on the certitude that the individual does not exist without the familial community, which is sacred if the community obeys the practices of worship. Whoever is at peace in this community is sacred because it is the gods, represented first and foremost by the head of the family, who protect and guarantee this peace. If, for one reason or another, this peace is broken, as phrased so well by the old Swedish law ("If a man is struck and the peace he carries within is broken . . ."), he is no longer *fridheilagr*—he is no longer sacred because his peace has been disrupted. He no longer enjoys the protection of the law; he has sinned or someone has caused him to lose his inviolability. And thus there will be no rest for him until he has restored and recovered this peace, taking note however that this peace applies as much to him as to any of his descendants.

He then returns and harasses the living so that the law promoted by his ancestors is respected and so that the order for which the gods serve as guarantors can be reestablished. Speaking on this point is the finely crafted myth that tells us why and how the god Tyr (which simply means "god") consents to place his right hand inside the jaw of the wolf Fenris to maintain the order of the world. It is also through law that the survivors strive to dispel the threat. It is the curious practice (curious only in appearance—in fact, it is rigorously logical) of *duradómr* ("door court," tribunal of the dead) in which the dead individual—in this case, always a criminal that a man has executed—is judged in order to convince him that he deserves his fate . . . that his death was the logical result of his actions. In short, the judging convinces the revenant that he made himself *úheilagr* (desanctified) and is legally condemned to accept his fate. The *Saga of Snorri the Godi* (*Eyrbyggja Saga,* chapter 55) is perfectly clear on this point. In other cases, when the draugr who was a wicked individual in life, as often proved to be the case in reality, continues to abuse physically or harass people after his passage to the otherworld, he will have to be overcome by duly listed and codified means. Finally, in the case where his legal basis to reappear is intact because the familial community has not observed the law of the clan, his interventions will come to an end only when the legally reprehensible cause of the discord has disappeared. We can never ascribe too much import to the extent to which a society manages to establish an ideal of order founded on peace and actively nurtured by the members of a community that is first and foremost familial. The draugr, ghost, or revenant is either a troublemaker or is an indignant witness and righter of disorder.

These are a few of the thoughts that were inspired by my reading of Claude Lecouteux's splendid book that skillfully combines his vast erudition with an extremely pertinent consideration of the very essence of his subject matter. I will not linger over the tonic and distinctly

metaphysical aspect of his sound work. It would be appropriate though
if our era that is in complete disarray, especially when it comes to this
essential theme, would relearn from the Middle Ages a certitude—and
more precisely, a spirit—that it has lost. In the final analysis, ghosts and
revenants are only a literary affabulation of a faith in life that makes
sport of our tiny, derisory twentieth-century fears. (And this is the
implicit lesson that Claude Lecouteux teaches us, however discreetly
because he prefers to let the evidence burst out of the texts.)

Two runic inscriptions found in Denmark, each a thousand years
old, sum up these thoughts. On them we read: "Enjoy your tomb
(*kuml*) well" (D.R. 239) and "Enjoy your tomb (*thormódr*) fully" (D.R.
211). In both we can hear the verb *njóta* (to enjoy) and the noun *kuml*.
Enjoy connotes "be at peace because it was in the order of things that
you left us, or because your descendants managed to maintain the peace
and order that were your family's honor" and also "do not come back,
for this would be a sign that some flaw has come to alter yours and our
inviolability." A grave is of course the physical place where we rest, but
it is also the "tomb"—speaking as the "tomb" of Edgar Allen Poe or
the "tomb" of Couperin—that has been raised in our memory by those
who have succeeded us, whether they have done so orally or in writing
or through their conduct and works. It has been raised by the survivors, who are just as alive as dead.

RÉGIS BOYER

Notes

Preface

1. Régis Boyer, *La Mort chez les anciens Scandinaves* [Death and the Ancient Scandinavians] (Paris: Les Belles Lettres, 1994).

2. Alexandre Micha, *Voyages dans l'au-delà d'après les texts médiévaux (IVe–XIIIe siècles)* [Journeys into the Beyond Based on Medieval Texts (4th to 8th Centuries)] (Paris: Klincksieck, 1992).

3. Jacqueline Amat, *Songes et visions. L'au-delà dans la literature latine tardive* [Dreams and Visions: The Beyond in Later Latin Literature] (Paris: Études agustiniennes, 2000), 175, 184, 266–80. See also Marie-Laure Le Bail, "Le mort sur la vif" [The Dead—Live], in *Hésiode 2* (1994): 157–77, especially page 165 on the medieval wills that often counseled gravediggers to carry the cadaver gently for fear of harming it.

4. Claude Lecouteux, "Zur anderen welt" [The Other World], in W. D. Lange, ed., *Diesseits und Jenseitsreisen im Mittelalter* [Voyages Here and in the Beyond in the Middle Ages] (Bonn/Berlin: Bouvier, 1992), 79–89.

5. Martin Illi, *Wohin die Toten gingen. Begräbnis und Kirchhof in der vorindustriellent Statdt* [Where the Dead Were: Funeral and Cemetary in the Preindustrial City] (Zurich: Chronos, 1992).

6. Himmel, Hölle, Fegefeuer, *Das Jenseits im Mittelalter* [The Beyond in the Middle Ages], ed. Peter Jezler (Zurich: Verlag Neue Zürcher Zeitung, 1994). See pages 123–32, 248, and 268, and illustrations, 120, 251, and 309.

7. Danièle Alexandre-Bidon, Cécile Treffort, *A réveiller les Morts. La Mort au quotidien dans l'Occident medieval* [Waking the Dead: The Dead in Everyday Life in the Medieval West] (Lyon: Presses Universitaires de Lyon, 1993), with a fine presentation by C. Treffort on funeral furnishing, 207–21.

8. Jean-Claude Schmitt, *Les Revenants: les vivants et les morts dans la société medieval* [Ghosts in the Middle Ages: The Living and the Dead in Medieval Society] (Paris: Gallimard, 1994). This publication has a nice collection of illustrations.

9. Henri Bresc, "Folklore et théologie: le revenant de Beaucaire chez Gervase de Tilbury, *Otia imperialia*" [Folklore and Theology: The Beaucaire Revenant in Gervaise of Tilbury's *Otia imperialia*], in *Razo* 8 (1988): 65–74.

10. Danièle Régnier-Bohler, "Béances de la terre et du temps: la dette et le pacte dans le motif de mort reconnaissant au Moyen Age" [Gaping of the Land and Time: Debt and Covenant on the Grounds of Death Recognized in the Middle Ages], in *L'Homme* 29 (1989): 161–78. See also Danièle Régnier-Bohler, "La largesse du mort et l'éthique chevaleresque: le motif de mort reconnaissant dans les fictions médiévales du XIIIᵉ au Xvᵉ siècle" [The Largess of Death and the Chivalrous Ethic: The Grounds of Death Recognized in Medieval Fiction from the 8th–15th Centuries], in Michel Zink, Xavier Ravier, eds., *Receptions et Identification du conte depuis le Moyen Age* [Receptions and Identification of Stories Since the Middle Ages] (Presses Universitaires du Mirail Toulouse, 1987), 51–63; Felix Karlinger, *Portugiesische Legenden, Studien und Texte* [Portuguese Legends: Studies and Text] (Salzburg: Bibl. Hispano-Luso 5, 1995), 83–88; and L. Röhrich, "Der dankbare Tote" [The Grateful Dead], in *Märchenspiegel* (1995): 1–3 (with illustrations).

11. Arnolt Buschmann, Claude Lecouteux, *Dialogue avec un revenant* [Dialogue with a Revenant] (Paris: Presses de l'Université Paris-Sorbonne, 1999).

12. Stuart J. Edelstein, *Biologie d'un mythe: reincarnation et génétique dans les tropiques africains* [Biology of a Myth: Reincarnation and Genetics in the African Tropics] (Paris: Sand and Tchou, 1988). See especially pages 89–116, which provide confirmation for everything brought out in my various studies.

13. André Levy and René Goldman, "L'Antre aux fantômes des collines de l'Ouest" [The Ghosts of Antre Hills of the West], in *Connaissance de l'Orient*, vol. 21 (Paris: Gallimard, 1987).

14. Anatole Le Braz, *La Legende de la Mort* [The Legend of the Dead] (Marseille: 1982).

15. G. Grober-Glück, "Muster räumlichen Verhaltens bei Vorstellungen des Volksglaubens" [Patterns of Space Behavior with Respect to Folk Belief Representations], in *Ethnologia Europaea* 8 (1975): 227–42; L. Petzold "Die Botschoft aus

der Anderswelt. Psychologie und Geschichte einer Wundererzählung" [Messages from the Other World: Psychology and Stories], in *Märchen, Mythos, Sage* (Marburg: Elwert, 1989), 101–44; Arnold Angenendt, *Heilige und Reliquien* [Saint and Relic], (Munich: C. H. Beck Verlag, 1994), 108–19.

16. Felix Karlinger, "Das Gastmahl der freundlichen Toten" [Feast of the Friendly Dead], in *Scritti in Memoria si Sebastiano Lo Nigro* (Catania: Universitá degli Studi, 1994) 143–48, to be compared to my study on the fairy meal (*Mediävistik* 1 [1988]: 87–99); Felix Karlinger, *Zauberschlaf und Entrückung. Zur Problematik des Motivs der Jenseitszeit in der Volkserzählung* [Magic Sleep and Rapture: On the Problems of the Subject Beyond the Time of Folktales], Vienna: Museum für Volkskunde, (1986) Raabser Märchen-Reihe vol, 7.

17. Charles Joisten, *Le Monde Alpin et Rhodanien* [The Alps and Rhone] (Isere: Centre Alpin et Rhodanien Ethnology,1988), 217.

18. Marcel van Den Berg, *De Volkssage in De Provincie Antwerpen in De 19de En 20ste Eeuw* [Folktales in the Antwerpe Province in the 19th and 20th Centuries], 3 volumes (Gand: Koninklijke Acadmie voor Nederlandse Taal- en Letterkunde, 1993), vol. 3, 1648–66; Van den Berg also examines animal ghosts (vol. 3, 1610–30). Unfortunately, this study totally fails to take diachrony into account.

19. I. Müller, L. Röhrich, "Der Tod und die Toten (*Deutscher Sagenkatalog*)" [Death and the Dead (German Catalog of Legends)] in *Deutsches Jahrbuch für Volkskunde* 13 (1967), 346–97. See mainly motifs C1, D4, G14, J27, K2, M1, M2, M4, N3, all of which are confirmed in my work. See also L. Röhrich, "Das Verzeichnis der deutschen Totensagen" [The Index of German Legends], in *Fabula* 9 (1967) 270–84.

20. See the Motifs Index by A. Aarne, Antti Aarne, and Stith Thompson, *The Types of the Folktale: A Classification and Bibliography* (Helsinki: The Finnish Academy of Science and Letters, 1961), 184. In these lists, we can find this material under the references E200–E599, to which we can add E700–E799 (external soul). For the *exempla* of Christian literature, we can refer to Frederic C. Tubach, *Index Exemplorum: A Handbook of Medieval Religious Tales* (Helsinki: Suomalainen Tiedeakatemia, 1969), FF Communications, 204, see references 354, 575, 1464a, 1465, 1643, 2452, 2944H, 3358, 4635, 4696, 5256.

21. I was able to reap a rich harvest in Jean Gobi, *Scala coeli,* ed., Marie-Anne Polo de Beaulieu (Paris: 1991), nos. 263, 441A, 632, 649, 736, 738, 740 (written between 1323 and 1330). For more on the Infernal Hunt, see nos. 95, 626, 627.

22. Claude Lecouteux, *Les Nains et les Elfes au Moyen Age* [Dwarves and Elves in the Middle Ages] (Paris: Ed. Imago, 1988).

23. Jobbé-Duval, *Les Morts malfaisants, Larves, Lemures, d'après le Droit et les Croyances populaires des Romans* [The Wicked Dead: Larvae and Lemurs Based on the Law and Folk Beliefs of the Romans] (Paris: Léon-Tenin, 1924). See *supra*, footnote 1.

24. Claude Lecouteux, *Démons et Génies du terroir au Moyen Age* [Demons and Earth Spirits in the Middle Ages] (Paris: Ed. Imago, 1995).

25. Claude Lecouteux, *Fées, Sorcières et Loups-Garous. Histoire du Double au Moyen Age* [Fairies, Witches and Werewolves: History of the Double in the Middle Ages] (Paris: Ed. Imago, 1988); Claude Lecouteux, *Witches, Fairies, and Werewolves: Shapeshifters and Astral Doubles in the Middle Ages*, trans. Clare Frock (Rochester, Vt.: Inner Traditions, 2003).

26. Claude Carozzi, *Le Voyage de l'âme dans l'au-delà d'aprè la literature latine (Ve-XIIIe siècle)* [The Soul's Voyage into the Beyond Based on the Latin Literature (5th through the 13th Centuries)] (Rome: Collection de l'École française de Rome, 1994), 189.

27. Ibid., 176–79, 214. The author was unfortunately unaware of the work of H. Lixfield on the subject he examines in these pages. See for example "Die Guntramsage (AT 1645A). Volkserzählungen vom Alter ego in Tiergestalt und ihre schamanistische Herkunft" [Folktales (AT1645A) from the Alter Ego in Animal Form and Shamanistic Descent], in *Fabula* 13 (1972) 60–107.

28. Claude Carozzi, *Le Voyage de l'âme dans l'au-delà d'aprè la literature latine (Ve-XIIIe siècle)* [The Soul's Voyage into the Beyond Based on the Latin Literature (5th through the 13th Centuries)], 105.

29. Phillipe Walter and I organized study days on this subject in November 1995 for which the information was published. A monograph on the Infernal Hunt as seen by the preacher Johann Geiler von Jaiserberg appeared in *Études germaniques*, no. 4 (1995).

30. See Claude Lecouteux and Philippe Marcq, *Les Esprits et les Morts: croyances médiévales* [Spirits and the Dead: Medieval Beliefs] (Paris: H. Champion, 1990), essay 13; Claude Lecouteux, *Mondes parallèles. L'Univers des croyances du Moyen Age* [Parallel Worlds: The Universe of Medieval Beliefs] (Paris: H. Champion, 1994), essay 14. A volume of my articles devoted to this subject is scheduled to come out in the beginning of 1996 with Presses Universitaires de Paris-Sorbonne. [This was published by H. Champion in 1994. —*Trans.*]

31. K. T. Nilssen, *Draugr, De norrøne forestillingene om fysiske gjengangere* (Oslo: Oslo University, 1993). My thanks to the author for sending it to me.

32. See K. Köster, "Alphabet-Inschriften auf Glocken" [Alphabet Inscriptions on Bells], in Rudolf Schültzeichel, *Studien zur deutschen Literatur des Mittelalters*

[Studies of German Literature in the Middle Ages] (Bonn: Bouvier, 1979), 371–422 (with an iconographic survey).

33. See Gerard Harrie Buijssen, *Durandus' Rationale in spätmittelhochdeutscher Übersetzung* [Durandus' Rationale in Late Middle German Translation], 4 vols. (Assen: van Gorcum and Prakke and Prakke, 1983), vol. 1, 274, *"Affer eczlich sprechen das si schollen anhaben hozzen mit preyzschuech en den fuezen, in soleicher maynnung daz si peraitt sein zu dem gericht."*

34. See A. Bratu, "Du pain pour les âmes du purgatoire. A propos de quelques images de la fin du Moyen age" [Bread for the Souls in Purgatory: Concerning Some Images from the End of the Middle Ages], in *Mabillon* Revue 65, no. 4 (1993): 177–213, page 213 here.

35. See Ludwig Pauli, *Keltischer Volksglaube. Amulette und Sonderbestattungen am Dürrnberg bei Hallein und im eisenzeitlichen Mitteleuropa* [Celtic Folk Belief: Amulets and Special Burials at Dürrnberg in Hallein and Iron Age Central Europe] (Munich: Der bayerischen Akademie der Wissenschaft, 1975), 63, 205 (with reproductions).

36. Cécile Treffort, "Le corps et son linceul" [The body and its shroud], in *A réveiller les Morts. La Mort au quotidien dans l'Occident medieval* [Waking the Dead: The Dead in Everyday Life in the Medieval West], 180–206, here 205.

37. Wolfgang Irtenkauf, *Fridolin, der heilige Mann zwischen Alpen und Rhein. Ein deutsches Fridolinsleben, gedruckt in Basel um 1480* [The Holy Man between the Alps and the Rhine: A German Fridolin Life, Printed in Basle in 1480] (Sigmaringen: Jan Thorbecke, 1985). This story has been abundantly illustrated in sculpture, painting, and stained glass, see P. Jezler, *Das Jenseits im Mittelalter* [The Beyond and the Middle Ages], 120, 249–51.

38. See the discussion of the problem by A. Vauchez, "La foi des laïcs vers 1200: mentalités religieuses féodales" [The Faith of the Layman 1200: Feudal Religious Mentality], in *Les Laïcs au Moyen Age* (Paris: Éditions du Cerf, 1987).

39. See F. Feydit, J. Obéli, "David de Sassoun, epopee en vers" [David de Sassoun,Epic in Verse], in *Connaissance de l'Orient*, vol. 32 (Paris: Gallimard, n.d.), 141.

40. T. Arnold, ed., *Symeonis monachi opera omnia*, vol. 1 (London: Rolls Series LXXV, 1882), 3–135, see especially 114–16.

41. Jane H. M. Taylor, *Le Roman de Perceforest, première partie* [The Book of Perceforest, part one] (Geneva: Librairie Droz, 1979), 303.

42. F. Dubost, *Aspects fantastiques de la littérature narrative médiévale, XIIe, XIIIe siècles). L'autre, l'ailleurs, l'autrefois* [Fantastical Aspects of Medieval Narrative Literature, 12th and 13th centuries: The Other, Elsewhere, and Other Time],

2 vols. (Paris: H. Champion, 1986), vol. 2, 821, note 9; 970, note 21. We can also find an excellent analysis of the word *fantosme* and its uses in vol. 1 of this series, 49–55.

43. Pierre-Yves Lambert, trans., *Les Quatre Branches du Mabinogi et autre contes gallois du Moyen Age* [The Four Branches of the Mabinogion and other Welsh tales from the Middle Ages] (Paris: Gallimard, 1986), 280.

44. See D'Arbois de Jubainville, *Le cycle mythologique irlandais et la Mythologie celtique* [The Irish Mythological Cycle and Celtic Mythology] (Paris: Ernest Thorin Libraire du College de France, 1884), vol. 4, 235, nos. 37, 51, 52.

Introduction

1. Edgar Morin, *L'Homme et la Mort* [Man and Death] (Paris: Seuil, 1970), 149–59.

2. Jacques Chiffoleau, *La Comptabilité de l'Au-delà: Les hommes, la mort et la religion dans la région d'Avignon à la fin du Moyen âge, vers 1320-vers 1480* [The Bookkeeping of the Beyond: Men, Death, and Religion in the Avignon Region at the End of the Middle Ages, from 1320 to 1480] (Rome: Diffusion de Boccard, 1980), 403–7; Alain Groix, *La Bretagne aux XVIᵉ-XVIIᵉ siècles: La Vie, la Mort, la Foi* [Britanny in the 16th and 17th Centuries: Life, Death, Faith] (Paris: Maloine, 1981) II, 1058; Jean Delumeau, *La Peur en Occident* [Fear of the West] (Paris: Fayard, 1978), 75–87.

3. Jacques Le Goff, *La Naissance du Purgatoire* [The Birth of Purgatory] (Paris: Gallimard, 1981), 241–46.

4. Jean-Claude Schmitt, *Les Revenants dans la société medieval* [Revenants in Medieval Society] (n.p.: Le Temps de la Réflexion, 1982), 285–306.

5. M. Vovelle, "La Religion populaire: Problèmes et Méthode" [Popular Religion: Problems and Method], in *Le Monde Alpin et Rhodanien* (1977): 28.

6. Régis Boyer, *La Saga des Chefs du Val au Lac (Vatnsdaela Saga)* [Saga of the Chiefs of Lake Valley] (Paris: Payot, 1980), 7. See also Régis Boyer, *Les Sagas Islandaises* [The Icelandic Sagas] (Paris: Payot, 1979); E. O. Sveinsson, *Les Sagas Islandaises* [The Icelandic Sagas], in *Archives des Lettres Modernes* 36 (1961), 3–64. For the literary and foreign influences: Régis Boyer, *La vie religieuse en Islande (1116-1264)* [The Religious Life of Iceland (1116–1264)] (Paris: Payot, 1979), 141–268.

7. J. Benediktsson, ed., *Lándnámabók*, 2 vols. (Reykjavik: University of Iceland, 1968, Íslenzk Fornrit I). French translations of the most important passages from Régis Boyer, trans., *Le Livre de la Colonisation de l'Islande* [The Book of Iceland Colonization] (Paris: Mouton, 1973), 10.

8. J. Strange, ed., *Dialogus miraculorum,* 2 vols. (Cologne: H. Lempertz and Co., 1851); K. Ruh et al., eds., *Die deutsche Literatur des Mittelalters* [German Literature of the Middle Ages] (Berlin: Walter de Gruyler, 1992), vol. 2, col. 1363–66.

9. See E. von Seimeyer and E. Sievers, *Die althochdeutschen Glossen* [The Old High German Commentary] 5 vols. (Berlin: 1879–1922); Taylor Starck and John C. Wells, *Althochdeutsches Glossenwörterbuch* [Old High German Dictionary] (Heidelberg: Carl Winter, 1972–90).

Chapter 1. The Fear of the Dead and the Dread of Revenants

1. Books worth reading on this include Jacques Fontaine, *La Littérature latine chrétienne* [Latin Christian Literature] (Paris: Que Sais-je?, 1970) and Maurice Hélin, *La Littérature latine au Moyen Âge* [Latin Literature of the Middle Ages] (Paris: Que Sais-je?, 1972).

2. For the complete development of this, see the important study by Emile Jobbé-Duval, *Les Morts malfaisants, Larves, Lemures, d'après le Droit et les Croyances populaires des Romans.*

3. Ovid, *Fastes,* II, 533.

4. See Cicero, *Tusculans,* I, 16, 36.

5. Jobbé-Duval, *Les Morts malfaisants, Larves, Lemures, d'après le Droit et les Croyances populaires des Romans,* 51. See also, in Book 6 of the *Aeneid,* how Virgil relates Aneas's meeting with the drowning victim Palinure: ". . . or else throw dirt on top of me," this latter asked, ". . . or else stretch out your hand to a victim of misfortune and carry me with you through these waves, so that at least in death I may rest in a peaceful home," M. Rat, trans., *Aeneid* (Paris: 1965, 139). Another example can be found in *Ode XXVIII* by Horace.

6. *Epistolae* VII, 25, 5.

7. Jobbé-Duval, *Les Morts malfaisants, Larves, Lemures, d'après le Droit et les Croyances populaires des Romans* 45–47.

8. Ibid., 54.

9. Cited from J. Delumeau, *La Peur en Occident* [Fear in the West] (Paris: Hachette, 1977), 85.

10. Césaire d'Arles, *Sermo XIII: In parochiis necessaries,* ed. CCL 103, 64–68; *Vita Eligii,* ed. MGH SS *rerum Merovingium* IV, 705–8, page 706 here; Martin de Braga, "De collectione rusticorum," ed. C. W. Barlow, in *Martini episcopi Bracarensis opera omnia* (New Haven: Yale University Press, 1950), chapter 16.

11. A common comment in texts from the seventh to twelfth centuries. See D. Harmening, *Superstitio* (Berlin: E. Schmidt Verlag, 1979), 273.

12. G. Jecker, ed., *Dicta du singulis libris canonicis* (Münster: 1927), chapter 22.

13. Ed. H. J. Schmitz in: *Die Bussbücher,* 2 vols. (Düsseldorf: 1898), vol. 1, 611–45.

14. See Claude Lecouteux, "Paganisme, Christianisme et Merveilleux" [Paganism, Christianity, and the Marvelous], in *Annales E.S.C.* (July/August 1982): 700–16, page 704 here.

15. On this point, see Jan de Vries, *Altgermanische Religionsgeschichte* [Germanic Religion], 2 vols. (Berlin: W. De Gruyter, 1956), vol. 1, 83; Régis Boyer, *La Religion des anciens Scandinaves* [The Religion of Ancient Scandinavians] (Paris: Payot, 1981), 47; Hilda R. Ellis, *The Road to Hel* (Cambridge: University Press, 1943), 7–29.

16. E. Metzger, "La Mutilation des Mort" [The Mutilation of the Dead], in *Mélanges Andler* (Paris: Librairie Istra, 1924), 257–67.

17. E. Morin, *L'Homme et la Mort* [Man and Death] (Paris: Seuile, 1970), 150.

18. Tacitus, *Germania* XII.

19. For more on these points, see Rudolf His, *Der Totenglaube in der Geschichte des germanischen Rechts* [The Faith of the Dead in the History of German Law] (Munster: Aschendorff, 1929).

20. These examples are taken from Metzger, *La Mutilation des Morts,* 267; and His, *Der Totenglaube in der Geschichte des germanischen Rechts,* 5.

21. Delumeau, *Le Peur en Occident,* 86.

22. In volume 3 of Jacob Grimm, *Deutsche Mythologie* [German Mythology], ed. E. H. Meyer (Darmstadt: 1965), Meyer provides a list of more than two thousand six hundred superstitions from which I extracted these examples. See nos. 439, 664, 721, and 699.

23. Ibid., nos. 36, 681, 1049.

24. Caesarius of Heisterbach, *Dialogos miraculorum* XI, 56.

25. K. Müllenhoff, *Sagen, Märchen, Lieder aus Schleswig-Holstein* [Legends, Folktales, and Songs of Schleswig-Holstein], (Kiel: 1845), no. 237.

Chapter 2. The Funeral Rites

1. See, for example, E.Ó. Sveinsson, ed., *Laxdaela Saga* (Reykjavik: University of Iceland, 1939, Íslensk Fornrit V), chapter 17. There exists a French translation of the text by F. Mossé (Paris: 1914). It is extremely rare, and a copy of it is owned by the Bibliothèque Nationale. [Several translations of this saga are available in English. —*Trans.*]

2. E. Ó. Sveinsson and M. Thordarson, eds., *Eyrbyggja Saga* (Reykjavik: University

of Iceland, 1939, Íslensk Fornrit IV), chapter 54. Translated into French and edited by Régis Boyer as *La Saga de Snorri le Godi* [The Saga of Snorri Godi], (Paris: Aubier Montaine, 1979, Bibliothèque de Philologie Germanique), 24. [The source for the English translation of this citation is Hermann Pálsson and Paul Edwards, trans., *Eyrbyggja Saga* (London: Penguin Books, 1972), 37. —*Trans.*]

3. Ibid., chapters 11, 38.

4. Ibid., chapters 33, 92.

5. Ibid., 93.

6. S. Nordal, ed., *Egills Saga Skallagrimssonar* (Reykjavik: University of Iceland, 1939, Íslensk Fornrit II). [The source for the English translation of this citation is Hermann Pálsson and Paul Edwards, trans., *Egils Saga* (London: Penguin Books, 1977). —*Trans.*]

7. F. Jónsson, ed., *Gisli Saga Surssonar* (Halle: Altnordische Sagabibliothek, 1903), 10. [The source for the English translation of this citation is Martin Regal and Judy Quinn, trans., *Gisli Sursson's Saga and the People of the Eyri* (London: Penguin Books, 2003), 23. —*Trans.*]

8. *Dialogus miraculorum*, XII, 20. See later narrative, page 118.

9. Régis Boyer, *La Religion des anciens Scandinaves*, 13.

10. F. Jónsson, ed., *Edda Snorri Sturlusonar, Gylfaginning* (Copenhagen: 1931), chapter 51. The most important texts were translated by R. Boyer, see R. Boyer, *Les Religions de l'Europe du Nord* [The Religions of Northern Europe] (Paris: Payot, 1974). [The *Edda Snorri Sturlusonar*, has been translated into English by Jesse Byock as *The Prose Edda* (London: Penguin Books, 2005), 72. —*Trans.*]

11. *Eyrbyggja Saga*, chapter 51, 133.

12. *Decretum I, interrogatio* 54, Cologne, 1548: "There are people who during the night sing diabolical poems in the presence of the deceased, eating and drinking as if celebrating his death." See also x, 34.

13. The editor for this collection of texts was B. Thorpe, *Ancient Laws and Institutes of England*, 2 volumes (London, 1840); Ecgbert, vol. 2, 154 and 258; Theodore, vol. 2, 32; Aelfric, vol. 2, 157 and 356.

14. *Edda Snorri Sturlusonar, Gylfaginning Völuspá*, strophe 52.

15. Jan de Vries, *Altgermanische Religionsgeschichte*, vol. 1, 190.

16. *Eyrbyggja Saga*, 24. [The source for the English translation of this citation is *Eyrbyggja Saga*, Hermann Pálsson and Paul Edwards, trans. (London: Penguin Books, 1972), 137. —*Trans.*]

17. Complete text in R. Boyer, *La Religion des anciens Scandinaves*, 176. On the

horse frequently found in tombs, see L. Malten, *Das Pferd im Totenglauben* [Horses in Death Art] (Berlin: Jahrbuch des Deutschen archäolog, Instituts 29, 1914), 179–256.

18. For more on boat tombs, see Hilda R. Ellis, *The Road to Hel*, 39–50.

19. F. Jónsson, ed., "Prologue of the Ynglinga Saga," in the *Heimskringla* (Copenhagen: STUAGNL, 1898–1901), vol. 1, *The Chronicle of the Kings of Norway.*

20. Ibid., endnote 5.

21. Hilda R. Ellis, *The Road to Hel*, 39.

22. Burchard, "Decretum" XIX, 5, 179, ed. H. J. Schmitz, in *Die Bussbücher*, 2 volumes (Düsseldorf: 1898), vol. 2, 448.

23. "Laws of the Gulathing," in Kayer and Munch, eds., *Norges gamle Love* [Norway's Old Love], 2 vols. (Christiana: 1846), chapter 23.

24. M. Gravier, ed. and trans., *La Saga d'Eric le Rouge* (*Eiríks Saga Rauöa*) [The Saga of Eric the Red]; *Le Récit des Groenlandais* (*Groenlendinga thattr*) [The Greenlander Account] (Paris: Aubier Montaine, 1955), Bibliothèque de Philologie Germanique 17. [The source for the English translation of this citation (and following quotes) was Kereva Kunz, trans., *The Vinland Saga* (London: Penguin Books, 2008), 38. —*Trans.*]

25. Berthold of Regensburg, *Berthold of Regensburg: Complete Edition of His German Sermons,* eds. F. Pfeiffer and J. Strobl, 2 vols. (Vienna: 1862–1880), vol. 1, Sermo VIII.

26. For more on this point, see P. Sartori, *Die Totenmünze,* Archive f. Religionswissenschaft 2 (1899): 202–25. On the rights of the dead, see H. Schreuer, *Das Recht der Toten,* Zeitschrift f. vergleichende Wissenschaft 33 (1916): 333–423; 34 (1917): 1–208.

27. *Egil's Saga,* chapter 58; *Laxdaela Saga,* chapter 26.

28. G. Jónsson, ed., *Grettis Saga Ásmundarsonar* (Reykjavik: University of Iceland, 1939, Íslensk Fornrit V), chapter 18. English translation: George Ainslie Hight, trans., *The Saga of Grettir the Strong* (London: J. M. Dent and Sons, 1913). Régis Boyer notes: "A tenacious belief (still in evidence in Denmark at the end of the last [nineteenth] century) held that flames burned through the night over hidden treasures and on the mounds where men had been buried with their riches" (*Les Religions de l'Europe du Nord,* 529).

29. *Landnámabók, Hausbók* 6. Translated into French by R. Boyer as *Le Livre de la Colonisation de l'Islande* 6, with an important commentary.

30. Petersens, ed., *Jómsviking Saga* (Copenhagen: 1832), chapter 12. Translated into French by R. Boyer as *La Saga des Vikings de Jomsburg* [Saga of the Vikings of Jomsburg] (Caen: Presses Universitaires de Caen, 1982).

31. *Indiculus 2, MG Capitularia reg. Franc. 2*, I, 222. *De sagrilegio super defunctos, id est dadsisas.* Other texts confirm this practice.

32. *Epistolae* 23, 291.

33. *Sacrificia mortuorum defuncta corpora apud sepulchra illorum,* says a sermon interpolated into the *Vita Eligii,* 705–8), but the sixth sermon of the *Pseudo Boniface* (*De capitalibus peccatis et praecipuis Dei*) adds "or" (*vel*): . . . *defuncta corpora vel super sepulchra* (ed. Migne, *Pat. Lat.* 89, col. 855). In fact, clerics had a tendency to confuse the ceremonies performed at the home of the deceased, those made at the tomb, and posterior oblations.

34. *Eyrbyggja Saga,* chapter 54, 137–38.

Chapter 3. The Church, Ghosts, and Revenants

1. G. H. Waszink, ed., *De anima* (Paris/Amsterdam: 1934), chapters 51 to 57.

2. Jacques Le Goff, *La Naissance de Purgatoire.*

3. R. Howlett, ed., *Continuatio chronici Willelmi de Novoburgo,* in *Rerum Britannicarum Medii Aevi Scriptores* (London: 1885), 409–583, page 572 here.

4. *De anima,* 51, 6–8.

5. Ibid.

6. Ibid., 57, 10.

7. St. Augustine, "On the Care of the Dead," ed. CSEL, 51, 621–60, in Jacques Le Goff, *La Naissance de Purgatoire,* 111.

8. Ibid.

9. Ibid., 244.

10. Ibid.

11. Gregory the Great, *Dialogues,* ed. V. Thalhofer, Kempten (n.p.: 1873). See the fourth book in particular.

12. Jacque Le Goff, *La Naissance de Purgatoire,* 126.

13. Ibid., 126.

14. Ibid., 170–73, and O. G. Oexle, *Die Gegenwart der Toten,* in *Death in the Middle Ages,* 25.

15. Jacque Le Goff, *La Naissance de Purgatoire,* 162, and Jacobus de Voragine, *The Golden Legend,* chapter 163.

16. *Liber de spiritu et anima,* [Free the Spirit and Soul], ed. Migne, *Pat. Lat.* 140, col. 779–882, col. 799 here.

17. *De Miraculis* [The Miracle], ed. Migne, *Pat. Lat.* 189, col. 851–954.

18. O. G. Oexle, "Die Gegenwart der Toten" [The Dead in the Present], in H. Braet

and W. Verbeke, eds., *Death in the Middle Ages* (Louvain: Mediavalia Lovaniensa, 1977), 1/ix.

19. T. Graesse, ed., *Legenda aurea* [The Golden Legend] (Breslau: 1890), chapter 163 (*De commemoratione mortuorum*), 728.

20. *Rationale divinorum officiorum* VII (Madrid: 1775), 38.

21. For more on changelings, see G. Piachewsky, *Der Wechselbalg. Ein Beitrag zum Aberglauben der nordeuropäischen Völker* [The Changling: A Collection of Superstitions of Northern European People] (Breslay: 1935); J. C. Schmitt, *Le Sant Lévrier* [The Holy Greyhound] (Paris: Flammarion, 1979), 109–18.

22. *Bonum universale de apibus,* chapter LVII, no. 20–21, Douai, 1627.

23. Ed. M. R. James, *De nugis curialum* (Oxford: 1914), II, 13, page 78; IV, 8, page 173.

24. See H. Achterberg, *Interpretatio christiana. Verkleidete Glaubensgestalten der Germanen auf deutschen Boden* [Christian Interpretation: Faith-Disguised Forms of the Germans on German Soil] (Leipzig: 1930), Form und Geist 19.

Chapter 4. The False Revenants

1. E. O. Sveinsson, ed., *Vatnsdoela Saga* (Reykjavik: University of Iceland, 1939, Íslensk Fornrit VIII), chap. 41. Translated into French by Régis Boyer as *La Saga des Chefs du Val au Lac* (Paris: Payout, 1980), 115.

2. *The Vinland Saga,* 37.3, chapter 6, 136, chapter 13.

4. *Eyrbyggja Saga,* chapter 33, 93.

5. F, Jónsson, ed., *Flóamanna Saga* [Saga of Floi's Folk] (Copenhagen: 1932), chapter 13.

6. *Hallfredar Saga vandraedaskalds,* chapter 7.

7. See F. Jónsson, ed., *Skjaldedigtning,* 2 vols. (Copenhagen: 1912–1915), vol. 1, 339 (*Anonymous* 6). Analyzing the relations between beyond the tomb and the otherworld, E. Le Roy Ladurie writes in *Montaillou, village Occitan* (Paris: Gallimard, 1982), 595: "The dead are cold. They shall get warm at night in houses where a large reserve of logs are stored. . . . The dead do not eat, but they do drink wine."

8. *Eyrbyggja Saga* [no page number].

9. *Edda, Helgakvida Hundingsbana* II, 153. Translated into French by R. Boyer as *Les Religions de l'Europe du Nord,* 232. [Translated into English by Carolyne Larrington from *The Poetic Edda* (Oxford: Oxford University Press, 1996).]

10. *Dialogus miraculorum* XI, 36.

11. Wace, *The Ascending Chronicle of the Dukes of Normandy,* 3 vols., ed. A. J. Holden (Paris: 1970–1973, SATF), part 1, verses 250–56.

12. Ibid., part 3, verses 275–336. Holden incorrectly titles this episode *The Devil in the Church,* unintentionally echoing the clerical interpretation.

13. L. Brandin, ed., *Foulke Fitz Warin* (Paris: 1930, CFMA), 4.

14. S. Nordal and G. Jónsson, eds., *Viga-Styrs ok Heidarviga Saga* [The Saga of Styr the Murderer or the Battle on the Moors] (Reykjavik: University of Iceland, 1938, Íslensk Fornrit III), chapter 7.

15. *Eyrbyggja Saga,* chapter 51, 133–34.

16. R. Boyer, *La Saga de Snorri le Godi,* 215.

17. *The Saga of Grettir the Strong,* chapter 18.

18. *Landnámabók, Sturlubók,* 6.

19. S. Haft, ed., *Hardar Saga Grímkelssonar* (Lund: 1960), chapter 15.

20. *Hromundar Saga Greipssonar,* cited by H. J. Klare, 14.

21. *Landnámabók, Sturlubók,* 52.

22. *Jóns Saga Helga* I, 49, cited from R. Boyer, *La vie religieuse en Islande,* 391.

23. J. Grimm, *Deutsche Mythologie,* 199 (no. 176).

24. *Divinae institutions,* ed. Migne, *Pat. Lat.,* 6, col. 336. See also *Epitome divinarum institutionarum,* chapter 23, ed. CSEL 19, 673–761.

25. Hincmar, *De divortio Lotharri et Tetbergae reginae,* interrogatio 15, ed. Migne, *Pat. Lat.* 125, col. 718; Ivo, *Decretum pars* XI, c 66, ed. Migne, *Pat. Lat.* 161, col. 760, and *Panormia* VIII, 65, ibid., col. 1318; Hugues, *Didascalion* c. 15, ed. C. H. Buttimer, *Studies in Medieval and Renaissance Latin* 10, 1939; John of Salisbury, *Polycraticus* I, 12, ed. Webb, Oxford, 1909; Gratien, "Decretum," pars 11, causa 26, quaaestio 2, can 7, eds. Richter and Friedberg in *Corpus iuris canonicus* I–II, Leipzig, 1879, 1023.

26. *Etymologies* VIII, 9, 11, ed. Migne, *Pat. Lat.* 82. That strange things were done with the dead is undeniable: the Frisian laws of Hausing Canton prescribed a fine of seven times seventy-two schillings to whoever ties a corpse to a ladder and stands it against the wall of a church, see W. J. Buma and W. Ebel, *Das Hunsingoer* (Göttingen: 1969, Altfriesische Rechtsquellen 4), 89.

27. *De magicis artibus,* ed. Migne, *Pat. Lat.* 110, col. 1098.

28. *Historia scholastica, Lieber Deuteronomi,* chapter 8, ed. Migne, *Pat. Lat.* 198, col. 1253.

29. I am using the remarkable work R. Jente, *Die mythologischen Ausdrücke im atlenglischen Wortschatz* (Heidelberg: Carl Winter, 1921, Anglistische Forschungen 56), 1–344, page 263 here.

30. See Claude Lecouteux, "Les Revenants germaniques" [The German Revenants], in *Etudes Germaniques* 39 (1984); H. Wesche, *Der althochdeutsche Wortschatz im Gebiete des Zaubers und der Weissagung Halle* (Saale: Max Niemeyer, 1940).

31. *The Poetic Edda, Groagaldr.*

32. J. Mansi, ed., *Concil. Iuliobonense* c. 34, in *Sacrorum conciliorum nova et amplissima collectio,* 31 vols. (Florence/Venice: 1757–1798), vol. 20, 563.

33. See "Aeldre Gulathing Lov" [Aeldre Gulathing's Law], in Kayer and Munchs, eds., *Norges gamle Love,* vol. 1, 19, chapter 32, and "Gulathing Christenret," [Gulathing's Christian Law] in Kayer and Munchs, eds., *Norges gamle Love,* vol. 2, 308.

34. *Heimskringla, Ynglinga Saga,* chapter 7.

35. *The Poetic Edda, Baldrs draumar* [The Dreams of Balder], 243.

36. *Hervarakvida,* in trans. R. Boyer, *Les Religions de l'Europe du Nord,* strophe 11, 527–34.

37. For more on this figure, see Georges Dumézil, *Du Mythe au Roman* (Paris: PUF, 1970), 21.

38. J. Olrik and H. Raeder, eds., *Gesta Danorum* I, vi, 4 (Copenhagen: 1931).

39. "Hervarakvida," in trans. R. Boyer, *Les Religions de l'Europe du Nord,* strophe 15.

40. Ö. Halldorsson, ed., *Faereyinga Saga* (Reykjavik: 1978), chap. 41. Translated into French by J. Renaud (Paris: 1983), 83.

41. J. Árnason, *Íslenzkar Thjodsógur og Aefintyri,* 2 vols., vol. 1, 317, in A. Ohlmarks, *Totenerweckungen in den Eddaliedern,* Archive f. Nordissk Filologi 52 (1936): 264–97, page 297 here.

Chapter 5. The True Revenants

1. Artemidorus, *Onirocriticon* I, 3 and II, 25, trans. A. Festugière (Paris: 1975).

2. Macrobius, *Commentarii in Sommium Scipionis* I, 3, 4–9, ed. F. Eyssenhardt (Leipsig: 1893). See also Jacques Le Goff, "Les Rêves dans la Culture et la Psychologie collective de l'Occident médiéval" [The Dreams in the Culture and the Collective Psychology in the Medieval West], in *Pour un autre Moyen Age* [For Another Middle Age] (Paris: Gallimard, 1977), 299–306.

3. Gregory, *Dialogi* IV, 48, ed. Migne, *Pat. Lat.* 77, col. 499. See also Claude Lecouteux, "Paganisme, Christianisme et Merveilleux," *Annales E.S.C.* (July–August 1982): 700–716.

4. *Admonitio* c. 65, ed. M. G. Leges 2 I 58, *Capitulare c.* 40, ed. M. G. Leges 2 I 104.

5. *Capitulare* c. 8, ed. Hartzheim I, 36.

6. *Admontio,* ed. M. G. Leges 3 II 669.

7. *Heimskringla, Saga of Halfdan the Black,* chapter 7.

8. *La Saga des Vikings de Jomsburg,* 18 (chapter 2).

9. *Saga of Gisli Sursson* (Paris: Gallimard, 1987), chapter 14.

10. E. Tonnela, trans., *Song of the Nibelungen* (Paris: Bibl. De Philologie Germanique 6, 1945), 92.

11. S. Sigfússon, ed., *Ljóvetninga Saga* (Reykjavik: 1940, Íslenzk Fornrit X), chapter 21.

12. E. O. Sveinsson, ed., *Brennu-Njáls Saga* (Reykjavik: 1940, Islenzk Fornrit XII), chapter 62. Translated into French by R. Boyer as *La Saga de Brennu-Njal* (Paris: Presse de l'Université-Sorbonne, 1976), 125. [Translated into English by Sir George W. DaSent as *Njal's Saga* (London: E. P. Dutton, 1861).]

13. See also *Flóamanna Saga* [*Saga of Floi's Folk*], chapters 20–21, in which the god Thor appears to Thorgils two times in a dream, and B. K. Thórolfsson and G. Jónsson, eds., *Fóstbreodra Saga* [*Saga of the Sworn Brothers*] (Reykjavik: University of Iceland, 1943, Íslenzk Fornrit VI), chapter 26 in which the god Odin appears to Grim and asks him to come to the aid of his skald Thormod.

14. Anne Heinrichs et al., eds., *Olafs Saga hins Helga* (Heidelberg: 1982), with German translation.

15. Ibid., chapter 96.

16. Ibid., chapter 98.

17. See Claude Lecouteux, "Introduction à l'Étude du Merveilleux médiéval" [Introduction to the Study of Medieval Wonders], in *Etudes Germaniques* 36 (1981): 273–90.

18. Heinrichs, *Olafs Saga hins Helga,* chapter 101.

19. *Landnámabók, Hausbók* 21; Boyer translation, 13.

20. *Laxdaela Saga,* chapter 76.

21. *Gunnlauga Saga,* chapter 13; W. Baetke, ed., *Hoensa-Thóris Saga* (Halle: 1953), Altnort, Textbibl. 2, chapter 10.

22. *Landnámabók, Hausbók* 60; Boyer translation, 20.

23. H. J. Klare, *Hromundar Saga Greipssonar,* 7.

24. Ibid., 7.

25. Ibid.

26. G. Jónsson, ed., *Islendinga Sögur* [Book of the Flat Island] IV (Reykjavik, 1946), 383–87, page 383 here.

27. B. Sigfússon, ed., *Reyksdaela Saga* [Saga of the Dwellers in the Valley of Smoke] (Reykjavik: University of Iceland, 1940, Íslensk Fornrit X), chapter 19.

28. *Faereyinga Saga,* chapter 56.

29. Jacobus de Voragine, *The Golden Legend,* 2 vols., trans. J. B. M. Rose (Paris: 1967), vol. 2, 328.

30. *Saga of the People of Floi,* chapter 22.

31. Ibid., chapter 13.

32. Jobbé-Duval, *Les Morts malfaisants, Larves, Lemures, d'après le Droit et les Croyances populaires des Romans,* 202.

33. *Laxdaela Saga,* chapters 17 and 24.

34. K. von Amira, *Die germanischen Todesstrafen. Untersuchung zur Rechtsund Religionsgeschichte,* Abhandl. D. Bayer. Akademie d. Wissenschaften, Phil.–hist. Classe, XXXI. 3 (1922): 1–415, here pages 121, 130, and 141.

35. *Heimskringla, Saga of Olaf Tyggvason,* chapter 63.

36. B. Thórólfsson, ed., *Book of Settlements* (Reykjavik: University of Iceland, 1940, Íslensk Fornrit VI), chapters 2–3.

37. *De nugis curialium* IV, 12. For more on this point, see Claude Lecouteux, "Das bauchlose Ungeheur," *Euphorion* 71 (1977): 272–76. In C. A. Thomasset, ed., *Dialogue de Placides et Timeo* (Geneva/Paris: 1980), TLF 289, 184, § 331 I (originally written in the thirteenth century), we see a fragment of the legend. This story enjoyed great success at the end of the Middle Ages because it was inserted in C.W.R.D. Moseley, ed. and trans., *The Travels of Sir John Mandeville* (London: Penguin Books, 1983), vol. 2.

38. *Eyrbyggja Saga.* Here I am using the Sveinsson edition and the Boyer translation conjointly.

39. Walter Map, *De nugis curialium* I, II. For more on this legend, see Jean-Claude Schmitt, "Temps, Folklore et Politique au XIIᵉ siècle. A propos de deux récits de Walter Map," [By the Way of Two Stories by Walter Map] in *Le Temps chrétien de la Fin de l'Antiquité au Moyen Age (IIIᵉ–XIIIᵉ siècles)* [The Christian Times at the End of Antiquity in the Middle Ages (3rd to 8th Centuries] (Paris: CNRS, 1984, Colloques Internationaux du C.R.N.S. 604), 489–515.

40. V. Ásmundarson, ed., *Svarfdaela Saga,* (Kostnadarmadur: Sigurdur Kristjansson, 1898), chapters 22–23.

41. Ibid., "The Soul."

42. *Grettir's Saga.* Here I am using the F. Mossé translation and the Boyer edition conjointly.

43. For more on this point, see R. Boyer, *La Saga de Snorri,* 201 and 216. We can note that the dead are treated like the living here, and death does not prevent them from being subject to the laws.

44. *Edda Snorra, Gylfaginning,* chapter 48.

45. See Claude Lecouteux, "Zwerge und Verwandte" [Dwarfs and Relatives], *Euphorion* 75 (1981) 366–78.

46. *Sy thaet ylfa the him sie, this him maeg to bote,* O. Cockayne, *Leechdoms, Wordcunning and Starcraft of Early England,* 3 vols. (London: Public Record Office, 1864–1866), vol. 2, 290. See also the charm, *Contre un Nain (Wid Dweorh)*

[Against a Dwarf], in which the dwarf represents a convulsion, and H. Stuart, "The Anglo-Saxon Elf," *Studia Neophilologica* 48 (1976): 313–20, page 315 here, from which I pulled the following phrase: "Then he (an asthmatic) shuddered as if a dwarf was clutching him tightly" (*hwile he rith a swylce he on dueorge sy*).

47. See J. Grimm, *Deutsche Mythologie,* vol. 1, 364.

48. See the graduate thesis by Laurence Chudacet, *Les Nains et les Morts dans la religion germanon-scandinave* [Dwarves and the Dead in Germano-Scandinavian Religion], Paris-Sorbonne, 1982.

49. See Claude Lecouteux, "Zwerge und Verwandte," 378.

50. *Laxdaela Saga,* chapter 18.

51. Georges Dumézil, *Le Festin d'Immortalité* [The Feast of Immortality] (Paris: P. Geuthner, 1924).

52. G. Neckel, *Sagen aus dem germanischen Altertum* [Speaking from Germanic Antiquity] (Darmstadt: Wissenschaftlich Buchgesellschaft, 1966), 66, 95.

53. M. R. Graves, ed., "Twelve Medieval Ghost Stories," in *English Historical Review* 37 (1922), 413–22. James published twelve tales but there are thirteen.

54. Ibid.

55. Gervase of Tilbury, *Otia imperialia* III, 62. Her is how Gervase depicts it: a horse-shaped spirit walking upon its back hooves; its appearance is the sign that heralds an imminent fire.

56. Graves, "Twelve Medieval Ghost Stories," 413–22.

57. Ibid.

58. During the nineteenth century, a revenant appeared in the form of a burning flame near Rothwisch (Schleswig-Holstein), see K. Müllenhoff, *Sagen, Märchen, und Lieder aus Schleswig-Holstein* (Kiel: 1845), no. 350. The flame is one of the traditional forms taken by revenants in rural beliefs. See T. Dömötör, *Volksglaube und Aberglaube des Ungarn* [Folk Belief and Superstition of Hungary] (Budapest: Corvina Kiado, 1982), 107.

59. Graves, "Twelve Medieval Ghost Stories," 413–22.

60. Ibid.

61. Tekla Dömötör, *Hungarian Folk Beliefs* (Bloomington: Indiana University Press, 1982.)

62. *Ekkehardi Urgausiensis Chronica,* ed. MG SS VI, 207–48.

63. J. Grimm, *Deutsche Sagen,* 284.

64. *Dialogus miraculorum* XII, 20.

65. Compare my stories to those of the anthology A. Boucher, trans., *Ghosts, Witchcraft and the Other World* (Reykjavik, 1978).

66. Aniela Jaffé, *Geistererscheinungen und Vorzeichen* [Ghost Apparitions and Omens] (Zurich/Stuttgart: Rascher Verlag, 1958), 104–28.

67. *Dialogus miraculorum* XII, 20,

68. Claude Lecouteux, "Hagazussa-Strigo-Hexe," in *Etudes Germaniques* 38 (1983): 161–78.

69. H. Gröchenig, *Reuner Relation und Vorauer Novelle,* facsimile ed. (Göppingen: 1981, Litterae 81).

70. Michel Beheim, "Von dem van Wirtenperg," eds. H. Gille and Ingeborg Spreiwald, in *Die Gedichte des M. B.* (Berlin: 1968, DTM 60), 366.

71. Franziska Heinzle, ed., *Der Württemberger* (Göppingen: 1974, Göppinger Arbeiten z. Germanistik 137).

72. *Dialogus miraculorum* XII, 18.

73. See the excellent synthesis by L. Röhrich, Dankbarer Toter in K. Ranke, *Enzyclopädie des Märchens* (Berlin/New York: 1980), vol. 3, col. 306–22.

74. F. H. von der Hagen, ed., "Rittertreue," in *Gesamtabenteur* (Stuttgart: 1850), vol. 1, 105–28.

Chapter 6. The Name of the Revenants

1. R. Hildebrandt, ed., *Summarium Heinrici,* 2 vols. (Berlin/New York: 1974–1982), *manie quidam monstra i.e., insanie.* See also G. Goetz, *Corpus glossarum* (Leipzig: 1896), vol. 6, 676 ("mania").

2. Cornelius Celsus, *De medicina III,* 18. See also Nonius Marcellus, *Compendiosa doctrina* I, 64, ed. Lindsay (1903).

3. Palladius, *De agricultura,* I, 35: *De remediis horti vel agri* 11. Another synonym: *monstra noxia.*

4. Here I am using Steinmeyer and Sievers, *Die althochdeutschen Glossen* (Berlin: Weidmann, 1975). For a more technical approach, I refer you to my study "Les Revenants germaniques," in *Etudes Germaniques* 39 (1984).

5. See Jean-Claude Schmitt, *Les Revenants dans la Société féodale,* 287.

6. See T. Wright, *Anglo-Saxon and Old English Vocabulary,* second ed., revised by R. P. Wülker, 2 vols. (London: Trubner, 1884), 466.8 and 494.36.

7. O. Cockayne, *Leechdoms, Wordcunning and Starcraft of Early England,* vol. 1, 374.

8. Ibid., vol. 1, 350. See also vol. 1, 360; vol. 2, 64 and 2888; and vol. 3, 204.

9. Horace, *Epistolae* II, 2.

10. *Summarium Henrici,* vol. II, 124, no. 72; 348, no. 28, *Goetz,* vol. vi, 635 ("lemures"). The incorporation of all these beings into demons obscured their proper nature. Fortunately, texts are available to confirm the information. In the

third century, Porphyrion writes: "They believe that night lemures are the wandering souls of men who died prematurely, thus are dangerous" (*Commentarii* XI, 2, 209).

11. Steinmeyer and Sievers, *Die althochdeutschen Glossen,* vol. 3, 320, 11; 412, 36.

12. Wright, *Anglo-Saxon and Old English Vocabulary,* 29, 8; 33, 30; 442, 30; Steinmeyer and Sievers, *Die althochdeutschen Glossen,* vol. 4, 178, 27.

13. *Germania,* 43.

14. E. G. Graff, *Althochdeutscher Sprachschaatz,* 6 vols., vol. 6, (Graz, 1954), 577.

15. See Du Cange, *Glossarium mediae et infimae aetatis* (Graz, 1954), 365 c ("umbra"); G. Durand, *Rationale divinorum officiorum* VII (Paris: 1672), 8.

16. *Edictum Rothari* c. 108, ed. MG Leges 1 IV.

17. Jan de Vries, *Altnördisches etmyologisches Wörterbuch* (Leyden: E. J. Brill, 1962), 134.

Chapter 7. Questions and Answers

1. Schröder, Halle, ed., *Halfdanar Saga Eysteinssonar* (Saale: Max Niemeyer, 1917), 122.

2. Cicero, *De divinatione* I, 27, 57; Titus-Levy III, 58, 11.

3. *Edda, Sigurdthakvida in Skamma* [Brief Song of Sigurd], strophe 44, 209.

4. See Jobbé-Duval, *Les Morts malfaisants, Larves, Lemures, d'après le Droit et les Croyances populaires des Romans,* 74.

5. See *Hamlet* I, 4, the words of Ghost: *So art thou to revenge, when thou shalt hear . . .*

6. Kristjansson, ed., *Viga-Glams Saga* (Reykjavik: University of Iceland, 1956, Íslensk Fornrit IX), chapter 19.

7. *Haraldskvedi,* strophe 6, in R. Boyer, *La Religion des anciens Scandinaves,* 172.

8. See for example C. Joisten and C. Abry, "Du 'Roi chasseran' au Réchéran scieur de Têtes: un avatar de la Chasse sauvage en Savoie" [An Avatar of the Wild Hunt in Savoy] in *Mélanges Ernest Schüle* (Berne: 1983), 286–328.

9. R. Boyer, trans., *Edda, Helgavida Hundingsbana* II, strophe 51, 156.

10. *Landámabók, Hauksbók* (Ingolf) and 73 (Thorolf).

11. *Vatnsdaela Saga,* chapters 10, 12, and 14 and *Landámabók, Hauksbók* 145. In the *Hauksbók* 164, Hreidar refuses to throw the posts of his high seat into the sea. He instead invokes Thor and leaves the decision in his hands.

12. *Landámabók, Sturlubók* 29.

13. Ibid., *Hauksbók* 120, 151, 161, and 162.

14. Ibid., 166, 198.

15. *Sturlubók* 93.
16. *Laxdaela Saga,* chapter 17; *Hoensa-Thoris Saga,* chapter 17.
17. See J. Brunner, *Geschichte der Grenzstadt Furth im Wold,* Furth I/W, 1932, 90.
18. "Thorsteins Thattr Shelks," in *Flateyarbók* (Christiana: G. Vigfússon and C. R. Unger, 1860), vol. 1.
19. "Thorsteins Thattr Baearmagnis," in *Fornmanna Sögur* (Copenhagen: 1825–1837), vol. 3, 197.
20. "Thattr Thorvalds," in *Vidfórla,* chapter 2.
21. "Óláf's Saga Tryggvasonar," in *Flateyarbók,* vol. 1, 421.
22. Heinrichs, *Óláf's Saga hins Helga,* chapter 67.
23. See R. Boyer, *La vie religieuse en Islande* (1116–1264) (Paris: Payot, 1979), 390.

Chapter 8. Revenants, Death, and the Beyond

1. As stated in *Fridthjofs Saga ins Fraekna,* in *Fornaldar Sögar* III (Reykjavik: 1959), chapter 3, 71–104), Ran owned a hall; according to Snorri Sturluson (*Skáldska-parmál,* chap. 31), she captured men who fell into the sea with her net.
2. *Edda Snorra, Gykfaginning,* chapter 49, in trans. R. Boyer, *Les Religions de l'Europe du Nord,* 445. [Translated into English by Jesse L. Brock as *The Prose Edda* (London: Penguin, 2005). —*Trans.*]
3. *Edda, Vafthrúdismál,* strophe 43, in trans. R. Boyer, *Les Religions de l'Europe du Nord,* 468.
4. Ibid., strophe 38, Boyer translation, 483. Nidhogg is a dragon who lives in the kingdom of the dead. He gnaws at the roots of Yggdrasil, the World Tree (see *Grímnismál,* strophe 32).
5. *Edda, Baldrs Draumar,* strophe 5, in trans. R. Boyer, *Les Religions de l'Europe du Nord,* 536.
6. *Edda Snorra, Gykfaginning,* chapter 48, in trans. R. Boyer, *Les Religions de l'Europe du Nord,* 445. [Translated into English by Jesse L. Brock as *The Prose Edda. —Trans.*]
7. *Edda, Grímnismál,* strophe 8.
8. Benediktsson, ed., *Landnámabók, Sturlubók* 85, in trans. R. Boyer, 25. See also *Sturlubók* 68, in which it is the same for Sel-Thorir, and 197, in which it is the same for Kraku-Hreider, who "chose to die in the Maelifell" (*Hann kaus at deyja í Maelifellm,* vol. 2, 233).
9. Trans. R. Boyer, *Edda,* 56.
10. For more on this point, see O. Huth, "Der Glastberg der Volksmärchens," *Symbolon* 2 (1955): 15–31.

11. A detailed study can be found in Claude Lecouteux, "Aspects mythiques de la Montagne au Moyen Age," in *Le Monde Alpin et Rhodanien* (1982): 43–54.

12. *Edda, Helgakvida Hundingsbana* II, 146–57, strophe 38, in trans. R. Boyer, *Les Religions de l'Europe du Nord*, 220–34.

13. *Moralia* VI, 15 ed. Migne, *Pat. Lat.* 75, col. 740 c: *Homo itaque, quia habet commune/esse cum lapidibus/vivere cum arboribus,/sentire cum animalibus/(. . .) recte nominee universitatis exprimitur.*

14. Text and translation, Claude Lecouteux, *Les monstres dans la litterature allemande du Moyen Age* [Monsters in the German Literature of the Middle Ages] (Göppingen: 1982), vol. 1, 19.

15. *Edda, Vafthrúdismál*, strophe 21, in trans. R. Boyer, *Les Religions de l'Europe du Nord*, 464.

16. I quote only a representative sample, see J. Grimm, *Deutsche Mythologie*, vol. 3 (appendix).

17. *Landnámabók, Sturlubók* 355, in trans. R. Boyer, *Le Livre de la Colonisation de l'Islande*, 90.

18. Ibid., 121.

19. Ibid.

20. *Thorsteins Thattr Uxafóts*, in *Flateyarbók*, vol. 1, 253, or in *Islendinga Sögur* X (Reykjavik, 1947), 341–70, chapter 6.

21. *Thorsteins Thattr Baearmagnis*, in *Fornmanna Sögur* 3, 181.

22. G. Jónsson, ed., *Bardar Saga Snaefellsáss*, in *Fornaldar Sögur* 3, chapter 20.

23. *Hromundar Saga Gripssonar*, in *Fornaldar Sögur* 3, chapter 3.

24. *Egils Saga einhanda ok Áamundar*, in *Fornaldar Sögur* 3, 323–65, chapter 6.

25. I must cite the testimonies collected on site by my friend Felix Karlinger. A glimpse of them is provided in F. Karlinger and E. Turczynski, *Rumänische Sagen und Sagen aus Rumänien* [Romanian Legends and Tales from Romania] (Berlin: 1982), 43–48.

26. Claude Lecouteux, "Hagazussa-Strigo-Hexe," 161–78.

27. See *Áns Saga Bogsveigis* [Saga of An the Bow Puller], in *Fornaldar Sögar* 2 (Reykjavik: 1954), chapter 6. Thorir appears *all blodugr, ok stud sverd í gegnum harn* (all bloody and the sword sticking out of him).

28. *Fridthjof's Saga*, chapter 11: *Haugr minn skal standa hjá drdinum. En skammt mun okkar thorsteins í millum verda, ok er vel, at vit köllumst á.*

29. *Laxdaela Saga*, chapter 33.

30. I am inventing nothing; all these elements are provided by the *Lay of the Lance* in *Burnt Njal's Saga*, chapter 137 and by the *Saga of the Vikings of Jomsberg*, chapter 7.

31. *Göngu-Hrolf's Saga,* in *Fornaldar Sögar* 3, chapter 16.

32. Ibid., chapter 32.

33. *Hromundar Saga,* chapter 4.

34. *Fridthjof's Saga,* chapter 3: *Tha maelti Fridthjof Nu er vist, at till Ránar skal fara, ok búumst vaskligo, ok skal hverr gull hafa á sér* (Fridthjof then says: "As we know we are going to Ran's home to stay, each of us should have gold on our persons").

35. A. Potthast, ed., *Liber de rebus memorabilioribus sive chronicon Heinrici de Hervordia* (Göttingen: 1859), 279. For the year 1348, Heinrich indicates the appearance of three men of fire (277). We can note the peculiar atmosphere that emanates from this text: Reyneke—and we see only his hand—becomes an individual like any other for the narrator.

Chapter 9. The Soul

1. *Svarfdaela Saga,* chapter 26.

2. *Vatnsdaela Saga,* chapter 3.

3. *Laxdaela Saga,* chapter 63.

4. Jaan de Vries, *Altgermanisches Religionsgeschichtes,* vol. 1, 182.

5. See also *Thorgils Saga Skarda,* chapter 62. In the presence of Thorgils's qualities, the free peasants of the Skagafjord "believed that Kolbeinn had returned *(aftr kominn)* and been reborn *(endrborinn),* cited from R. Boyer, *La vie religieuse en Islande (1116–1264),* 388.

6. I am using the studies that R. Boyer devoted to the subject in various books and articles: "Hamr, Fylgja, Hugr: L'Ame pour les anciens Scandinaves," *Heimdall* 33 (1981): 5–10; *La Religion des anciens Scandinaves* (see the key words cited in the index, pages 241–45); *Les Religions de l'Europe du Nord,* 12–56; *La Saga des Chiefs du Val au Lac,* 25–30. See also Jan de Vries, [*Altgermanisches Religionsgeschichtes*], vol. 1, 220–28. Bibliographical information is available in all these works.

7. *Vatnsdaela Saga,* chapter 36.

8. Robert Cook, trans., *Njal's Saga* (London: Penguin Books, 2001), chapter 23, 40.

9. *Saga of Gisli Surrson,* chapter 14.

10. *Brennu-Njáls Saga,* chapter 12.

11. *Gunnlauga Saga,* chapter 2.

12. *Laxdaela Saga,* chapter 4.

13. *Gisla Saga,* chapters, 22, 30, and 33. We should note that Gusli is called *draumamádr ok berdreymr,* meaning "man who has significant and premonitory dreams."

14. *Laxdaela Saga,* chapter 67.

15. *Brennu-Njáls Saga,* chapter 41.

16. Ásmundarson, ed., *Draumr Thorsteins Sidu-Hallssonar,* n.p.

17. *Hallfredar Saga,* chapter 11.

18. R. Boyer, "Hamr, Fylgja, Hugr: L'Ame pour les anciens Scandinaves," 8.

19. Ibid., 9. *Svá segir hugr mér; hafa e-t í hug; renna hug sínum; komma hug a e-t; leggja hug á konu; e-m rennr hugr til e-s.* In the *Poetic Edda,* one of the god Odin's ravens is named Huginn. He goes out into the world and returns to tell Odin what he has seen . . .

20. Ibid., 9.

21. Jan de Vries, *Altgermanische Religionsgeschichte,* vol. 1, 220.

22. *Saga of the Sworn Brothers,* chapter 26.

23. *Laxdaela Saga,* chapter 31.

24. *Edda Snorra, Ynglinga Saga,* chapter 7, in trans. R. Boyer, *Les Religions de l'Europe du Nord,* 539.

25. On this point, see P. Buchholz, *Schamanistische Zuuge in der altisländischen Überlieferung* (Munster: 1968).

26. Paulus Diaconus, *Historia Langobardorum* III, ed. MGH SS rerum (Hanover: Lang and Italic, 1878), 34.

27. Ibid., VI, 6.

28. *Edda,* Helgakvida Hiorvardssonar, prose following strophe 5, 137.

29. Ibid., *Hávamál* strophe 155, in trans. R. Boyer, *Les Religions de l'Europe du Nord,* 176.

30. *Vatnsdaela Saga,* chapter 12.

31. Ibid., chapter 12, and *Landnámabók, Sturlubók,* 179.

32. *Landnámabók, Sturlubók,* 76 (Thorain), 251 (Vékell), 259 (Odd), 289 (Lodmund), 344 (Dufthak), and 377 (Olaf). We should recall that the gods and giants had the ability to shapeshift. See Frigg/Freyja, whose metamorphosis is rationally attributed to falcon (*valshamr*) plumage, and the Valkyries, who possess the shapes of swans (*álptarhamr*).

33. *Völsunga Saga,* chapter 7. See Claude Lecouteux, *Les Monstres dans la littérature allemande du Moyen Age,* vol. 2, 164.

34. Wulfstan, *Homelia* XLI, ed. A. Napir (Berlin: 1883), 191; Knut, *Laws,* ed. R. Schmid, I § 26; R. Schmid, *Gesetze der Angelsachsen* (Leipzig: 1858), 270; Burchard, *Decretum* XIX, 10; Gervais of Tilbury, *Otia Imperialia* I, 15.

35. *Landnámabók, Sturlubók* 350, in trans. R. Boyer, 89. This information coincides exactly with that from the *Hausbók* and the *Melabók.*

36. Ibid., 259, in R. Boyer, 72. "For sorcery and magic" is an addition of the *Hauksbók* 223.

37. Ibid., 289, in R. Boyer, 76.

38. The glosses in Old High German give *hugu* for *animus*. See Sievers and Stein-meyer, *Die althochdeutschen Glossen,* vol. 1, 144, 21; 145, 21; and 210, 11.

39. E. Grunewald, ed. "The Knight of Staufenberg" (Tubingen: Aldeutsche Text Library 1979), ATB 88, v. 498. Another manuscript provides an expanded les-son: *wo das ich wil do bin ouch ich* [Where I want to be, there I am too].

40. J. Rychner, ed., *Lay of Lanval* (Paris/Geneva: 1958, TLF 77), v. 163–68. All the manuscripts offer the same lesson.

41. See *Göngu-Hrolf's Saga* and *Gull-Thoris Saga.*

42. *Bardar Saga Snæfellsássm,* chapter 18, in *Islendinga Saga* III.

43. *Laxdaela Saga,* chapter 42.

Chapter 10. The Dead, Revenants, and the Third Function

1. *Heimskringla, Ynglinga Saga,* chapter 10, in trans. R. Boyer, *Les Religions de l'Europe du Nord,* 143.

2. For more on Frotho, see Georges Dumézil, *Du Mythe au Roman* [From Myth to Novel] (Paris: PUF, 1970), 179–84.

3. Tacitus, *Germania* XL.

4. *Flateyjarbók,* vol. 1, 337.

5. *Heimskringla, Hálfdanar Saga Svarta,* chapter 9.

6. *Flateyjarbók,* vol. 1, 456.

7. *Landnámabók, Hausbók,* 19. According to Jan de Vries (*Alternordisches Etymolo-gisches Wörterbuch,* page 299 b), we must start with the root *gembhna,* "bud," to understand *Kambann.*

8. *Landnámabók, Sturlubók* 75; *Hausbók* 63.

9. *Laxdaela Saga,* chapter 66. Translated into English (London: Muriel Press, Tem-ple Classics, 1899).

10. *Kristni Saga,* chapter 2, in *Altnordische Sagabibliothek* XI (Halle, 1905).

11. *Heimskringla, Hákonar Saga Goda,* chapter 11.

12. *Tháttr Thorvalds ens Vidförla* [Old Norse Magic and Gender], chapter 2, in *Alt-nordische Sagabibliothek.*

13. E. Ó. Sveinsson, ed., *Kormaks Saga* (Reykjavik, 1939, Íslenzk Fornrit VIII), chap-ter 22.

14. *Landnámabók, Hausbók* 268, in R. Boyer, 78.

15. Ibid., *Sturlubók* 330, in R. Boyer, 85.

16. See Jan de Vries, *Altgermanisches Religionsgeschichte,* vol. 1, 232; Ó. Briem,

Heidinn Sidur á Íslandí (Reykjavik: 1945), 187; R. Boyer, *La vie religieuse en Islande (1116–1264)*, 392. [Translated into English by Diana Whaley in *Sagas of the Warrior-Poets* (London: Penguin Books, 2002), 107. —*Trans.*]

17. *Landnámabók, Sturlubók* 329, in R. Boyer, 84.

18. D. Strömbäck, *Island. Bilder fran gammal och ny Tid* (Yppsala: 1931), 60–62.

19. Heinrichs, *Olafs Saga hins Helga,* chapters 3–6.

20. Ibid.

21. For trolls, see E. Hartmann, *Die Trollvorstellungen in den Sagen und Märchen der skandínavischen Völker* (Stuttgart/Berlin: 1936, TGA 23).

22. See Dreams in *Old Norse Literature and Their Affinities in Folklore,* with an appendix containing the Icelandic texts and translations (Cambridge: 1935), 41.

Chapter II. Disguised Revenants

1. F. Holthausen, ed. and trans., *Beowulf* (Heidelberg: Carl Winter, 1908), 190.

2. Ibid.

3. E. Mogk, *Altgermanisches Spukgeschichten,* 114.

4. F. Mossé, trans., *The Saga of Grettir,* xxxi.

5. F. Holthausen, ed., *Beowulf,* 190.

6. Ibid., verse 104. For more on this point, see S. Crawford, "Grendel's Descent from Cain," *Modern Language Review* 23 (1928), 209 and 24 (1929) 63; O. Emerson, "Legend of Cain, Especially in Old and Middle English Literature," *Modern Language Association of America* 21 (1906): 831–929.

7. *Grettir Saga,* chapters 32–35. I refer to the following remark (chapter 64, 210): "Grettir had the habit of annihilating ghosts and revenants" (*reimleikun edu aptrgongum*).

8. *Grettir Saga,* chapter 66. See F. Mossé, xxx–xlii, on the comparisons between this saga and *Beowulf.*

9. *Grettir Saga,* chapters 64–65, 213: *Thetta er sogn Grettis, at trollkonan step dysk f gljúfrin vid, er hon fekk sdrit, en Bárdardalsmenn segja, at hana dagadi uppi, tha er thau glimdu, ok sprungit, thá er hann hjó af henni hondina, ok standi that enn I konuliking á bjarginu.*

10. *Grettir Saga,* chapter 66. See F. Mossé, xxx–xlii, on the comparisons between this saga and *Beowulf.*

11. J. Wilson, ed., *Samsons Saga Fagra* (Copenhagen: Sammfund til udgivelse af gammal nordisk Literature LXV, 1953), chapter 8.

12. See M. B. Landstad, *Norske Folkevisor* (Christiana: 1853), no. 1, Asmund Frae-degaevor, strophes 30 and 43. In song no. 4, that of Steinfin gefinson, we read:

"He drew the trolls from the mountain to the light of day" (*lokkad han alle dei bergetrolli uti dagin ljose*).

13. R. Boyer, *Les Religions de l'Europe du Nord*, 53.

14. *Edda, Helreid Brynhildar*, strophe 14.

15. Ibid., *Voluspá*, strophe 50: *Naglfar losnar. / kióll ferr austan / koma muno Muspellz / um log lydir; kióll* can be understood as "a boat" or "the boat," which would then designate Nagalfar. See R. Boyer, *Les Religions de l'Europe du Nord*, 480.

16. Ibid., strophe 52;, in R. Boyer, 486.

17. Steinmeyer and Sievers, *Die althochdeutschen Glossen*, vol. 2, 492, 15; 645, 28 and 44.

18. T. Wright, *Anglo-Saxon and Old English Vocabulary*, 36, 15 and 459, 31.

19. *Dialogus miraculorum* XII, 19. Notable is the noise preceding or accompanying the apparition.

20. *Edda, Alvíssmál*, strophe 2.

21. Snorri Sturluson, *Ynglinga Saga*, chapters 4 and 7. In the *Voluspá* [Poetic Edda], strophe 22, Mimir guards the spring of supreme wisdom, which gushes forth at the foot of Yggdrasill, the Cosmic Tree.

22. *Edda, Vafthrúdnismál* [no page number].

23. Jan de Vries, *La Religion des Celtes* (Paris: Payot, 1963), 91. Interesting parallels between Celtic and Norse literature can be found here.

24. See Caesar, *De bello Gallico* VI, 18, 1.

25. *Ynglingatal*, strophe 2.

26. Preface in prose of A. von Keller, ed., *Book of Heroes* (Stuttgart: 1867), St LV 87. In the Johann Prüss edition, Strasbourg, the dwarf does not appear (see folio 5v°).

27. For more on these kinds of beings, see Claude Lecouteux, *Les Monstres dans la litterature allemande du Moyen Age* [Monsters in the German Literature of the Middle Ages], vol. 2, 5.

28. "Book of Sturla," ed. and trans. L. C. Stern, *Revue Celtique* XIII, 12–17.

29. Dimock, ed., *Topographica Hibernica* III, 2, 141.

30. *Wigalois, Der Ritter mit dem Rade*, ed. J. M. N. Kapteyn (Bonn: Rheinische Bieträge, 1966), 9.

31. Martin Wierschin ed., *Eckenlied* (Tubingen: Neimeyer Verlag, 1974, ATB 78), strophe 23.

32. Johann Prüss, *Heldenbuch* (Strasbourg, ca. 1483), folio 214r°-v°.

33. D'Arbois de Jubainville, *Le cycle mythologique irlandais et la Mythologie celtique*, 337–43.

34. Ibid.

35. B. Woledge, ed., *The Perilous Hearth* (Paris: 1936), CFMA 76, verses 1131–443.

Chapter 12. Perspectives

1. K. Müllenhoff, *Sagen, Märchen, Lieder aus Herzoghümer Schleswig-Holstein* (Kiel, 1845), no. 260.

2. Jacob Grimm, *Deutsche Sagen* [German Legends] (Darmstadt: Wissencshaftliche Buchgesellschaft, 1974), no. 286.

3. Ibid., no. 285.

4. Müllenhoff, *Sagen, Märchen, Lieder aus Herzoghümer*, no. 266 B. See also Mackensen, *Niedersächsische Sagen* [Legends of Lower Saxony] 1 (Leipzig/Gohlis, 1923), no. 55.

5. *Omnis possessio tres sylvanos habet: unus domesticus, possessioni consecratus; alter dicitur agrestis, pastoribus consecratus; tertius dicitur oreientalis, cui est in confinio lucus positus* (Keil, ed., *Grammatici latini veteres*). I thank Christian Abry (Grenoble) for sending this text.

6. Steinmeyer and Sievers, *Die althochdeutschen Glossen*, vol. 1, 268, 26; vol. 4, 194, 23.

7. J. Earle, *Two of the Saxon Chronicle* (Oxford: 1865). The *Parker Chronicle*, and the *Land Chronicle* mention the event, anno 547.

8. R. Boyer, *La Saga de Snorri le Godi*, 203.

9. R. Boyer, *Le Livre de la Colonisation de l'Islande*, 139. The technical term is *örskotshelgi*.

10. Claude Lecouteux, "Hagazussa-Strigo-Hexe," 174.

11. Mackensen, *Niedersächsische Sagen*, no. 49.

12. Ibid., no. 64.

13. Ibid., no. 54.

14. Ibid., no. 53.

15. Ibid., no. 50.

16. Müllenhoff, *Sagen, Märchen, Lieder aus Schleswig-Holstein*, no. 347.

17. H. Lohre, *Märkische Sagen* [Mark of Brandenburg Saga] (Leipzig/Gohlis: 1921), no. 172.

18. J. Müler, *Sagen aus Uri* (Basel: G. Krebs, 1929), vol. 2, 327.

19. Sven Grundtvig, *Danmarks gamie Folkeviser*, 5 volumes (Copenhagen: 1853–1878), no. 92, in L. Pineau, *Les Vieux Chants populaires scandinaves*, 2 vols. (Paris: 1898–1901), vol. 1, 122.

20. Lohre, *Märkische Sagen*, no. 40.

21. A. Hass, *Rügensche Sagen und Märchen* [Rügensche Legends and Fairytales] (Leipzig: 1896), no. 22.

22. Mackensen, *Niedersächsische Sagen,* no. 65.

23. See *Le Chevalier au cheval gris* [The Knight on the Grey Horse] by Theodor Storm, for example.

24. F. H. von der Hagen and V. Höttger, *Lesebuch der deutschen Volkssage* [The German Folk Legend Reader] (Berlin: 1963), no. 29/2.

25. Kahlo, *Niedersächsische Sagen* 1 (Leipzig/Gohlis: 1923), no. 50.

26. Lohre, *Märkische Sagen,* no. 11.

27. A. Haas, *Rügensche Sagen und Märchen,* no. 11.

28. Grundtvig, *Danmarks gamie Folkeviser,* no. 89B.

29. Ibid., no. 90.

30. Le Pineau, *Les Vieux Chants populaires scandinaves,* vol. 1, 128.

31. The motif is known to folklorists as *Tränenkrüglein.* See also E. T. Kristensen, *Gamle Viser i Folkemunde* (Copenhagen: 1891), no. 68; Grimm, *Kinder und Hausmärchen,* no. 107; and Mackensen, *Niedersächsische Sagen,* no. 48.

32. Grundtvig, *Danmarks gamie Folkeviser,* no. 92. We should note that Gertrude uses a book and a wand.

33. Lohre, *Märkische Sagen,* no. 35.

34. I. von Zingerle, *Sagen, Märchen und Gebräuche aus Tirol* (Innsbruck: 1859), no. 400.

35. Mackensen, *Niedersächsische Sagen,* no. 42.

36. Ibid., no. 43.

37. Müllenhoff, *Sagen, Märchen, Lieder aus Schleswig-Holstein,* no. 349.

38. Lohre, *Märkische Sagen,* no. 38.

39. Ibid., no. 14.

40. Mackensen, *Niedersächsische Sagen,* no. 59.

41. Aniela Jaffé, *Geistererscheinungen und Vorzeichen, Eine psychologische Deutung.*

42. Cited from Samivel, *L'Or de l'Islande* [The Gold from Iceland] (Paris: 1963), 293–96. Notable are the behavior of the dog and the conclusions Kristjan Thorolfsson draws from it.

Index

Books of Related Interest

Witches, Werewolves, and Fairies
Shapeshifters and Astral Doubles in the Middle Ages
by Claude Lecouteux

Witchcraft Medicine
Healing Arts, Shamanic Practices, and Forbidden Plants
by Claudia Müller-Ebeling, Christian Rätsch, and Wolf-Dieter Storl

Seeing the Dead, Talking with Spirits
Shamanic Healing through Contact with the Spirit World
by Alexandra Leclere

The Green Witch Herbal
Restoring Nature's Magic in Home, Health, and Beauty Care
by Barbara Griggs

Being a Pagan
Druids, Wiccans, and Witches Today
by Ellen Evert Hopman and Lawrence Bond

The Pagan Mysteries of Halloween
Celebrating the Dark Half of the Year
by Jean Markale

The Dreamer's Book of the Dead
A Soul Traveler's Guide to Death, Dying, and the Other Side
by Robert Moss

The Seeress of Prevorst
Her Secret Language and Prophecies from the Spirit World
by John DeSalvo, Ph.D.

INNER TRADITIONS • BEAR & COMPANY
P.O. Box 388
Rochester, VT 05767
1-800-246-8648
www.InnerTraditions.com

Or contact your local bookseller